THE ORIGINAL
Wild Ones

TALES OF
THE BOOZEFIGHTERS
MOTORCYCLE CLUB
EST. 1946

BILL HAYES

WITH

JIM "JQ" QUATTLEBAUM

FOREWORD BY DAVE NICHOLS
EDITOR-IN-CHIEF, EASYRIDERS MAGAZINE

motorbooks

First published in 2005 by MBI Publishing Company and Motorbooks, an imprint of
MBI Publishing Company, 400 First Avenue North, Suite 300, Minneapolis, MN
55401 USA

Motorbooks titles are also available at discounts in bulk quantity for industrial or
sales-promotional use. For details write to Special Sales Manager at MBI Publishing
Company, 400 First Avenue North, Suite 300, Minneapolis, MN 55401 USA.

To find out more about our books, join us online at www.motorbooks.com.

ISBN-13: 978-0-7603-3537-6

Editor: Darwin Holmstrom
Designer: Tom Heffron

Printed in the United States of America

BILL HAYES is an avid motorcyclist whose articles, columns, and fiction have
been published in Easyriders, Thunder Press, and Biker magazines. His column in Real
Blues magazine has run for many years, and several of his feature articles on martial arts
have appeared in Black Belt magazine. Bill writes passionately about the things he loves
and knows best: motorcycles, the blues, and martial arts.

JIM "JQ" QUATTLEBAUM, BFMC National Historian, generously
contributed his time and attention to this project on behalf of the club, supplying a
wealth of photographs, memorabilia, and writings from the club's archives. Jim is quite
a storyteller in his own right.

"Everyone must believe in something. I believe I'll have another drink."

—W. C. Fields

"WINO WILLIE"

This is the story about the Original Wild Ones, the Boozefighters
In a little town outside of San Jose,
Just some boys havin' some fun,
Wanted to live their own way,
They were fussin' and fightin',
Drinkin' at Johnny's Bar . . .
Just back from the war,
Became a rebel,
And a rider,
That knew how to play the game . . .
Willie Forkner was his name

Started a movement,
Outside of San Jose,
In the town, Hollister, USA

(From the CD *Freedom* by Charlie Brechtel)

CONTENTS

FOREWORD

This is a story that is as old as humankind; it is a true story about men, boundaries, brotherhood, society, and freedom of expression. It is a tale of rebellion; of fire and magic, remembrances and embellishments that make legends. Yes, these tales walk hand in hand with myth, for you see, American bikers are the last of a breed. Free thinkers all, and proud defenders of free thought, bikers are the last Vikings, the last frontiersmen and mountain men, the last pirates and outlaws, the final breed of the wild ones who made this country. Woe to the world when the last biker rides into Valhalla, for the world we all were born to will be long gone. The wolves will have gone and the sheep will inherit the earth in a bleating, vacant-minded void of dreamless, meaningless sleep.

While reading of this book is best done aloud with close friends 'round a campfire while intoxicated, it is also fully enjoyable in one's living room accompanied by Bob Seger on the stereo and a bottle of Jack Black. While these tales of the open road, of the wind in your hair and unadulterated freedom are indeed true, we bikers are known to flavor our tales with a bit of spice. However, we'll leave it to you to believe them or not.

You are about to enter a world unlike the weakened down version currently filled with cell phones, stock traders, and Volvo-driving moms transporting their kids to soccer practice. The world we will now enter is based on a creed of conduct and honor that goes back to the time of knights in slightly tarnished armor. Now, the members of this biker brotherhood would laugh out loud at any similarity drawn between their grizzled selves and such men of valor, but until you've seen 50 bikers blasting past you in formation on their chopped iron steeds, chrome straight pipes thundering, well, you haven't lived. And once you have experienced such sights and sounds of utter freedom, only then will you realize that you have been living a diminished existence.

I once knew a biker that I'll call "Spider," who lived large to the extent that it was hard to believe the world could contain such a free spirit. He loved to laugh, drink, fight, and fool with the ladies more than any human being I've ever known. He was a massive 6 foot 5 inches and nearly 300 pounds of muscle, the very stuff of biker lore. He had been in so many fights that his nose was less a functioning feature than a mass in the center of his face. The thing about this brother was he loved pain. I once saw him get into it with another dude, who gave him all he had right in the nose. Spider just spat out blood and smiled with a truly insane glee. "That's the way I like it!" he bellowed, and meant it.

But images can be deceiving.

The very same mountainous scooter tramp could also be poetic; he sang with a beautiful voice and grew misty eyed when speaking of a lost love: his 1954 Harley Panhead. He could also stop a fight before it started by filling his opponents with a visual image so shocking that they would rethink their challenge, no matter how drunk they were. Even his "in the heat of battle" phrases had their own brutal poetry. For instance, while being sized up by three would-be troublemakers, he completely diffused what would have been a very messy fight in a club brother's bar by simply asking, "Have you boys ever tried to pick your bloody teeth off the floor with a broken hand?" The men backed down, and before the night was through, all of them were drinking and laughing with Spider like lifelong friends.

I don't know what ever became of my old brother Spider, but I sincerely hope that he went out blazing with a sword in his hand against the wolves of winter, in the best Viking tradition. See you down the road, bro.

So, with these bikeresque word pictures ablaze in your fertile imagination, may I suggest you sit back with your beverage of choice and perhaps raise a toast to those free spirits who have come and gone before you. In particular, here's to Wino Willie Forkner, the Original Wild One, who was Hollywood's model for Lee Marvin's character "Chino" in Stanley Kramer's *The Wild One*. But Wino Willie was the real thing, and so are the men you're about to meet. May the tales of their two-wheeled exploits fill your heart with yearning for adventure on open roads that never end.

Here's to The Wild Ones. OWOF.

—Dave Nichols, editor-in-chief, *Easyriders* magazine

PREFACE

This is not a history book. That has been done. Many times.

Meticulous writers like Tom Reynolds (*Wild Ride*) and Brock Yates (*Outlaw Machine*) have already exhumed the skeletal remains of early biker culture from the historical tar pits of post–World War II America and neatly reassembled them into an enormous, impeccably clean, and highly detailed fossilized model.

This monster looms over much of modern mainstream society like a hungry T-rex hovering and salivating over frightened and quivering prey.

We, however, are going to put some flesh on those bones. We are going to breathe life into the beast. We are going to discover if the brute existed—and *still* exists—only to run amok, trying to satisfy an insatiable, antisocial blood lust, or if there really is a lot of gentleness in this roaring giant.

Acknowledgments

Bill Hayes and Jim Quattlebaum would like to thank the true bikers and their supporters who have helped to make this book a reality:

Gil Armas, Les Haserot, Jack Lilly, Jim Cameron, Dago, Johnny and Jeannine Roccio, Vern Autrey, Fritz Clapp, Darwin Holmstrom, Mike Council, Charlie Brechtel, Dennis Sanfilippo, Bobby Reynoso, "Grump," Randy "Scarface" Mills, Dave Nichols, "Big John" Rogers, Doug "Duke" Barron, Carl "Big Daddy" Spotts, Brian "Snowman" Trum, Panhead Jimmy, R. J. "Cowboy" Carter, Mark Gardiner, Michael Schacht, Markus Karalash, Norm "Raoul" Flynn, Paula Hayes, Pat Quattlebaum.

This book is dedicated to "The Original Wild Ones"—the first generation members and associates of the Boozefighters MC

"Wino" Willie Forkner	Les "Baja" Haserot
Vern Autrey	Jim "Tex" Hunter
"Fat Boy" Nelson	"J. D." John Cameron
Johnny Roccio	Jim "Smiley" Cameron
"Crocker Jack" Lilly	George "Herkemer" Manker
"Red Dog" Dahlgren	"Little" Bobby Kelton

Benny "Kokomo" McKell	Tommy Cook
Walt Porter	Jimmy Morris
"Dink" Burns	Jim Morrison
Gil Armas	"Red"
C. B. Clausen	"Fearless"
Johnny Davis	"Smoe"
Jim Smith	"Chuck"
'Pedro Roy	"Womp"
"Sleepy"	"Goldie"
"Burrhead"	Andy Burk
Al Orr	Bill Miller
Lance Tidwell	"Grover"
Teri Forkner	Jim Hicks
Jeannine Roccio	Joe Anchanado
Virginia "Dago" Day	Al Jordanelli
Jack Jordan	Earl Carlos
Jimmy Kimball	Lee "Bear" Nolan
Dick Carroll	

(and to "Yoyo" and all those mentioned in "The Tale of the Mysterious Lost Boozefighters' Stories" and to any brothers, sisters, or associates that we—*or time*—may have forgotten)

Chapter 1

The Tale of Grandpa and the Bottle of, uh, Milk . . .

Long before a spate of chopper-building programs flooded cable television, before one-percenter motorcycle clubs blurred the distinction between fame and infamy, and even before those outlaw clubs became targets for federal undercover agents in search of contraband and lucrative book deals, the Boozefighters Motorcycle Club—the original wild ones—backfired onto the American motorcycle scene like a fat-jetted Harley V-twin engine. These young men, restless World War II veterans eager to exercise the freedom they had risked their lives to preserve, fueled by hootch and pretty girls, unconsciously established the archetype of "biker."

One summer weekend in 1947, the BFMC gunned the stroked engines of their hopped-up Indians and Harleys and set out in search of a little fun. Instead they made history. A sensation-seeking press exaggerated their boisterous antics at the Fourth of July celebration in the sleepy little town of Hollister, California, and in the process created the biker lifestyle.

A few grizzled old bikers who participated in this seminal event are still alive today. A few of them even continue to ride motorcycles and wear the fabled patch of the Boozefighters MC: the three-starred bottle.

Sometimes they have a little explaining to do. A grizzled old biker usually observes the world in a slightly different light than a five-year-old girl.

Usually.

"Grandpa, why do you have that bottle of milk on the back of your vest?"

Old 'n grizzled wasn't about to begin a long, morally tinged ramble about the difference between milk and moonshine, which one's good for you, which one's not, and why. Instead he answered with a smile and a kid-like shrug that simply said, "Just because." And to a little girl that was OK, that was reason enough. Her grandpa is a member of the original wild ones: The Boozefighters Motorcycle Club. The "bottle" is the centerpiece of the patch, a sacred green icon that symbolizes a brotherhood and a heritage that few are ever fortunate enough to experience. Is it actually supposed to be a bottle of milk? Probably not. But that really is left up to the imagination. The Peter Pan eye-of-the-beholder that is the fanciful essence of an innocent five-year-old is, in many ways, what also fuels the Boozefighters.

The truth is that the founding fathers of the original wild ones were really just big kids themselves, simply trying to recapture some of the youthful fun they lost out on due to the innocence-destroying interruption of a very adult evil known as World War II.

There were no excuses, no laments, no protests. The country needed young soldiers. They went. War changes everyone. And everything. When young vets like Willie Forkner, Robert Burns, and George Manker returned home, it was difficult to forget the horrors of what they had seen. It was hard to shake off the ingrained military regimentation. It was impossible to shed some of the cold-sweat guilt that comes with surviving while so many others did not. And there was an unnerving restlessness in trying to adapt to the calmness and serenity of "normal" living after drowning in chaos. It was easy, however, to adopt an "I don't fit in" kind of attitude. It was easy for returning vets to feel more comfortable with one another than with those from "the outside."

The recipe had been written. The mix was almost complete. All that was needed was the addition of a potent ingredient to spice up the social soup. Something like, say, racing fast motorcycles. The races and rally organized by the American Motorcyclist Association Gypsy Tour in 1947 boiled the soup into a fiery jalapeno-laced stew.

The green stitched bottle that the five-year-old asked her old gramps about was very different from the real bottles that were gathered from the streets of Hollister by an energized photojournalist during that infamous weekend. The image on that patch is very different from the horde of broken

Tommy Cook (second from left) and Jim Hunter (far right) were among the World War II veterans who helped to establish the Boozefighters MC and the entire biker culture.

and empty bottles that were carefully arranged around the seemingly drunk and woozy non-Boozefighter (identified as Eddie Davenport or Don Middleton, depending on the source) by San Francisco Chronicle photographer Barney Peterson.

The resulting picture was not exactly a work of art that might have emerged from the all-American portfolios of Ansel Adams, Norman Rockwell, or Grant Wood. No. Instead, we were treated to an urban-ugly portrait of the tipsy "model," astride a "nasty, fire-breathing, Milwaukee-steel dragon," viciously framed by those stale-smelling empties and jagged glass shards.

When that twisted version of American Gothic leaped out at the sophisticated readers of *Life* magazine's July 21, 1947, issue, a frightening chill blew through the calm kingdom air. Some of the common village folk wanted to head for the hills, and some wanted to take up pitchforks, sickles, and torches against the strange new beast.

Some wanted to tell the whole story. Sort of. Filmmaker Stanley Kramer produced The Wild One six years later, and the snarling cat was out of the bag. The question is, of course, just how sharp were that cat's claws really?

But more than a half-century has already passed, and the legend has grown. The embroidered green bottles went on in 1946, Hollister swept up all that busted brown glass in 1947, The Wild One rolled out on black and white celluloid at the end of 1953, and the always colorful stories, tales, and traditions have never stopped.

Today, as in 1946, surviving BFMC members are more concerned with carrying on the most important Boozefighter tradition of all: Having fun. One of the early members, Jack Lilly, has a credo that is woven into the very fabric of that holy green patch when it comes to having a good time: "Do it now!" They did. And they still do.

When that cat flew out of the bag, the popularized fear was that he was bent on shredding and hunting prey. In reality that fast, sleek animal was just living up to his reputation for curiosity and playful prowling. For wanting to sniff out every aspect of life. Eat, drink, fool around, chase an occasional mouse, cough up a hairball or two after a tad too much consumption, and, in general, just enjoy the heck out of living.

"Every original Boozefighter I've met," club historian Jim "JQ" Quattlebaum says, "—Wino, J. D. and Jim Cameron, Red Dog, Jim Hunter, Roccio, Les, Gil, Lilly, and Vern Autrey—all exhibit signs that they are made of common threads: Spirited and daring character, challenging competitiveness,

The sacred club "patch" is more than just skin deep.

strong bonding friendship, a caring and giving nature, the love of motorcycling, and brotherhood with bikers. They're honest and law-abiding citizens, but not beyond the embellishment of a good story." Even in their old age they've stayed active. No rocking chairs for them! Still riding motorcycles as long as their health and bodies would allow.

"Yeah, they let off a lot of steam, partied hearty, got jailed for getting drunk, got a lot of speeding tickets, and occasionally duked it out with redneck bar patrons that hassled them . . . and sometimes they fought with each other. Then they'd sit down together and laugh about it over a beer.

"But no original ever got put in jail for a serious crime like murder or drugs. They got along with all other MC clubs, sponsored races, baseball games, and different events with other clubs. They never considered themselves outlaws the way that term is used today. This was a term that the AMA applied to riders and clubs who didn't follow the structured AMA racing rules back in the 1940s.

"And the originals didn't discriminate toward any ethnic, religious, or political group. Wino said, 'We fought side by side for all Americans to have freedom of choice.'

"That freedom also extended to the members' choice of bikes to ride, as long as they could keep up! Indians and Harleys were the most available, so they were the most used. However, many old BFers started acquiring the Triumph because of its improved racing speed. Hendersons and other pre-World War II bikes were used, too. When the BSA was introduced in the

1950s, it became the bike of choice for the still-racing BFers, like Jim Hunter, Jim Cameron, Ernie and Johnny Roccio.

"Present day BFMC requires members to ride an American or World War II-allied brand of bike. But some exceptions are made in some chapters for special consideration. 'Brooklyn' is allowed to ride a touring Moto Guzzi in honor of his grandfather, who fought with the Italian underground resistance against the Germans.

"The present-day Boozefighters revere our originals and the club's founders for their intent, purpose, and priorities: Family, job, and club brotherhood. We're family men, engaged in legitimate businesses and careers, enjoying getting together as a social group for parties, rides, and special events. We're into this thing strictly for having harmless, good clean fun. We couldn't care less about 'territory' and things like that.

"We don't push religion on anyone but we do have a national chaplain, 'Irish Ed' Mahan, who, in a nondenominational way, conducts Bible study class every Tuesday night, performs legal marriages and funerals, and visits members that request special counseling or have illness issues. He also conducts Easter sunrise services at our clubhouse every year. It's attended by a lot of friendly clubs.

"And we're involved in giving back to society through fund-raising, toy runs, March-of-Dimes, Wish With Wings and such. We have a blood bank for members. We're active in motorcycle rights organizations, and many of us are state delegates to our respective political parties.

"We believe in peaceful coexistence with all clubs, but we don't wear support patches for any other organization. And we don't believe in displaying any antisociety or anti-American items."

Apparently some of the original members' priorities and the club's eventual evolution based on those principles were neglected just a bit in The Wild One. But, with another shrug of the shoulders, that, too, is OK. The Boozefighters are comfortable with who they are. And who they were. They're very proud of their founders. And they're happy with the continuance of the all-important "fun" tradition.

They're content with their personalities being somewhere in between Brando's "Johnny," Marvin's "Chino," and the brilliant 1940s/1950s abandon of, oh maybe, a Red Skelton or a Jackie Gleason.

In a letter dated September 18, 1946, the San Francisco Boozefighter prez, Benny "Kokomo" McKell, wrote to the L.A. chapter to order four club sweaters for his newest members. They had just passed the rigorous series of seven tests required of a "prospect":

1. Get drunk at a race meet or cycle dance.
2. Throw lemon pie in each other's faces.
3. Bring out a douche bag where it would embarrass all the women (then drink wine from it, etc.).
4. Get down and lay on the dance floor.
5. Wash your socks in a coffee urn.
6. Eat live goldfish.
7. Then, when blind drunk, trust me ("Kokomo") to shoot beer bottles off of your heads with my .22.

Would Johnny or Chino do all that?

No.

Would Skelton or Gleason?

Probably.

Would the Boozefighters?

Just ask 'em.

So, are all of the tales and legends in this book the sworn gospel?

JQ answers that (more or less) in an interesting discussion about memory and motorcycle lore:

"If you ask me today what I did last night, I'd be hard pressed to remember all the details precisely right. I know I started off with 65 or 70 dollars in my pocket and got home with about 7. For the life of me I can't remember what I spent the money on. But to get the story more accurate, that doesn't count that $100 bill I had stashed away for an emergency. Man, I hope I didn't blow that, too . . .

"Ask the original wild ones what happened fifty years ago and they, too, are hard pressed to remember the precise facts. Once, sitting with three such old-timers, I witnessed a heated—but friendly—debate about what club one of them raced for during the Hollister melee. They finally all agreed on one thing: Whether it was the 13 Rebs, Yellow Jackets, or Boozefighters, they all had one heck of a good time, excluding the jail time for rowdiness, of course.

"I had a good time last night, too. (That is, unless I can't find my $100 bill.)

"But anyway, if Patrick Henry had said, 'If I don't get my rear end outta here, I'm gonna get it shot off,' and some historical writer quoted him as actually saying, 'Give me liberty or give me death,' then what kind of respect would you have for that writer? As historian, I've had to dig deep into the facts about the Boozefighters, and there are times I wished I hadn't found out that some stories just weren't so. But then again, the more I dug, the more I found out that there are great stories that were never told.

"They need to be told, so we'll tell them. Some are fantastic, but I'll let the listener or reader sort out what they want to believe. Most importantly, though, the telling of these stories will be geared to the essence of truth as the old-timers wanted to remember it."

And the heart of that truth—those stories—beats with the same wide-eyed wonder that drives the fertile imagination of that inquisitive five-year-old.

Is there milk in that bottle, some 90-proof hooch, or a genie that will pop out and take us directly into a unique and exotic land, a growling jungle that members of the button-down, mainstream, overly protected, boy-in-the-bubble society fear, envy, and would give their eye teeth to journey into?

Maybe it's all three.

CHAPTER 2

The Tale of "The Bats"
(Thank God They Didn't Fly)

The history of the world, American culture, and humanity in general is a lot better off because certain inventive and imaginative minds actually *forgot* or *gave up on* some specific ideas or thoughts.

Sure.

We're grateful, of course, for guys like Thomas Edison, Henry Ford, and whatever medieval lush came up with the concept of bottling up a bunch of grain, hops, and yeast and letting it sit for a spell. Those boys stuck to their guns, and the entire universe is better off for it.

But we can also thank the good Lord up above that some notions fizzled on the launch pad.

Civilized society, for example, only had to endure a short time sharing the world with Milli Vanilli. Brazil's "Amazonas" never became quite as popular a motorcycle as, say, Harley-Davidson. The Hondells only had one hit. Emu burgers never really caught on. The Spice Girls starred in just one flick. And we only did the Macarena for about a week.

We can say a *special* prayer of thanks, however, that Wino and the originals didn't name their new motorcycle club the Bats.

The Bats? The *Bats*? It just doesn't roll off the tongue. It doesn't really have that rugged feel of the rough and tumble, postwar, still-industrializing, good ol' U. S. of A.

It almost happened, though. The Henchmen was also in the running. And so was The Characters.

"Actually," says original wild one Jack Lilly, "A lot of us were riding together as early as 1939. We had a riding group called 'The Characters.' We even had our club name printed up on our belts but someone misspelled it, so we became known as the 'Caracters Club.' "

But, through what was almost assuredly an act of divine providence, Walt Porter came down from the sacred mountain that was the bar at the All American Cafe in the holy land of South Gate, California, with hallowed stone tablets that read: "It is written, the name shall be 'the Boozefighters.' " OK. Maybe there's a bit more to it than that. Yeah, actually he was drunk and the originals more-or-less agree that he raised his head up from the bar and said something to the effect of, "Ya might as well call yourselves 'the B-B-B-Boozefighters,' 'cause all you do is sit around the bar and fight that booze!"

Everyone thought that Walt was passed out and that he hadn't even been listening to the conversation about a handle for this bunch. After the laughter died down, Wino said that right then and there they decided to use the name that Walt had slurred out.

Another original added a twist: that name had actually been brought up before.

"We were not really satisfied with Walt's selection but we had been jokingly calling each other an 'ol' booze fighter' when someone got really drunk anyway. Kinda like you'd call someone an 'old sot' nowadays, but we kept trying to think up a more dignified, macho name for the club. After all, back then the term 'booze fighter' meant a man with a drinking problem or an alcoholic. That described us, of course, but it was embarrassing to be called that." A lot of ex-GIs fell into that category. But it was still the wild west. Helmet laws, noise ordinances, random sobriety road checks, and the tame, emasculating, proper-salad-fork, turn-the-other-cheek social grace of a modern new order had not yet settled in.

Frank, Dino, and Sammy could still get up onstage with a smoke in one hand and a tumbler of Scotch in the other and sing about good-lookin' dames, drinking, or the shapely legs on some cute blonde. They didn't have to worry then about being arrested for smoking indoors, blowing a .08, or offending some gender-neutral group. Neither did the Boozefighters. They had paid their dues defending America's freedom and they had some catching up to do.

Their new name fit just fine.

Ironically, Walt Porter was never an actual member of the club he named. He was described as a "young drunk who rode an old Army surplus Harley 45." He was a regular, however, along with the rest of the originals, at the Big A—the All American Cafe & Bar.

Wino regarded Porter as "the king of the one-liners. When you least expected it, Walt popped up with something witty and kept everyone laughing all of the time." Although not voted into the club, Porter was accepted as "more-or-less an honorary member of the Boozefighters. After all, he never missed a 'meeting.' He was always at the Big A."

Maybe the name didn't actually descend from the blessed mountain etched in consecrated stone, but—according to legend—its permanence was indeed written forever in the sanctified dirt of a racetrack in Riverside. "Shortly after the name was thought up," relates one of the originals, "the group went to some race event, Riverside, probably, and one of the guys was hot-dogging around the parking area when he ran into a patch of sand and slid down in a huge cloud of dust.

"Two girls were walking by, saw this mess, and got to laughing. They found their way through the dust and asked our guy on the ground, 'So what motorcycle club are *you* with?' He was still kinda shaken and came up with the first thing he could think of, our new name, 'The Boozefighters!'

" 'That figures,' they said with a smirk. Then they set off to warn everyone to watch out for those drunken Boozefighters from L.A.!"

Between the soggy, high-level powwows at the Big A, and the dust and disgusted chicks at Riverside, the name stuck. Just to be sure, Wino asked the group once more "what they thought of the name and just going with it, since no matter what, people were gonna call us that anyway."

They all agreed. But there was one more important detail that Wino had to deal with.

"Well, if we're gonna be known as a drinking club," Wino declared, "we might as well come up with a bottle of good booze for our logo patch!" The genesis of the legend was truly in high gear. Good thing he wasn't trying to come up with an image of a *bat*. "The Bats . . ." It just doesn't roll off the tongue, like good booze.

CHAPTER 3

The Tale of Evil Images:
"Typical Speed Demons, "The Riverside "Riots," An Honest Sheriff, Wild Red Hair, and the Electric Seat

"Our first club run as the East Bay Dragons MC pack was Memorial Day 1959. We rode 40 miles to Alum Rock Park near San Jose. We left Oakland at about nine that morning, stretched out from Seventy-Ninth Avenue to Eighty-Second. It took us five hours to go forty miles. On the way, we picked up our riding buddy, Heavy Evans, who was living in Menlo Park at the time.

"When we showed up at Alum Rock, we scared the holy hell out of the families barbecuing in the park with their kids. The minute they saw us ride up on our Harleys, they packed up their picnic baskets, loaded up their station wagons, and made a beeline for the exit gate. People were even more scared of us after they saw the movie The Wild One *with Marlon Brando."*

—Tobie Gene Levingston, President, East Bay
Dragons MC, from the book, *Soul on Bikes*

Images are hard to shake, and once they've taken a media-driven stranglehold on your personality, all bets are off. "Hard" becomes "impossible," and basically—if the image is bad—you're sunk. You're stuck with it. You might as well be branded like one of Ben Cartwright's steers or have a neon-scarlet "A" that glows in the dark carved directly into your forehead. It's permanent and it just ain't gonna change.

Ever.

Don Knotts, for example, is the pure embodiment of an everlasting media *image*. He was destined to have a lifelong career as various incarnations of Barney Fife, Mr. Furley, and the Incredible Mr. Limpett. I'm pretty sure that his phone never rang with offers from tough-talking, raspy producers just begging him to get outfitted with tight, sleeveless camouflage muscle jerseys and start learning testosterone-laden lines for the character of *Big Doc the Ice Pick Maniac* in the next "Terminator" flick.

Don Knotts could've gained 150 pounds, chiseled himself into Mayberry's answer to Lennox Lewis, chugged steroids like Tic-Tacs, and he still would have been Barney Fife in everybody's mind. His ground-in image was set in stone. Period.

And *image* is, of course, the root of the word, *imagination*.

Another example: I'm sure that sports fans find it hard to look at Marv Albert in men's clothing now. The *imagination* immediately rockets us back to his *other wardrobe*, with or without the rug.

Another: It's difficult to see the lovely and talented Monica Lewinski standing straight up. The *imagination* tends to visualize her a little more . . . *relaxed*.

Images like these are locked in. There's nothing that can be done. No erasing. No "delete" button. No laser removal operations. No going back.

And some images continue to grow, to get even more and more intense. They not only transcend the "delete" button, but they shatter the whole machine as they leap through the monitor, rise from the pages, or drop down from the silver screen. Barney and his one-bullet "nipping things in the bud," Marv slipping out of his Armani in favor of something more *comfortable*, and Monica reaching quickly for the Kleenex are *not* the kind of images that *grow*. They simply *are*.

But the image of the American biker is different. Very different. It has never stopped expanding. It has never stopped growing.

The image of the three-piece-patch wearing biker—*especially in numbers*, in an unstoppable, invincible group—is as starkly rattling to most people as having a Vise-Grip locked around their Adam's Apple. The media learned this truth very early on and they learned how to cash in on it. The visual power of a long, seemingly endless line of steel and chrome V-twins, surrounded by a deafening roar, descended on a nervous, unsuspecting public many years ago like the crazed, fiery stallions from the Apocalypse, and this metal-edged snowball has never stopped rolling.

The classic *Life* magazine photo of the funeral of Sacramento Hells Angels president, James "Mother" Miles, the writings of Hunter Thompson, the low-budget exploitation biker flicks of the 1960s, and even scenes in the ultramodern, slick 2003 film *Leather & Iron,* all center on the mass movement of an urban army of *implied* bad men on bad machines.

A *pack.*

In any encounter there are always strategic aspects, but nothing—*nothing*—can take the place of the fear and cold-sweat awe that is generated by sheer and overpowering *numbers.* "Bikers Take Over a Town" was the kind of official headline hook that kicked the image into gear over a half-century ago. And it worked. It sold newspapers, magazines, and drive-in movie theater tickets. Vicarious thrills are always popular. But there are degrees. Most people who are comfortable with their given niche in methodic, *normal* society aren't connected to organizations that are even *capable* of "taking over a town."

> *American Dental Association Convention Erupts Into Brutal Rioting: Drunken Hygienists Seize Eight Floors of Chicago's Palmer House*
>
> *Bourbon Street Reduced to Rubble by Knife-Wielding Rowdy Rotarians: Louisiana National Guard Called In to Take Back 'The Big Easy' From Convention Partiers in Funny Hats*

No, these headlines are never seen. And neither are the ones about bikers anymore. At least not very often. But they *could be,* and there's the difference. The media fear factor that began back in 1947 is still on a roll, precisely because the image has never changed. And it never will. Motorcycles are not for everybody. The lifestyle is not for everybody. And *everybody* knows this. But the air of mystery is profound. That is what makes the biker world so titillating. We all know how Monica stained her dress. On the other hand, most people don't have a clue as to how it feels to ride in the wind at 70 miles per hour, side-by-side in solid brotherhood with other bikers. They don't know what it's like to pull up in front of joints like Johnny's in Hollister, the All American in South Gate, The Crossroads or Cook's Corner, or any other bona fide biker bar, past or present. They've never casually parked their bike in line with all the others and comfortably strolled in for a cold one, just like in the movies.

There are 4,560,424 registered motorcycles in this country, according to the latest available stats (2001) published by the Motorcycle Safety Foundation in Irvine, California. The population of the U.S. (according to the national census conducted the year before, in 2000) was listed at 281,421,906. Simple math boils the percentage of the populace on two wheels down to around 1.6 percent. Eliminate the kids on the "crotch rockets," and the sedate "touring motorcycle enthusiasts" on their Gold Wings and the like, and you have a very, very elite group. Along with elitism go the seductive mysteries that accompany any such "secret society."

Although 1947 was a long time ago, to this day whenever Mr. and Mrs. Wholesome in the family Saturn sedan are even remotely close to a long, two-by-two procession of perceived motorcycle madness, they pray that the savages aren't hungry for even more human flesh.

IMAGE

The Boozefighters MC has fallen into one of the strangest, most oddly ironic social situations in the entire history of civilized, postindustrial human existence. They started a lifestyle that they were never really a part of. It's kind of like finding out that the Pilgrims didn't eat turkey on Thanksgiving.

Kind of . . .

Are the Boozefighters real "bikers?" Yep. They are genuine, pure, and authentic, no questions asked. But the *image* that shotgunned out of Hollister in 1947 redefined that word before it even had a chance to make Webster's, and the "biker" *definition* is the shaky social fulcrum that this whole image thing balances on. It is a definition that remains as subjective as the recipe for the perfect Bloody Mary. Following the Hollister "event," Frank Rooney's short story (*Cyclist's Raid*), and Stanley Kramer's production of *The Wild One*, however, the media's idea was forged in solid steel; the definition began to take on a life of its own.

Talking with the remaining Boozefighters "originals" is like fine-tuning an old analog tube radio. As you slowly and carefully move the dial in just the right way, suddenly all the static and fuzziness clears up. Gradually, everything becomes clear. A distorted *image* glides into straight-razor focus. Sitting face to face with surviving BFMC pioneers like Jack Lilly, Johnny and Jeannine Roccio, Gil Armas, Jim Cameron, Les Haserot, and Vern Autrey, one thing is undeniable—the Boozefighters definitely had a purpose in mind when they banded together, whether they formally voiced it or not.

Did they know that they were about to rip an enormous hole into the social fabric of America?

No.

Was their intention to flex some aggressive, post-wild-west, high-noon muscle, forcing meek and mild townspeople in small burgs everywhere to cry and beg for mercy? Did they intend to ride into town after town, swilling the mayor's finest whiskey (after kicking in his front door, of course), caging up all of the women under 25, so they could be used as cheap chattel by drunken "gang" members?

Please . . .

The originals all have one thing very much in common: They smile and they laugh. When you ask them about what "really happened" in Hollister—and the early days in general—they all get the same sheepish, kicking-the-stone grin that Opie had when Andy asked him why he put the frog in the school marm's desk drawer.

"Aw, Pa, I wuz just havin' some fun . . ."

Why did the originals climb on those bikes? Because it was fun. The *purpose* was pretty uncomplicated and basic. Did they think about seizing the shaking souls of an entire town? Did they think about the regal glory of commanding large sectors of concrete "turf?" Did they imagine their "club" as a conduit for drug peddling, violence, extortion, and gun running?

Let's revisit the first two requirements of an early Boozefighter prospect for some answers:

1. Get drunk at a race meet or cycle dance.
2. Throw lemon pie in each other's faces.

Now, unless they were communicating in some secret club code, it appears that they pretty much wanted to drink, ride motorcycles, and, yeah Pa, just have some *fun*. And it seemed like a fairly simple goal at the time. But there are many definitions of "fun." Your basic sloppy drunken pie toss didn't provide particularly good fuel for a profitable media fire, so guys like Barney Peterson, Frank Rooney, and Stanley Kramer reached into *Cap'n Billy's Whiz Bag* and came up with "trouble with a capital T" to rope in the poor, timid citizenry of River Cities everywhere.

One of the most visible events of the Hollister episode was Jim Cameron riding his Indian into Johnny's Bar. It's a bit of a stretch to imagine that this was the first act in a series of vicious, calculated strikes designed to soften up the town before the actual "take over." According to the always-smiling Jim, "I rode it into the place and leaned it against the bar. I had to have *someplace* to put it. They were pretty nice about it . . . didn't think much of it . . . just asked me to lean it against the wall instead of the bar, so people could still have room to drink. OK, no problem."

Still grinning, Jim recently commented on a present-day Boozefighter's description of the legend of Hollister: "I think you've learned it better than any of us lived it . . . " And what most people have learned is a lot about something that never happened. It's been well over 50 years since Hollister, yet present-day websites like something called *Whole Pop Magazine* still carry accounts that state: "The Hell's Angels are the biggest gang, but they were not the first. 'The Booze Fighters' (sic) were the first of a new breed of motorcyclists, the outlaw gang. During a fourth (sic) of July revelry in 1947, they lived down to their name and terrorized an agricultural town, Hollister, California, getting themselves into the news and their story eventually into the movies (*The Wild One*)."

Even the venerable Hunter Thompson lapped up the hype. In his 1966 documentary epic, *"Hell's Angels,"* Thompson talks about the predecessors of the HAMC: "Many of the Angels are graduates of other outlaw clubs . . . some of which, like the Booze Fighters (sic), were as numerous and fearsome in their time as the Angels are today. It was the Booze Fighters (sic), not the Hell's Angels, who kicked off the Hollister riot, which led to the filming of *The Wild One*."

Let's look at "numerous." In 1966, when Thompson's book was published, the Hells Angels had an estimated 463 members, based on statistics compiled by then California State Attorney General Thomas C. Lynch and other California law enforcement agencies. (This figure is also mentioned in Thompson's book.) In "their time" of 1947, the Boozefighters membership was approximately 60 members within three chapters, according to original wild one Vern Autrey. Then we come to "fearsome." The actual hand-written minutes of the Boozefighters' meeting of July 9, 1947, immediately following the "Hollister riot," were as follows: "July 9 Big meeting and a line of clatter about the rally (Hollister). Reading all about it in the papers. Big discussion on sprockets-handlebars etc. Red (Dahlgren) will be on a three months (probation). Not to miss no meetings for any reason or is to be automatically out."

The entire Hollister extravaganza was reduced to "a line of clatter" and "reading about it in the papers." Then it was on to a "big discussion" of "sprockets" and "handlebars." Oh, and by the way, Red better not miss "no meetings" again. This was sure enough an ominous powwow of "fearsome" desperados. The next month's minutes were equally terrifying: "Aug 27 (1947) Had a dandy beer bust Sat night & Sun. Plenty drunk—a good time was had by all . . . "

Frank Rooney's story had not yet been published when Riverside, California, hosted two post-Hollister motorcycle events; rallies on Labor Day of 1947, and the Fourth of July 1948. But Barney Peterson's photo had already been seen by most of America. Fertile seeds of dread instilled into "normal, God-fearing citizens" were already beginning to sprout and spread. The beast was alive!

The two Riverside events are often confused with one another, probably because they were held so close together and because they both occurred within a year of Hollister. Street racing, some fighting, and a lot of drinking in the local bars were certainly a part of both of these wingdings in Southern California's "Inland Empire," but the second event, Fourth of July 1948, really got the presses rolling.

RIVERSIDE AGAIN RAIDEDBY GANG: ONE DEAD, 54 ARRESTED AS MOTORCYCLISTS STAGE RIOTS

This article featured what has become the second most famous photo ever connected with the Boozefighters: Vern Autrey and "Fat Boy" Nelson sitting on their parked bikes drinking bottles of beer. Teri Forkner was perched behind "Fat Boy." The caption read:

CYCLISTS TAKE OVER TOWN — As townspeople watch from the relative safety of the sidewalk, three motorcyclists whose sweaters read "Boozefighters Motorcycle Club," stop for a beer on one of Riverside's (Calif.) streets. More that 2,000 cyclists, in town for racing at a nearby track, took over the town and rode wildly about the streets. With one dead and 54 arrested in the second outbreak of rowdyism by motorcyclists in 11 months, Sheriff Carl F. Rayburn said he will sponsor no more motorcycle races in Riverside.

Okay, except that the picture wasn't taken in Riverside. Teri, the late wife of Wino Willie, was quick to identify the photo as having been taken in Hollister. "We were proud of that picture," she said, "but we were ticked off that it wasn't used in the *San Francisco Chronicle* story or in *Life* magazine, instead of that other picture that was staged with the drunk on the bike with the beer in each hand. This picture was actually taken in Hollister, July 4, 1947."

And the photo definitely made the rounds within the "biker as beast" press.

The December 1957 issue of the gossip tabloid *Top Secret* featured some pretty eminent literary landmarks, like *"SHOCKING NEWS FROM THE A-LABS: HUMAN SPERMS FOR SURVIVAL,"* and *"WHY NEGRO WOMEN SAY . . . 'WHITE MEN ARE BETTER LOVERS.' "*

The magazine also included a "hot" exposé of high-profile, high-priced society call girl Pat Ward. Among her tawdry attributes was the fact that she was—gasp—a "biker!" Much of the text in the article, I believe, was ripe for a Pulitzer. This is serious literature. Pat Ward's former lover, Manny Trujillo—described as an "admitted spy, a former loyal student at a Communist Party school, and a black-leather-jacketed tough"—had a lot to say concerning his former "ol' lady":

> "She wouldn't bathe for days on end," he declares. "When she stayed in my place, the room smelled like something had died." Manny claims that Pat was a violent nymphomaniac, an insatiable lover who delighted in engaging in weird sexual acts. Whenever Trujillo refused—or was unable—to satisfy Pat's raging lust, the girl went into fits of screaming fury."

Naturally the only picture in the entire universe that could go along with the acrid spice of *Top Secret's* article was—yep—the recycled shot of Teri, "Fat Boy," and Vern. But this time the Boozefighters logo on the jackets had been surgically removed with whatever photographic technology an upper-echelon outfit like *Top Secret* had available to them at the time. And then there were those little, clandestine, taboo '50s "blackout" strips applied across the eyes of the villains, so as to not reveal the true identity of the devil himself. The caption above the picture dug deep into Hades: " . . . motorcycle gang of typical speed demons."

Sure! The very same "demons" that "took over" Riverside!

Well, not exactly . . .

On July 17, 1948, Roger L. Abbott, undersheriff of Riverside County, released a notarized open letter to any and all news and press outlets concerning what *really* happened at the second "Riverside riot." I've not tampered with Undersheriff Abbott's document in any way—no grammatical corrections, nothing—this is his letter, pure, straight ahead:

As beautiful and cultured Riverside, painfully emerges torn and bleeding from the wreckage and devastation of a three day 4th of July celebration of several thousand motorcycle enthusiasts attending the Novice, Amateur, and National Championship 100 mile motorcycle races held under the auspices of the Riverside County Sheriff's Training Center, Incorporated, sponsored by the Bombers Motorcycle Club of Riverside and sanctioned by the American Motorcycle Association, one asks, "just what is the extent of damage caused by these hoodlums and tramps, these uncivilized demons, who ride exploding and fire-belching machines of destruction with abandon, hell-bent on destroying the property and persons of Riverside citizens, according to the newspapers?"

Well, an awning got torn on a down-town business house. A city park plunge office was entered and a flashlight stolen. Swimming suits were left lying on the bottom of the plunge. Motorcyclists? Maybe.

An automobile, driven by an impatient citizen was set upon by victims and their friends who resented being knocked down by this car and its driver when it was driven into their midst for failing to yield the right of way. The body of the car was dented and some of its glass was broken.

A bottle fell or was dropped out of a hotel window, a man's wallet was taken from his pocket, and three motorcycles were reported stolen, one of which has been recovered.

A city park official got a bloody nose during an altercation with a motorcyclist who wanted to sleep in the park, and who had imbibed too freely. This motorcyclist submitted peacefully to arrest by an officer and has plead not guilty to charges of assault and battery. The courts must decide on the issues involved.

That is the official total of damage to persons and property in what the newspapers have screamed nationally to be "a weekend of terror, resulting from an invasion of Riverside by hoodlums and their molls on motorcycles rioting in the streets and wrecking the city."

In order to clinch the matter, and to make sure that the wire services would carry the story to the entire nation, the news articles added the spicy bit that, "the invasion left forty-nine arrested and one killed." It was convenient to omit, for the sake of sensationalism, that this one person killed in all of Riverside County on that week-end was nearly a hundred miles from Riverside at the time he ran into a bridge abutment on the highway and was killed and at the time he ran into the abutment, according to authentic reports, was not going to or from the Rally in Riverside. As a matter of police record, there were no traffic accidents in the City of Riverside from Saturday afternoon July 3rd at 4:05 o'clock until Monday afternoon July 5th at 1:15 o'clock. There were no accidents at any time during the entire week-end in the city in which motorcycles were involved. It is doubtful if many cities of fifty thousand inhabitants in the nation can boast of such a record over that week-end.

Forty-nine persons arrested! Well, almost—46 to be factual, and 8.7 percent of these were Riverside residents.

These people came to Riverside that weekend on a holiday. Some of them took on a too heavy cargo of beer and other drinks—and having become uninhibited, performed obediently for the hundreds of Riverside citizens who had come out of their homes to enjoy the fun. When the police decided it was time to put an end to the confusion and noise, they simply walked in and ordered the celebrants to disperse. If they could not, they were arrested and lodged in jail—if they did not, they were arrested for failure to disperse. Thirty minutes, and the job was accomplished. A number were arrested throughout the weekend for shooting fireworks, intoxication, drinking in public, and disturbing the peace. These were the methods used by the police to control the situation.

The following arrests have been used by news articles to point the finger of shame at Riverside's seduction, violation, and disgrace:

Drinking in public, 4 persons arrested

Drunk, 8 persons arrested

Drunk Driving, (motorcycle) 2 persons arrested

Drunk Driving, (automobile) 1 person arrested

Shooting Fireworks, 9 persons arrested

Disturbing the Peace, 12 persons arrested

Assault and Battery, 1 person arrested

Failure to Disperse, 8 persons arrested

Interfering with an Officer, 1 person arrested

Total, 46 persons arrested

This tabulation indicates that the Riverside Police Department had control of the situation at all times and acted with effective efficiency.

The State Forestry did not enter into the enforcement program but did drive a pickup truck through town on their way to an assignment.

Contrary to newspaper sensationalism on a national scale—Sheriff Rayburn did not invite the motorcycle fraternity to Riverside. It was the Riverside County Sheriff's Training Center Inc., the members of which are full time deputy sheriffs and who hold such a fund raising event each year to construct and maintain a training center with training facilities where officers of the Sheriff's Department and other law enforcement agencies of the County of Riverside can receive training for their jobs.

Sheriff Rayburn did not get his "trousers torn off in the riots of motorcycle raiders."

Sheriff Rayburn did not say he "would never invite the motorcycle fraternity back to Riverside again."

To say that the news services have been guilty of gross exaggeration and sensationalism in their presentation of this 4th of July week-end and last Labor Day week-end in Riverside is an understatement. However, they may be given consideration on the basis that such news balloons are often set adrift by young, inexperienced, overzealous and perhaps frightened newspaper reporters who are correspondents for large metropolitan newspapers and have wire service at their disposal. I am certain it was not, or is not, the intent of the vast majority of news editors throughout the nation to condone such reporting as they well know the practice of it would bring them into the same ill repute, good and bad alike, that the motorcycle sport now is burdened with.

In spite of all this, however, law enforcement cannot condone the unlawful acts of the few, which bring discredit to the many through unfavorable publicity, exaggerated or not.

Certainly the American Motorcycle Association recognized motorcycle clubs and the "outlaw" motorcycle clubs should reach an understanding to ensure the future of motorcycle sports without making the host city the victim of ill-will between those clubs.

Certainly stricter concentrated enforcement and education must be undertaken to eliminate the use of devices intended to increase rather than decrease exhaust noise. It was this irritating noise made by a liberal estimate of perhaps one hundred motorcycles, which sound caused the din, some of these no doubt, normally would have not done this had it been the American custom to celebrate Independence Day with all the noise possible.

The use of streets and highways for drag races and other motorcycle games must be abandoned.

Most of the arrests were made in the downtown area while three thousand of the motorcyclists were several miles out of twon [*sic*] enjoying clean healthy games and contests sanctioned by the American Motorcycle Association. It cannot be overlooked that not a single arrest was necessary at the track either day of the races or at the night field meet.

In view of the reports received through the mail our sympathy is extended to the thousands of dealers throughout the nation whose life savings are affected and to worthwhile clubs who are suffering and in some cases quite badly from the injustice of the reports.

Definitely, a change in attitude and acts of the one percent of irresponsible, intemperate and sometimes vulgar motorcyclist hiding behind the cloak of decency of the ninety-nine per cent of motorcyclists must be accomplished.

In reviewing the evidence developed in this report one is compelled to acknowledge that the nation-wide sensational publicity given the 4th of July week-end in Riverside, California was neither honest nor factual—but will in all likelihood hasten the day of a clean name for motorcycling and honest press reporting.

(This article may be used for news or publication purposes)

(signed)

Roger L. Abbott

Undersheriff

Riverside County, California

(notarized)

Alrighty then . . . Seems like ol' Sheriff Roger wasn't particularly pleased about having his town (or as his old manual typewriter put it, *twon* . . .), and the good citizens of Riverside, being made into yet another field of poor, helpless grunion, flopping aimlessly and unprotected as the evil, heavy-booted bikers marched along the shore, stuffing them into buckets, only to be devoured later at some depraved bacchanalian orgy and drooling feast.

"*CYCLISTS TAKE OVER TOWN*"? Nope . . . just didn't happen. . . .

But let's go back to that *image* thing. One image was good for business, depending on the business you were in. And like a lot of businesses, the nuts and bolts are screwed together behind the scenes while the little people go on about their daily lives. Wander into your local grocery and ask the first person you see who's pushing a cart load of things like milk, bread, and a twelver of Bud, just what the NASDAQ mark is up or down to on the stock exchange today.

The same kind of thing was dead-on true in the early world of the biker. As one faction (the media . . .) began to turn the wheels of the commercial *image*, the people who actually made the whole shebang work (the real bikers) were living the *truth*, not acting out the more sensational *fiction*. The actual playing out of the media creation unfortunately came later. After the damage had been done. The original truth was all about *fun*. Fun that can sometimes get a bit messy, like a pie in the face. Fun that can even get somewhat out of hand, like when the rodeo clown gets a pretty good whack from a bus-sized, aggravated bull. But a pie is still a pie, and a clown is still a clown—we're not talkin' guns and SWAT teams here. Problem is that splattered lemon meringue and red noses don't sell the way mayhem and destruction do.

As I sat with some of the originals at Jack Lilly's home in the California desert—not far from where all the Riverside "activity" occurred—a strong,

Riverside Again Raided by Gang

One Dead, 54 Arrested as Motorcyclists Stage Riots

Riverside, Calif. —(AP)— As the last of "those wild motorcycle boys" chugged off, citizens of Riverside began sweeping their way today out of the dust and debris.

Sighs of relief were audible on all sides, but perhaps the loudest came from Sheriff Carl F. Rayburn, sponsor of the three-day meet which disrupted the city.

"That's the last time I'm inviting the motorcycle crowd," said the sheriff. "I don't think it's a good thing for a little town like Riverside."

Sheriff Rayburn, however, placed the blame on "a bunch of crazy kids," and said American Motorcycle association members were not responsible for the wild riding down main streets and fist throwing in sundry bars.

When the 2,000 cyclists departed, the box score stood one dead, one injured and 54 arrested.

The A.M.A. 100-mile tough track race on the Box Springs course was won by Ed Kretz of Wilmar, Calif.

The winner's time was two hours, 26 minutes and 2:15 seconds, which seemed a short race to some residents after the impromptu series of street dashes Saturday and Sunday nights.

Flying beer bottles, firecrackers and fists punctured near riots which brought all available police and sheriff's officers into action.

It was the second time in a year that Riverside dug itself out after a motorcycle invasion. Last Labor day two were killed, 15 injured and more than a score arrested.

CYCLISTS TAKE OVER TOWN—As townspeople watch from the relative safety of the sidewalk, three motorcyclists whose sweaters read "Boozefighters Motorcycle Club," stop for a beer on one of Riverside's (Calif.) streets. More than 2,000 cyclists, in town for racing at a nearby track, took over the town and rode wildly about the streets. With one dead and 54 arrested in the second outbreak of rowdyism by motorcyclists in 11 months, Sheriff Carl F. Rayburn said he will sponsor no more motorcycle races in Riverside. (AP wirephoto)

"Cyclists Take Over Town" during yet another riot—according to the media. The picture, supposedly of the Riverside incident, was actually taken in Hollister, according to Teri Forkner.

Told here for the first time is the inside story of a shadowy vagrant who tried to frame Cafe Society's notorious C-girl

"Manny" was — and is — Emmanuel Trujillo, an admitted spy, a former loyal student at a Communist Party school, and a black leather-jacketed tough who, until recently, was the swaggering boss of a dangerous American Nazi organization!

SIX WEEKS WITH PAT

"Mickey Jelke made me entertain men for money," Pat Ward testified in court. She gave her testimony in such a manner as to imply that she had been an inexperienced, innocent child led into a life of sin by the oleo-margarine-fortune heir.

Emmanuel Trujillo, with whom Pat lived in sin for six weeks in a dingy, rundown New York City tenement apartment, describes her much differently.

"She wouldn't bathe for days on end," he declares. "When she stayed in my place, the room smelled like something had died."

Manny claims that Pat was a violent nymphomaniac, an insatiable lover who delighted in engaging in weird sexual acts. Whenever Trujillo refused — or was unable — to satisfy Pat's raging lust, the girl went into fits of screaming fury.

"She walked around in front of my friends in the nude," he says. "If I didn't go to bed with her whenever she wanted, she would shriek and throw ashtrays and whatever else was available at me . . ."

Emmanuel Trujillo, who is a motorcycling enthusiast, one of those young toughs who drive their "bikes" at full

(Continued on Page 41)

During one of his rare appearances in the limelight (wearing a business suit with a tie for a change), Trujillo is shown (at left) with Lieutenant Dan O'Keefe of the District Attorney's office. At right, motorcycle gang of typical speed demons.

The December 1957 issue of the tabloid Top Secret *featured a scathing story about a call girl who was also a "biker." To epitomize biker trash, the magazine used a ten-year-old photo of Teri Forkner, Vern Autrey, and Fat Boy Nelson.*

warm breeze was dropping down from the foothills, stirring things up along the flats. It was the perfect ambient atmosphere to begin to twist time into reverse, the ideal raw setting to explore the foul and sleazy truth about how over 50 years ago a "motorcycle gang of typical speed demons" took over yet another quiet, peace-loving town of meek, God-fearing, once-happy *Father Knows Best* families, shattering their innocence, burning their Christmas trees, carving vile graffiti into the fine paint on their new DeSotos, and laughing like Attila the Hun while the blood of murdered children ran ankle deep through the streets.

"I remember when we first got there," recalled Jack. "The first couple of guys that got drunk—I think it might have been Wino and John Davis—well, they had this douche bag they filled with wine. They were walkin' down the middle of the street—they just stopped traffic and were walkin' down the middle—one of them holdin' the bag, the other had the 'nozzle' in his mouth . . .

"And we had this big water drum with us, carried it in the old Model T pick-up with the trailer that used to go with us on all our runs. The drum had three Xs painted on it. At first I thought some of the guys brought some water for drinking, but they never drank water. Then I thought it might have been for washing, but they didn't wash either."

"It was filled with wine!" said Johnny Roccio.

Jack Lilly nodded and smiled at Johnny. As he continued to relive the Riverside run I thought of a line from Charlie Brechtel's tribute tune to Wino Willie—*"They rode them old motor-sickles, didn't need no car . . ."*—the definition of a "real" biker.

"We got to Riverside," Jack remembered. "Havin' a good time, and I stayed too long. My wife was waiting for me up in Idyllwild. She'd given me a deadline to make it before dark 'cause I had a pretty weak battery on my VL. I could a bought a battery, too, 'cause I was workin' at the time, but I always tried to nurse these damned old batteries. I'd buy Electro-lites at Western Auto, and I'd nurse them along, charging them for a couple of days, put them back in my motorcycle. First time I'd use them at night, you could see the light just shrinkin' back into it, so I'd have to follow a car with bright lights."

"Just like my old Knucklehead!" said Johnny.

"Same thing, huh? Why they'd build a motorcycle with a 2-amp generator and it took 10 amps to run the damn headlight, I'll never know.

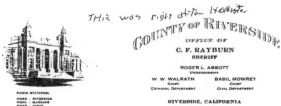

THIS was right after Hollister.

COUNTY OF RIVERSIDE
OFFICE OF
C. F. RAYBURN
SHERIFF

ROGER L. ABBOTT
UNDERSHERIFF

W. W. WALRATH
CHIEF
CRIMINAL DEPARTMENT

BASIL MOWREY
CHIEF
CIVIL DEPARTMENT

RADIO STATIONS:
KQPC · RIVERSIDE
KQHL · BANNING
KQAD · INDIO
KERO · BOX SPRINGS
KIDO · BLYTHE

RIVERSIDE, CALIFORNIA

July 17, 1948

As beautiful and cultured Riverside, painfully emerges torn and bleeding from the wreckage and devastation of a three day 4th of July celebration of several thousand motorcycle enthusiasts attending the Novice, Amateur, and National Championship 100 mile motorcycle races held under the auspices of the Riverside County Sheriff's Training Center, Incorporated., sponsored by the Bombers Motorcycle Club of Riverside and sanctioned by the American Motorcycle Association, one asks, "just what is the extent of damage caused by these hoodlums and tramps, these uncivilized demons, who ride exploding and fire-belching machines of destruction with abandon, hell-bent on destroying the property and persons of Riverside citizens, according to the newspapers?"

"Well, an awning got torn on a down-town business house. A city park plunge office was entered and a flashlight stolen. Swimming suits were left lying on the bottom of the plunge. Motorcyclists? Maybe.

An automobile, driven by an impatient citizen was set upon by victims and their friends who resented being knocked down by this car and its driver when it was driven into their midst for failing to yield the right of way. The body of the car was dented and some of its glass was broken.

A bottle fell or was dropped out of a hotel window, a man's wallet was taken from his pocket, and three motorcycles were reported stolen, one of which has been recovered.

A city park official got a bloody nose during an altercation with a motorcyclist who wanted to sleep in the park, and who had imbibed too freely. This motorcyclist submitted peacefully to arrest by an officer and has plead not guilty to charges of assault and battery. The courts must decide on the issue involved.

That is the official total of damage to persons and property in what the newspapers have screamed nationally to be "a week-end of terror, resulting from an invasion of Riverside by hoodlums and their molls on motorcycles rioting in the streets and wrecking the city".

In order to clinch the matter, and to make sure that the wire services would carry the story to the entire nation, the news articles added the spicy bit that, "the invasion left forty-nine arrested and one killed". It was convenient to omit, for the sake of sensationalism, that this one person killed in all of Riverside County on that week-end was nearly a hundred miles from Riverside at the time he ran into a bridge abutment on the highway and was killed and at the time he ran into the abutment, according to authentic reports, was not going to or from the Rally in Riverside. As a matter of police record,

ADDRESS ALL COMMUNICATIONS TO THE SHERIFF

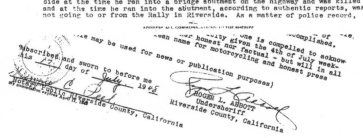

... e may be used for news or publication purposes)

Subscribed and sworn to before me
this ___ day of _____ 19 4 8

Notary Public, Riverside County, California
My commission expires April 11, 19

ROGER L. ABBOTT
Undersheriff
Riverside County, California

The July 17, 1948, letter from Riverside Undersheriff Roger L. Abbott presented quite a different picture of the Riverside "riot."

Anyway, I stayed way too late. I took off at dusk. I got halfway up the hill and the lights went out. I don't know if you've been up Idyllwild grade—if you have you know how twisty it is. Well, you don't want to go up there when there's no moon, no stars, and no headlight! I finally gave up and found a wide spot and pulled off. I thought, 'I'll sit here and wait for a car.' So here comes a car, and the son of a gun was a speed demon. I said, 'Hell, I can't catch *him*. I'll wait for the next one.' The next one came along and I followed him for a while, but all of a sudden he speeds up and leaves me. I wait for another one and the same thing happened. I finally figure that I was scaring the hell outta these people. They'd hear the sound of a motorcycle but couldn't see me following them! So they'd just speed off!"

"You shoulda waited for a truck!" said Johnny. "A loaded one!"

"I did! Finally! It was a pickup with a load of wood or something that he was taking up the hill . . . and *he* couldn't outrun me. Followed him all the way up the hill 'til the road splits at the end of town, where my wife was waiting for me in this nice cabin she had borrowed from a friend for the weekend. And she had fire in her eyes. Here it was about nine or ten o'clock, and I was supposed to be there before dark to take her out to dinner, but it took me forever to get up that hill in the dark!"

Evidently Jack left just before the remaining *"Cyclists Take Over Town,"* but he vividly remembers the barbaric ride into Riverside: hordes of cruel Boozefighters storming the gates of this placid Southern California community, teeth undoubtedly filed to fine points to more easily tear into human flesh, coal-black souls and hearts bursting with depraved lust.

"We all dyed our hair bright red. Well, not all of us—me and 'Red Dog' already had red hair—but everybody else, all the other guys, the ones with brown hair, and blond hair, and so on, all suddenly had really bright red hair. Here's this whole group ridin' down the highway, a sea of red, following this Model T Ford pickup truck with our club trailer hooked to it. I don't understand how they got enough power outta that thing to pull that trailer—the Model T had like 20 horsepower brand new, I think—and that was about an 18- or 20-foot trailer with our bunks in it and that goofy water drum filled with wine up on the roof."

Johnny's wife, Jeannine, also remembered the 1947–1948 version of the evil Trojan Horse: "The trailer . . . *the* trailer . . . with the bunks . . . they had several bunks they built into it so the drunks could lay in there and dry out . . . and they had cases and cases of beer underneath . . . "

All of the originals have fond memories of the trailer. "They had bunks built into it so the drunks could lay in there and dry out," said Jeannine Roccio. "And they had cases and cases of beer underneath."

Their arrival must have looked like Hannibal crossing the Alps . . . you could just sense the pending carnage in the air.

"There was one little hamburger stand that caught our attention as we rode into town," said Jack, "because just past the hamburger joint there was a vacant lot where we could park the trailer. Well, on the way to the lot, the trailer got a flat. Just so happened that in the lot there was a piece of road equipment of some kind so, naturally, we just swapped the wheels from the trailer and the road equipment, and everything was fine. Another thing I don't understand, though, was why we had those little Model T wheels and tires on that trailer in the first place. How they held up that trailer, the bunks, and all that beer is still a mystery."

"The truck," added Johnny, "had a 2-by-12 for the seat, just a piece of wood, and they pounded 16-penny nails through that thing that would stick up just a little bit when you sat on it. And underneath it they had it hooked up to the coil. And if they didn't like you or something or wanted to be funny they'd pull a switch and you'd definitely jump off that SOB. It was a real jolt! They'd pull all kinds of stuff like that!"

Except, evidently, "stuff" like taking over a town. I guess things like bright red hair and electric seats were just a lot more *fun.*

IMAGE

The genesis of the biker lifestyle was born very innocently into a restless world that apparently needed some fear served up with its smiles. Or at least the media thought it did.

Jack, Johnny, Jeannine, Wino and all the rest of the originals seemed to have a little bit better grasp on the truth, a better grasp on just what constituted real fun, a better grasp on the definition—*and the image*—of a real "biker."

CHAPTER 4

The Tale Of Vern Autrey, the "Shanghai Red" Bar, Too Much Fun at the All-American, Gas Girls, Cold Feet in the Stove, "The Toughest Corner in the World," and Teri and Wino's Bathroom

The founding Boozefighters—the original wild ones—definitely had an aura that primarily focused on good-natured fun, with all of the serious, antisocietal criminal behavior of, say, Spanky and Alfalfa with a pack of firecrackers.

However, there was never a question that they were tough. The entire generation that emerged from World War II was. They had to be. Just a look into the faces of FDR, Truman, or Eisenhower sets the tone for the times. It took a very hard line to land at Normandy, blast through the Pacific theater, and then come home to fire up a flathead or a Knuckle, grab a frosty Pabst, and head for the sunset.

But there is a special turn in the legends that surround BFMC members Dink Burns and Vern Autrey: They were *real* tough.

Robert "Dink" Burns gave both of his legs to the cause of freedom in 1942 when the naval ship he was serving on was blown up and sunk. But he never stopped riding. Through the use of some extremely creative 1940s-era artificial limbs, he and his Triumph and Arial motorcycles were regulars at the "Big A." Understandably, though, his attitude was a bit edgy after the war, and "Dink" became notorious for a temper that was somewhat less than tolerant.

Then there was Vern Autrey.

Then there was Vern Autrey. All of the toughness of the times, and all of the pure, no-BS grit and determination of an entire generation seemed to reach out from Vern.

All of the toughness of the times, all of the pure, no-BS grit and determination of an entire generation seemed to reach out from Vern. He had the stature of a white 1940s-style middleweight boxer, the kind that just aren't around anymore. You could almost see him as a younger man, sweaty and muscular, sipping water in his ring corner between rounds.

I felt a special affinity for Vern. He knew my Uncle "Bub," an unique name for an unique man. My uncle rode his Indians and Knucks all over the Long Beach area, just around the southern port end of San Pedro, just south of South Gate where the Boozefighters began. Vern remembered my uncle, even recalled where he worked. Those were tight-knit times. If you rode, you generally knew the others who did, too. Early in our conversation Vern showed me a picture of himself on the way to Hollister in 1947. The photo grabbed 'hold of me like a meat hook to the back.

The snapshot, black-and-white, of course, showed Vern with that cool 1940s hair blowing in the wind, the bike in motion, flying down the road, on his way to the turning point in the biker culture, scooting along a cow-path-looking thoroughfare that was one of the main drags into Hollister. Riding into history.

Although the All American Bar was their favorite hangout, some of the original Boozefighters occasionally found their way to other swanky lounges like Shanghai Red, a seriously tense joint at 5th and Beacon along the waterfront jungle of San Pedro. Having a drink in there often proved to be like living out the lyrics to "Frankie & Johnnie" and "Staggerlee" all at once.

"I was havin' a beer at the bar," recalled Vern. "This guy was sittin' next to me. In walks this babe, she pulls out a gun and shoots him three times! 'You'll never cheat on me again,' she yells as he's slumpin' over! Guess she was right.

"Another time some guy found a human head in a locker in the back room there. After all that we pretty much got the hell outta there! But ol'

The Shanghai Red bar, a "seriously tense joint" located at 5th and Beacon near the waterfront in San Pedro.

'Pedro (always pronounced 'peed-row') Roy, he was the head of the Boozefighters in San Pedro. Bald-headed guy, longshoreman—a strong SOB, looked like Marciano—all he had was his motorcycle. Rode it everywhere he went. I asked him one time, 'Don't you have a car?' 'I don't use them glass houses,' he says, 'I use my motorcycle.'

"Yeah, ol' 'Pedro Roy, he was somethin' else, and he was kind of a mean sumbitch, too. I asked him one time, 'Hey, where do you guys hang out down there?' He says, 'Well, we don't have any one place special. We do go to Shanghai Red a lot though . . . ' I said, 'That's far enough!'

"All those 'Pedro longshoremen, they'd all hang out together, and they were all pretty tough, but not a better bunch of guys you ever met in your life, man, give you anything, you know, no matter what it was."

The spirit of brotherhood was intense in Vern's eyes when he relived the early days of the biker lifestyle. He displayed a vitality that showed no age at all. And that's because this spirit—*his* spirit, the spirit of brotherhood, the spirit of the original wild ones, the essence of the biker culture—is timeless. It's a holy, ingrained potent part of the American ethos that is big and powerful. The love for the freedom that comes with being a part of this extraordinary and wholly inimitable way of living is synonymous with that rare rugged desire for adventure on the outside. Vern is a special man, a pioneer in a special way of life.

"And then we had a bar across the street from the Hollywood Park racetrack on Prairie there," Vern recalls. "The guy who owned it, he called it the Corral. It was a little beer bar. We'd ride from the All American to there once a week on the weekends and drink with those guys down there. Those guys were mostly 'Pedro guys. Then they'd come to the All American as a group, you know.

"There was 20 Boozefighters in 'Pedro, 20 in L.A., and 20 in 'Frisco, and that was about it. 'Frisco would come down to the races with us. Really they'd come down to race *us*! And our *sickles*!"

The absolute "genuine biker" aspect of Vern was now in high gear as he spoke. Like any extremely rare insight into something that is totally without pretension, there was no way to separate the original wild ones from their machines.

Boutique bike shops and expensive designer t-shirts were not yet considered obligatory connections to the biker lifestyle. Riding, however, still was. Knowing their *sickle* was.

"C. B. (Clausen), he didn't have a cradle frame Harley," explained Vern. "He had a hill-climber Harley—they're just a single frame. They only made about 10 of them. Well, he got hold of one and put a stroker motor in it, an 80, and he'd ride it once in a while when we'd go somewhere. But Sleepy, who was in the Boozefighters, he had the next one C. B. built, the stroker, and I had the one from Burrhead. When Burrhead retired I bought his. When the guys from 'Frisco and down south would come to race us I'd always be the one to race 'em 'cause I was always the third one in line. If I got beat, then the plan was to turn them on to Sleepy, and then on to C. B. 'cause they'd never be able to beat C. B. But I never got beat, so we didn't have to worry about it!

"C. B. was the first one to ever hit upon strokers. Nobody had a stroker. They'd come down from 'Frisco just to *look* at it. Then they'd say to me, 'Can we look at your motor?' 'Yeah,' I'd say, 'You can *look* at it—that's all—*look* at it.'

"Then it'd be parked out front and they'd ask me, 'Hey, when you gonna leave?' I'd tell 'em, 'Pretty soon,' and they'd wait around 'til I was ready to go and they'd say, 'Hey, hook that sumbitch on down that street right there, would ya?' And I'd lift the front end of that SOB and haul ass down that street, and they'd just shake their heads. They'd bring a motor, too. They weren't foolin' nobody, neither—they had a pickup truck with a motor on it, you know, all stripped down and ready to go, but they didn't want none of that stroker!

"That sumbitch was fast! I could get off a signal with my girlfriend on the back and I'd lift that front wheel from here to way down there, let it down, burn rubber in second gear with it. That SOB was a bad motor scooter!"

And some things just never change. Someone in the bar where Vern and I were sitting mentioned something about a Vincent Black Shadow. Vern's ears perked up like a sharp cat waking up at midnight to the sound of a potential snack.

"A Vincent Black Shadow? I nearly bought one of those just about 10 years ago, in fact. I saw it in the paper and I talked to the guy. I said, 'What is it . . . a Lightning or what?' 'No, it's a Black Shadow,' he says. I says, 'Well I want it!' He says, 'Well I got a guy comin' over . . . ' I says, 'Hey, I'm in L.A., you're in San Diego, I'm not comin' all the way down there without a promise.' He said, 'OK, I'll tell him it's sold and come on down.'

"Well, I jump on my damn bike and haul ass on down there. Right before I got to his street a motor went by me and I thought, 'That sumbitch sounded like a Black Shadow!' Well anyway, the house was only about a half block down . . . I get there and the sucker had sold the damn thing!'

"But I raced a Black Shadow goin' to Texas one time. I didn't have that stroker but I had a 74, all stripped down with 19-inch wheels on it, all ready to go to Daytona. Well, about 100 miles this side of Austin I was parked by a tree drinkin' a Coke and this guy rides up. 'What's a matter?' he asks. I said, 'Nothin.' He says, 'Oh. You goin' into Austin?' I said, 'Yeah, I'm just gettin' out of this seat for a while.' 'Yeah, I am, too,' he says. 'Do you know where the motorcycle shop is in Austin?' 'No, I never been there,' I says. Then he says, 'Man, that's a good lookin' Harley you got there!' I had it all stripped down, you know, painted red with all the good stuff on it. Well, I was about ready to go and he says, 'Hey, how about the first guy into the motorcycle shop buys all the beer?'

"And I says, 'Huh! You're on!' He says, 'OK . . . ' And I hooked that sumbitch on. It was actually a 68, a de-stroker that was awesome off the line! I took off and I wound that sumbitch out, ripped second, third, looked behind me figuring this SOB was probably a mile behind, looked behind and he was right on my ass. When I got into high gear he comes along beside me, 'See ya at the motorcycle shop!' Wham, that sumbitch took off and I never did see him again 'til we got to the motorcycle shop! Boy, you talk about a motatin' sumbitch in high gear!

"I didn't know that much about them Black Shadows but I did after that! They were wicked sumbitches, they'd just start to run at about a hundred miles an hour."

"I rode all the way to Daytona all by myself that year," Vern continued. "All I had was a flight jacket from the war. It rained hard all the way in and outta there, and I had this bobbed rear fender. All the rain and sand and stuff coming up that back tire took and cut this jacket right in half. Had to throw it away when I got down there."

"In those days we'd be drinkin' in the All American and some guy would say, 'Hey, let's go to Tijuana for a ham sandwich.' 'Let's go!' 'Bout 10 or 15 of us would jump on our bikes, ride down the coast highway all the way to Tijuana. Sit there, eat a couple of tacos, get four or five beers, mess with the girls, turn around and go back. We'd ride all the way back. Some of us would pull in front of the All American and sleep on our bikes 'til the bar opened, then we'd go in there and start drinkin' again.

"Now Cookie, who owned the All American, he was a hell of a guy. He put up with a lot of crap. I don't know how he did it as I look back. But he lived in a little house out back of the bar. And the storeroom is where we had all our meetings. Ol' Cookie, he had the will power of steel to put up with us. We'd be in a big fight in there and we'd knock the brand new jukebox over on the floor. He'd kind of look at it and sigh, 'Well, I'll just order another one . . .' He wouldn't get excited.

"There were a lot of guys from Hollywood and stuff like that, they'd hear about the All American and they'd come down there but they wouldn't stay in there very long. We'd run their asses out. We'd ask, 'Who are you?' 'Oh, we're from Hollywood. We just want to see what's goin' on around here.' 'Well, see it from the *outside* . . . now!'

"And the sheriff's substation was on Alameda down there, a couple of miles down the road. And whenever we'd start to fightin' we'd start inside and then it would always spill outside. The All American was on the corner, and Manchester was a hell of a busy street. Well, we'd be fightin' like sumbitches and then it'd be over as quick as it started, and everything was fine and here comes the cops with about four squad cars and night sticks and everything. They'd say, 'Where's the fight?' We'd tell 'em, 'Hell, it's all over. Everyone went to the hospital.' And we'd hear the cops say, 'Well, Goddamn it, that's the only time we have any fun, when we come down here and there's a fight!'

"We'd leave the All American on a Saturday and go to hill climbs in a real exclusive part of town where there was a big hill. And we'd hill climb like sumbitches on our bikes, then we'd get through and take off and hit Inglewood. One time I looked around and everyone was ahead of me. I could see one bike way up there. So I take off to catch 'em and this broad in a car pulls out and center-punches me. Broke my nose, broke both my thumbs, broke my ankle. I'm laying there bleedin' and this woman from the drive-in across the street brings out this blanket and puts it underneath my head and everything and here comes ol' Fat Boy Nelson—he was stragglin' behind—so here comes Fat Boy and he sees all this. He comes up and I'm layin' there bleedin,' he comes up and kicks me! 'Get up you sonofabitch, you ain't hurt. We got a lot of drinkin' to do down here!' And that woman with the blanket got so damned mad. She said to Fat Boy, 'What are you doin' there? I'll call the cops and have you locked up! Don't be kickin' him!' I said, 'Leave him alone! He's a friend of mine!' 'Oh my God . . .' she says.

"But in those days everything was kinda laid back, you know. You didn't make a big thing outta anything. Like when I went to the hospital that night they cut my brand new pair of boots off—had 'em custom made, too—and my windbreaker was all full of blood. But I got out and we all just went around to the bars drinkin'. I didn't have any boots or jacket but it just wasn't any big thing. We did it every day!"

"The All American was in a line of industrial buildings. George Manker worked in a machine shop near there—he's the guy who invented and patented the convex rear-view mirror. Tex & Art's motorcycle shop was right next to the All American. Across the street was the Bluebird Café, where we used to burn circles on Manchester. When we'd get tired of drinking beer we'd go across the street and drink Sauterne wine. That's where Jimmy Cameron got burned up on his motorcycle. That's where he got it. It didn't have a gas cap on it and we was burnin' circles, and somethin' happened and it burned the hell outta him.

"And then there was Signal Hill. I used to have a gas station right there on the corner, on Cherry. I remember Curly's bar, too. We used to go there. That was the only place where you could get your check cashed. Once Curly knew you, well, he really didn't have to know you. He'd cash your check anyway. But if you cashed a bum check on him he'd send some-body after you. You only did that once! That was a famous place, but there was another bar just before you got to Curly's on the opposite side. My gas station was near there on the corner before you got to Pacific Coast. In those days it was considered pretty risqué even if you had some gal unbut-ton her blouse in an ad or something. Well, I used to hire these broads with big boobs with no bras out there fillin' guys' tanks. So here comes the city management with the cops. The district attorney puts me in jail. But every time the girls filled the gas tanks I had a roll of tickets by the pump, and the girl would bend over and get a ticket for the guy. At the end of every month we'd have a drawing—the prize was a date with one of the girls. In those days I was only payin' those girls a buck an hour, but for the date I'd give 'em a hundred dollar bill. You and your date figure it out. 'Oh yeah, no problem,' they'd say.

"Well, we got caught, you know. Here we had this line of cars from the gas station on PCH and Cherry two blocks long, blockin' everything. The cops came and asked, 'What the hell are you doin'?' They couldn't figure it out for a long time. I guess none of 'em ever bought gas from my place.

"I'd ride my motorcycle from that gas station to the L.A. River when they were first paving the river bottom . . . I'd get down in there and ride all the way to Alhambra, where I was livin' at the time. It was a lot quicker than the roads.

"We used to go to the drags and race our motorcycles, but there were no stands or anything like that there. In fact, when C. B. raced his motor that time against Chet Herbert—Herbert had a motor called the 'Beast' and we had the 'Brute'—well, we lined up and he was runnin' fuel and we didn't know anything about that fuel. And we couldn't smell it. He had put it in before he got there. Five hundred dollars was at stake. Well, C. B. blew a barrel off that thing during the race. So Cookie, the guy that owned the All American, was standing next to me with his girl friend and there was some guy right next to them. When C. B. went by and that barrel blew it went right at that guy and blew a hole through his jacket. Cookie says, 'Okay, time to move.'

"Those were sure the good days, though. Sure, we got some tickets, naturally, and ended up in jail sometimes, but it was always for racin' or speedin', stuff like that. Our favorite place some nights on the weekends was the Pullman Café in downtown L.A. across from the Union Depot. The owner of that joint was named Chips. He and a bunch of his friends robbed a cocktail lounge called the Zeppelin Blimp at Florence and Figueroa. They robbed the owner of the joint of 500 grand of diamonds in this suitcase. So the cops trace it back, and Chips winds up just spending about a year or so in jail. But he still owned the Pullman. All of us guys would park our motors down the alleys and everywhere. That's where C. B. got his motor stolen. Three guys got their motors stolen one night. Someone picked 'em up and put 'em in a truck.

"Guys from 'Pedro, Long Beach, Santa Monica, when we knew we were gonna go down there we'd let 'em know and we'd all go down there and drink together. That was a hell of a bar!

"Old Chips took me in the back one time and there was this door, this little door. It was bricked up at one time. He opened it up and there was a steel door behind that. You could go from the Pullman down this little passageway all the way to the 102 Brewery. You'd have to bend way down, and every so often there were these little alcoves with like a vent full of Chinese chips that they'd get for their pay and boxes of 102 beer where the employees probably came down and drank. The passageway went forever. It came out where they loaded the hops at the brewery.

"Ferguson Alley was a famous alley right near there. Since year one in L.A it was like Shanghai Red. There were a lot of 'happenings' in that sumbitch. We used to go to Olvera Street all the time on our bikes. We'd ride our bikes right into Chips' place and just leave 'em there. Chips wouldn't say anything. Just something like, 'Hi guys, how's everything goin'?'

"Chips was a bitchin' guy. He understood what was goin' on, you know what I mean? Everybody knew each other in those days. And the guys you didn't like you just stayed away from. If they came lookin' for you, they'd get all they wanted, so it was six of one, half-dozen of the other. Weren't no big thing. It was a fun time then. Guys put up with stuff, but they weren't afraid of anything.

"I paid $450 for an 80 flathead back then. I didn't know enough to buy an overhead. That's what motorcycles cost. I'd buy a motorcycle if some guy got killed or something, trade it for something else. I had a guy who wanted to trade me two Indian Chiefs, full-fendered, one was almost brand new, one was repainted but the motor had been rebuilt, for one Harley-Davidson that I had paid $150 for. I said, 'I wouldn't have that ugly sumbitch in my garage!' That's what I told him! 'I wouldn't own that ugly bastard! I'm not into Indians, 'cept if they're girls!'

"Dink Burns had an Arial Square-Four. He had big megaphones on that sumbitch. Well, he'd go by the house of this fancy-Dan motorcycle rider that lived just about a half-block from the All American. His name was Aub LeBard and he always had all his AMA crap and all that stuff, and ol' Dink would go by, wind that sumbitch out in low gear, hit second gear, and go by Aub's and just vibrate the windows. Ol' Aub would be so mad! One day he got out there, was gonna flag Dink down. Dink says, 'That sumbitch jumps in front of my motorcycle he's gonna have a burnt rubber mark down him from head to toe!'

"So there goes Dink, and Aub runs out in the street yellin', 'Hey, wait a minute!' And Dink heads straight for 'im! He had to jump outta the way, screamin' that ol' Dink was a crazy sonofabitch! Next time we saw Dink he says, 'I wasn't the crazy sonofabitch—*he* was, for jumping in front of *my* motorcycle!' "

"Fat Boy and I packed double on my Knucklehead all the way to Chicago one time to see Dink after he got married and moved there. We were sittin' in the All American one day and Fat Boy says to me, 'What the hell are we gonna do? I'm bored!' I says, 'So am I.' He says, 'Let's go to

Chicago and see Dink!' 'Chicago? That's a long way, and it's winter time, too, you know.' 'What the hell's the difference?' he says. So I say okay. Then he says, 'Well, we ain't gonna make it on my motor.' I said, 'Well we'll make it on mine.' It was that Knucklehead, that 68 stroker. We had a pillion pad and one little army saddlebag, we had our toothbrushes and our razors, one T-shirt apiece, and that was it. And we took off for Chicago . . . in the winter. We went over the Cajon Pass, and lemme tell ya, it was so Goddamn cold. Damn, I'm *still* cold. That sumbitch was *cold*! We had to stop on the other side and get into a gas station and stick our feet into a stove a guy had inside there to thaw out 'cause I couldn't feel my feet and neither could Fat Boy. And then we took off and went all the way to Chicago.

"What a trip! Stopped at Fat Boy's cousin's house right before we got to the state line in Missouri. We slept in his house and nearby there was this hilltop café, motorcycles everywhere. Well, ol' Fat Boy was famous for burnin' circles with his feet on the pegs. 'Show 'em what you can do Fat Boy!' I says. So he starts burnin' all around and these guys were amazed! But when we went back to go to sleep his cousin gets my motorcycle and goes back to the bar. We wake up and Fat Boy says, 'Uh oh! Looks like someone took your motorcycle!' I says, 'They better not have 'cause otherwise you're walkin' to Chicago! I'm flyin'!'

"Well, his cousin finally comes back and we head out. On the way out of town, I'll never forget, there was a little wooden gas station, one pump. And there was a tall, young kid about 17 years old in that place. I pulled in there an' I told Fat Boy, 'We need to fill this up. I hear it's a long way to the next town.' And I asked this kid, 'How far is it to Chicago from here?' He says, 'I haven't got no idea.' I says, 'Where was you raised?' He says, 'Right here in this town, Murfreesboro.' I said, 'What, you ain't never been to Chicago?' He says, 'No, I never been farther than this gas station.' I looked at Fat Boy. 'We better ask somebody else.'

"We got back on the motor and headed in the direction of Chicago. We finally get there and there's ice all over the streets. It's snowing. I looked up as we're going down the street and the 3/4-ton truck in front of us is hittin' bumps and all four wheels are comin' off the ground. I yell back to Fat Boy, 'I better slow this sumbitch down!'

"So we get to Dink's. He lived by the 'el' there. We wound up staying there for about a month. We slept on the floor. He took us to where Dillinger got killed and we hit all the bars in Chicago, which was an experience in itself.

"Well, Dink's wife's sister was married to the guy upstairs and they'd come down to eat and stuff like that. She was an absolute doll! And this guy she's married to, well, you could put his whole life in a box. He'd walk to work, just across the street at this machine shop, work all day, come back the same way, get home, eat, take a shower, go to sleep. That was it. That was his life!

"So one day I told her, 'Hey honey, anytime you get rid of that sumbitch you let me know. I'll take you to California and show you what life's really all about!' She says, 'Oh man, I don't know. Don't say nothin' to my sister about this!' I says, 'I ain't sayin' nothin' to nobody. I'm sayin' it to you!'

"Ol' Dink, he was gettin' ready to graduate from truck weigh master's school. So after that when Fat Boy and I got ready to leave, Dink said he'd come back with us. And his wife was gonna stay there for a while. So we made a hitch for Dink's car so we could tow my motor back with us. We get back to California, and Dink decides to settle in Lakewood, near Long Beach, 'cause Dink's wife's *other* sister lived there. Well, Dink's wife came out not too long after that, and then here comes the sister that was in Chicago. Dink's wife called her and said, 'You better come out here to California. This is where it's at. No snow, no ice.' She says, 'OK.'

"So she takes the train all the way out. She gets here and I ride over to see her. I ask her, 'How was your train ride? That's a long way on a train, ain't it?' And she smiles and says, 'Not if you fool around with every good-lookin' guy on the whole train!' That's what she told me! So I told ol' Dink about what she said. I said to him, 'Is she for real?' He says, 'You ain't kiddin'. She didn't tell her sister but she told me, too! She said she wanted to make that train ride memorable!'"

Memorable . . . memory . . . these are the keys to this vintage ignition, the ticket to a rowdy ride back to a time when the free bird that many of us were destined to become had just begun to hatch.

"Now Johnny Roccio and I shipped out in the merchant marines together, went on the same ship out of 'Pedro. Johnny had been around, that's for sure. Johnny and his brother used to come down San Pedro Street with a roar, hit this old dirt lot, slide in, park their motors, and go into the school that we went to for the merchant marines. That's all they rode was them motorcycles.

"And we'd go to field meets and everything and they were always there. Johnny was a born racer. He knew what was shaking with a motorcycle. He went to England and rode speedway there, he and our other buddy, Don

Holly, who was a champion motorcycle racer here. All those guys went to England to race. Johnny's brother, Ernie, was killed over there. If you go over to Johnny's right now there's a whole garage just filled with motorcycles and pictures. That's all that was there.

"I was over at John's once and Jim Hunter shows up. He sat down on the arm of the couch—he and I were always fooling around. Well, us guys who weren't married lived for a while near the Goodyear Tire & Rubber Company on Central. There's a walkway across the street and there's this bar, and there's this hotel called the Gateway Hotel. We all lived there. We'd park all our motorcycles in the back. The place looked like a whorehouse, but we had more damned fun there! The bar downstairs had all professional fighters or ex-fighters for bartenders because it could be a mean sumbitch in there sometimes.

"*Life* magazine once had a picture of the bar and hotel that they took from across the street. They called it '*the toughest corner in the world!*' That place was somethin' else!"

"One time at the All American I ran into this chick named Vivian. She rode an Indian Scout. Well, she and I and Hunter and some of the others got jobs 'shagging prints'—that was a job delivering blueprints on our motorcycles. We'd sit on this bench and as the blueprints came up for delivery we'd take turns delivering them. They were paying us a dollar an hour plus mileage. Your average riding per day around downtown L.A., Hollywood, Hollywood Hills, and around there was about 200 miles, in traffic. Once a day a car would hit me! Once a day! I'd be going through parked cars and stuff and some clown would open a door or something. Once a day! Bang! Knock the hell outta everything.

"And I would deliver to Charlie Chaplin's studio off of LaBrea. I'd pull into that lot, slide my motor right in, run in, hand 'em the thing, get my paperwork signed, run back out, get my motorcycle, and haul ass! You had to if you wanted to make money! But anyway, one time I pulled in there and this guy comes out an' says, 'Mr. Chaplin wants to see you.' I said, 'Who?' 'Mr. Chaplin wants to see you,' he says again. I thought, great, what did I do now? He brought me in there. There was this guard at the door and stuff. The door opens and they bring me in and this guy stood up and says, 'Glad to meet you. I'm Mr. Chaplin.' I says, 'Yeah?' It didn't ring a bell with me. I really didn't know who he was. But he says, 'See this window here. I see you come in here. You come in at a hundred miles an hour and leave at a hundred and ten. I like people that don't screw around when they work. How would you like to work for me?' I said, 'I *got* a job.' He says, 'Not this kind of job. I got a job where you'll keep clean.' I said, 'Naw, I'm into motorcycles. I don't want no job where I'll be inside. This is a movie studio isn't it?' 'Well, it's supposed to be,' he says, 'I'd like to have everyone who works for me move as fast as you do but it's impossible. But I'll tell you what; I'll give you a card and my number. If you change your mind come on back and you've got a job.' I said, 'OK.' When I got outside I threw the card away and went back to delivering my blueprints.

"Vivian, she was always riding. She rode to the All American, to the Pullman—she used to hang out in there—and delivered those blueprints every day on her bike just like anyone else. And she was good-looking, too. She came down to the All American one day when I had my stroker there. She says, 'Is this that stroker the guys been talkin' about?' I said, 'Yeah.' It was all painted black then: black wheels, 19-inch, front and back, bent bars, all stripped down. She said, 'Why don't you give me a ride on that thing?' I said, 'Sure let me take you home.' She says, 'Nope.' She lived down on Pico, downtown L.A. Her uncle had left this huge house to her, 20, 30 rooms. She and her cousin—who was also beautiful—lived there. Well, I was gonna give her a ride anyway, so we get on the bike. Right in front of that Goodyear Tire & Rubber Company I see someone I knew. He says, 'Hey, bro, what's going on?' I say, 'Not much.' And it was just getting dark. He says, 'Crank that sumbitch on!' So I cranked it on. Vivian was just there on the pillion pad, so when I stood that thing up I dumped her on the street. There she went bouncin'— bam! bam! bam! I said, 'Oh hell!' So I turned around and went back there to pick her up. I was yellin', 'Get your ass up! You ain't hurt!' And she didn't say anything, just got back on the bike. Well here comes some guy from across the street and *he's* yelling, 'Are you looking for some trouble? What are you doin' to that girl?' So without even blinkin' I just hit him right in the mouth. I told Vivian, 'Well, let's go,' 'cause I'd knocked this poor sumbitch all the way over to the other curb. We cranked up that bike and hauled ass. That's just how we used to ride!

"But let me tell you about Vivian. She was something else, really a nice girl. She called me up at the All American one day, she says, 'Do you want a job tonight from the *Times*, the paper?' I said, 'Yeah!' because she used to deliver prints all over. She knew a lot of people. She said, 'We've got to go to the Hollywood Bowl for some event. We stay there until these photographers give us their pictures. We rush them back to the press room, and we'll get paid.' I says, 'Okay.' Then I got to wonderin' who was gonna be at the Hollywood Bowl. Well, it turns out to be Margaret Truman. She was supposed to sing there or something. So we get there and we just sit. Had to listen to Margaret Truman sing her whole damned concert. As soon as the photographers were finished, they started to dispatch us on our bikes. Me and Vivian head out about the same time. I tell Vivian, 'I'm gonna eat that little Scout up!' 'Maybe,' she says. 'Ain't no maybe about it!' I says. So we start haulin' ass from Hollywood to the *Times* building in downtown L.A. I pulled up in front of the place and looked around and here she comes right behind me. She knew Hollywood and the side streets better than anybody. She says, 'Well, I might not be as fast as you but I make short-cuts!' I says, 'I guess you do!' We turned those pictures in and we got fifty dollars each! Big bucks in those days!

"But that's how it was back then. Everybody knew and helped each other. If anyone needed a couple of bucks, there was always someone who'd put you to work. At one time, in fact, me, C. B., and Von Dutch (the legendary custom painter/pinstripe master) all worked together at Crocker's motorcycle shop."

I was having my last drink in the bar where Vern and I had met. Fittingly, we eased toward the end of our conversation with a tale about Johnny Davis, a man for whom Vern obviously had a great deal of respect, as far as being a *true* Boozefighter, and you could feel his love for Wino and Teri.

"Now Johnny Davis! He was a real Boozefighter! A good lookin' guy, a Dapper Dan from the Rio Grande, lived right around the corner on Central. There was a big lot near his mother's place and he'd be rebuilding his motorcycle out there. I got a picture of him coming into Hollister. I stopped and took pictures of all of us. Johnny was a *real* Boozefighter! Had his Boozefighter sticker on the back of his Scout. Tall, all the girls used to go for him. As the years went by, Johnny still went up north to see Wino quite a bit before he passed away. In fact, Johnny was talking to Teri just three days before she died, too.

"Along Central Avenue at about 96th Street, there was a curve near the power plant, and there was an old gravel road that went straight. Well, Teri and Wino got a house there. One day everyone was just hangin' around the All American. Walt Porter was there, too, and several of the gals. All of a sudden Wino looks at the gals and says, 'Look you lazy broads, I want you girls to go get some paint and paint the bathroom at the house!' There were about four girls or so—Teri and Manker's girl friend and a couple of others. 'Okay, okay, dammit!' they say and they got up and left. Ol' Wino said, 'Now we can settle down to some steady drinking, now that I don't have to worry about that bathroom!' So we start drinking and everything, and it went into the afternoon, you know. The phone rang and Cookie says, 'Here, it's for you, Wino!' And Wino says, 'Who is it!?' Cookie says, 'It's Teri.' 'Teri! She knows not to call me here!' So he picks the phone up and says, 'What d'ya want!?' 'Well, your damn bathroom is painted, Wino. I hope you like the sumbitch! We had to work our asses off and now we're cleanin' up the mess! So don't worry about nothing you lazy SOB! You're the one that was supposed to do this in the first place!' 'Okay,' says Wino, then he looks at us, 'C'mon, let's go see what kind of a painting job them broads did.'

"We ride over there and all the girls are sitting there with smiles on their faces. 'What's a matter?' says Wino. 'Nothing's a matter,' they said sweet-ly. 'C'mon in you guys,' says Wino. We walk into the bathroom. The ceiling, the walls, the floor, the toilet, and the inside and the outside of the bathtub was all painted black! They even turned the water off and painted the *inside* of the toilet black! Wino let out this roar! 'What did you do to this bath-room? he screamed. Teri says, 'You just told us to paint it. You didn't tell us what color!'

"He wound up having to *pay* somebody to paint the sumbitch white!"

As we left the bar and I watched Vern head for home, I remained hung in a very different time. I just wasn't able to snap back into the present. I looked all around. The modern building that we just left was suddenly cloaked in the brick and wood of places like the All American, the Pullman and Shanghai Red, the vehicles rollin' by were all fat-fendered with thick white-walls; they were Studebakers and Packards.

When I fired up my SuperGlide and rolled out of that parking lot, all I could think of is what Vern had said to me sometime through my second beer:

"We cranked up that bike and hauled ass! That's just how we used to ride!"

CHAPTER 5

The Tale of "Nine Toes," Hennessy's, and the Three-Star Bottle

The miserable animal was perched up on the roof. It was big, it was growling, it was hunched over and leering, like a hungry mutant buzzard eyeing some freshly sautéed road kill. "It's OK, he doesn't bite. He's just a big teddy bear!" Rottweilers are *not* teddy bears. In the core of his spleen, Meyers knew this, and the rotten bag of fur and teeth looking down at him was snarling and drooling and about to make some kind of horrible move. "Really, he doesn't bite." OK. Right. Words mean things.

"*She's a nice girl and a real good cook,*" means she looks a lot like Lyle Lovett.

"*I'd never sell it—it's in perfect shape—but we need the money because my wife really wants us to start a family and buy a house,*" means it's got a bent crank.

"*C'mon, it's only a hundred bucks. I'll pay you back as soon as I get my check on Friday,*" means . . . well, we *all* know what *that* means.

And, "*Really, he doesn't bite,*" means that Cujo is about to sink his fangs into your jugular.

The Rott leaped from the roof to the carport to his doghouse to the ground, like a wicked, sadistic emperor descending a long, ornate staircase at the Coliseum to give a "thumbs down" sign to some poor, unfortunate, beaten, and bloodied gladiator. The thing's head was all mouth, with nasty bicuspids and incisors that resembled sharpened clawhammers or the Devil's own ice picks. Its downward momentum had it moving like a Panzer tank, heading directly for Meyers' left leg.

This lazy afternoon was going south in a hurry.

Steve Meyers was a Boozefighters prospect. He was also a cop. The seamstress that owned the Rott was the club's Betsy Ross. She was sewing on Meyers' bottom rocker patch. Her dog had never gone after a *biker* before. But Meyers showed up at her door in his lawman uniform. Apparently, to the pooch, this was something completely different. Badges and colors were, evidently, not quite the same thing in his fuzzy little consciousness. He had, it seemed, *sorted some things out.* And now the mutt was closing in, its steely yap open like a bear trap. Meyers stepped back and drew his sidearm. The woman was screaming: "Just stand still! He won't bite you if you stand still!"

By now the thing looked like a Boa sizing up a bunny hors d'oeuvre for happy hour. Just as his shin was about to become Alpo, Meyers fired point-blank. A .357-caliber packs a pretty good wallop.

A lot is expected of prospects. They need to prove their loyalty. They need to psychically bleed for the brotherhood. They give their energy. They give their time. Sometimes they have to be gophers. Sometimes their dignity must take a back seat to duty. While times may have changed in the 50-plus years since "Kokomo" required his 'Frisco greenhorns to eat live goldfish and drink wine in public from a douche bag, then *and* now the idea of a prospect winding up as lunch for a big maniacal animal seems somewhat extreme.

And besides that, Meyers had already fulfilled a very important requirement: "Contributing something special to the club."

He had found "The Bottle."

In the Boozefighters' museum is a solid green shirt that was donated by Wino himself. According to Willie, this was the first club colors. It has the famous "three star bottle" stitched on the upper left sleeve, and his nickname misspelled as "Vino," over the heart. (Willie's seamstress was Italian.)

When Willie offered his cool prototype to the original group, the reception was cold.

"I took it down to a meeting and showed 'em. They didn't like it and voted on getting a zip-up turtleneck. Geez, ya just can't please everybody, ya know!"

But the bottle patch remained.

"Why the three-star bottle? Aw, it was just something funny to do. I figured if people were going to call us a drinking club I thought we ought to have a bottle."

A bottle? *The* bottle.

When Wino Willie passed away in 1997, it was feared that the exact origin of the three-starred jug would never be written into the club's lore, that the history of this storied fraternity might suffer a gap, an empty in the wine rack. A serious quest was launched, a dusty crusade, a search for the scooter tramp Holy Grail, a raid for the two-wheeled Lost Ark.

The originals were the first to be grilled for clues to the treasure map. Chronicles and notes began to be gathered with Colombolike precision and diligence. "The old-timers all had various vague answers. Some said they thought it was patterned after a beer bottle, a whiskey bottle, a wine bottle. Some stated, 'Damned if I can remember! We just always had it.'

"Even Wino's wife, Teri, the original Boozette, said that she didn't really know where the bottle came from. But why those three stars? 'I don't know. Willie just liked the looks of them.'"

But then the 100-proof plot began to thicken. Colombo's right hand was high in the air and his left was against his forehead, a sign of pending enlightenment! Of revelation! Of an answer!

Maybe.

Johnny Roccio's wife, Jeannine, an avid club historian and memorabilia collector, was about to solve the three-star riddle. "I'll tell you exactly what it was. It was a Hennessy's cognac bottle!" Excitement and electricity charged the hearts of the crusaders. Members rushed to the nearest liquor store!

There weren't three stars on the Hennessy's bottles. There weren't *any* stars on *any* of their bottles. An old guy ran the store and reaffirmed the fact that Hennessy's doesn't have, and never *did* have, any little twinkling orbs on their labels. The riddle's door slammed shut. The Scrolls rolled back into their cave. Revelation's light was turned out!

But never underestimate the power and resolve of a biker babe. Almost two years later, Jeannine got wind of what the guy at the liquor store had said. She wasn't happy. "No stars? I know damn well that they had them! Call the company! Ask someone who knows what they're talking about!"

OK. A rep at Hennessy's New York corporate reopened the dig. "Sure we used to have a three-star bottle. It was known as the premium cognac throughout the world. I've got a picture of that bottle right here on my desk. Due to copycat labeling by other brands, our company quit putting stars on the bottle by about 1953."

Teri was called. A bombshell like this called for a second opinion. Some memory dredging. Some shock therapy. "Teri, could the three stars have been from, maybe, possibly, a Hennessy's cognac bottle?" "Exactly! I had forgotten, but now that you mention it I remember that was the name. Willie liked the looks of those three stars so much that he put them across the barrel of the bottle!"

Indiana Jones may have known *about* the Lost Ark, but the real drama didn't start until that bad boy was actually rolled out into the open; winds began to howl, and people started to melt. One of those vintage 1953 carafes absolutely *had* to find its way into the BFMC museum. The circle must remain unbroken.

The stuff that Steve Meyers had been offering up as his "special contribution" to the club hadn't exactly bowled over any of the members. Yet. It was time for Indy to take out his whip. The bottle was described to Meyers. Mission impossible. *"If you choose to accept this assignment . . . "* There really wasn't much choice. Duty called. Within a couple of months Meyers came up with the two 3-star Hennessy's miniatures and a pint-sized bottle from the '40s that are now on display in the national museum.

His 10th toe, however, is not. The damned dog moved like Emitt Smith in his prime. He did a perfect end-run as the gun went off, avoiding the bullet like No. 22 slipping a tackle. Meyers' foot unfortunately moved more like a Barry Bonds home run pitch, hanging, slightly away, right in the zone.

CHAPTER 6

The Tale of Gil Armas, C. B. Clausen, the Daytona Hustle, "Where's My Bike?" and the Origin of the Stroker

Gil Armas is like a rascally kid with a grin and a secret. He's the one with the perpetual guess-what-I-did smile. He's the original wild one who bends the definition of "wild" to include an atmosphere of storytelling and yarn spinning that would make moonlit, dusty cattle drovers sitting around a prairie campfire proud, stories and yarns that always result in a head-shaking laugh.

Since the 1940s a million books, songs, and movies have made attempts at capturing the ultimate "road trip," the perfect spontaneous existential excursion into the soul of America: *On the Road, Fear and Loathing in Las Vegas, Kathy's Song, Five Easy Pieces, Easy Rider*. It's been written about, sung about, and filmed, but the original wild ones *lived* it.

"C. B. Clausen says to me," Gil begins, " 'You know, I want to go to Daytona, go there for the racing and stuff.' So we checked our pockets and we had about a dollar-and-a-half between us. I say, 'We can't get nowhere with this! How are we gonna get to Daytona?' We were sitting there at the All American, discussing it. "Gotta find a way,' we say. 'Can't we borrow some money somewhere?' C. B. asks. 'I don't know anyone who has that much money right now,' I say. And he didn't either! But he starts to thinking. Then he gets this *look* . . . 'I'll tell ya what we'll do,' he says, 'Nobody knows about

Gil Armas on the Panhead of BFMC friend, PanTanna.

these strokers! We'll start hitting some bars and clubs along the way and race for money! We can get enough for gas at least.'

"We left the All American and headed for Daytona with the buck-and-a-half and we stopped in San Diego first. Right away we seen a guy on a bike. We ask him, 'Hey, where's the hangout around here?' 'Follow me, I'll show ya!' he says. So away we go. He took us over to this bar and they were nice fellas, buying us drinks and everything. But C. B. was getting a bit impatient, the time's getting late and we're horsing around, drinking and everything, but then it started. Some guy comes in and says to us, 'You ridin' them old bikes out there?' 'Yeah,' we say. And they really didn't look like much. We had painted them with a paintbrush, black, and we left them all dirty. The Knuckleheads pumped oil anyway, so we just left the oil all over and the dirt got on it. They really were a mess. You'd look at 'em and you'd think, 'Well this thing can't even get out of its own way!'

"So we said to the guy, 'Yeah, they belong to us.' He says, 'Well, how far are you going?' 'Daytona.' *'Daytona?'* he says, *'On those?'* So then they all get talking about this friend of theirs who has this real fast bike. Me and C. B. looked at each other and we thought, 'Now's our chance!' Just then one of these guys comes up and says to us, 'You know, if you guys had a bike that would stay together we could get up a little race with this friend of ours. And he's never been beat, neither.' And he kept going on and on about this friend and his fast bike. C. B. looks at me and says, 'What do ya think, Gil?' 'Well,' I said, 'I don't know.' C. B. says, 'Oh, go ahead, give it a try.' 'Oh, all right,' I says.

"So now a bunch of guys are getting the bets up. Everybody matching our buck-and-a-half. We'd a been sunk if we'd a lost, 'cause we wouldn't a had even a dime for gas! The deal was simple: a drag race, whoever crosses the finish line first gets the money. So here comes their friend with his bike, a full-fendered job, windshield, everything! We looked at each other and thought, 'This is a *race*?' C. B. just grinned at me.

"What we figured on doing was to have C. B. stand right there next to the guy with the bet money. When I won, I'd just keep goin'. C. B. would grab the dough and split quick before they realized that we'd hustled them so bad like that. Well, I take off and it was no race! I'm lookin' around and this guy's way back there, but here comes C. B.! He's got all the money and he's yelling, 'Keep going, just keep going!'

"We finally get somewhere where we could pull over and count the money 'cause we didn't know how much we'd won. Forty bucks! Forty bucks!

I said, 'Geez! That'll almost get us all the way there! We took off from there and get to another town. We're gassing up at a station and here comes another biker. 'Hi, how you guys doing?' Everyone on bikes was pretty friendly in those days. The guy says, 'Where you going?' We say, 'Daytona.' 'Oh God,' he says. 'That's a long ways. Why don't you guys follow me? I'm going down to have a couple of drinks at a place where we all hang out around here.' 'Fine,' we say, as me and C. B. look at each other and smile. Here we go again.

"We go over there, and everybody's drinking and everything. And they offered us a place to stay. In those days if you needed someplace to stay, they wouldn't take no for an answer. Everybody was always willing to help out another guy on a motorcycle. Well, in walks some guy. 'Who owns those old junks out there?' 'Some other guy says, 'These two guys are riding them, going to Daytona.' '*Daytona? On those?*' That kind a made C. B. mad this time so he says, 'Our *junk* will blow your thing off!' 'Damn! Did you hear that?' the guy says to the others in there. Now they start to get the bets up. Here we go again.

"We put up twenty of our bucks. We sure didn't want to lose it 'cause we needed it for the trip and now we were getting pretty far from home. But we put up the twenty, everybody else is putting up money. I was a little nervous. 'What if they beat us?' I said to C. B. 'They ain't gonna beat us,' he says.

"This race was C. B.'s turn. 'You're gonna take this one. *I'll* wait with the money,' I said. So this guy's got the money in his hand, just holding it kind a easy like, waiting for the race to start. I waited 'til they were about halfway down the road. C. B. was eating this guy up, so I grabbed the money and ran. I went flyin' by the other guy and started catching C. B. He's yelling, 'Come on! Come on!'

"When we finally stopped after that one, I was tellin' C. B., 'Maybe you shouldn't beat them so bad. You shouldn't leave them so far behind. They're gonna get wise and start calling ahead and the next place we come to they're gonna beat the hell outta us!'

" 'OK,' he says, 'you're right. We'll skip the next town. Besides we have a good chunk of money now.' It was late at night when we went through the next couple of towns so we didn't even stop. But then we came to this town in Texas and we see this guy wearing this big cowboy hat riding a motorsickle. We asked him, 'Hey, how do you keep that thing on when you're riding like that?' 'Oh, like this,' he says, and shows us this big strap he has around it and under his chin. So we go with him and wind up at his local hangout with a bunch of nice guys all on bikes. We spent the night there. They put us up in

C. B. Clausen (left).

a place. The next morning as we were getting ready to leave I asked C. B., kind a quietlike, 'You think we should try it again here? These guys have been pretty nice to us and all.' But ol' C. B., he was pretty money hungry and he wanted to get another race goin'. But I told him, 'You know these guys might get ticked off and we've gotta come back this way!' 'Yeah,' C. B. says, 'but I've been talking to that guy over there, thinks he's got a real fast bike.' We looked at the guy's bike. Another full-fendered job. I whispered to C. B., 'This is like taking candy from a baby. We've already got enough money to get to Daytona.' 'But you're right,' he says. 'We won't be able to do this coming back. They'll be looking for us. We need to make the money now so we can get home after Daytona without stopping anywhere.'

"So he cooks up a race with this guy. But I'm thinking that this just doesn't look right. All these guys were really egging us on, telling us stuff like they really want to see us beat this guy 'cause he's always bragging about his bike and stuff. Everyone's getting the bets up. And C. B. was the one to race. He really wanted to race this guy after all the talk and stuff. So they take off. This time C. B. is kind a playing with the guy. He'd let him get close then move up a little, let him get close than move ahead. He waited 'til they were almost at the finish line then he cranked it on and just left this guy sitting. And that guy was mad! I grab all these guys' money in a flash, jump on my bike and I can't get it started! I'm jumping and jumping, nearly went right over the handlebars. Finally she starts. By this time C. B. is long gone. I can't even see him. I don't know where he's goin'. I figure he's gone off and left me, except I had all the money!

"Well, he finally stopped way up the road and waited for me and we went on into Daytona, stopping in some more towns for some more racing. We got to Daytona, saw the races, drank a lot, drank some more, and when it came time to leave we took another way back, kind of a detour, longer, but we figured that would be best considering all that went on in those other towns! When we got back to L.A. we headed straight for the All American. We're sitting there having a drink and I says, 'OK, C. B., do we have *any* money left?' Well, he starts pulling money out of all his pockets and stuff, and we start countin' it on the bar and everyone's looking at us and all this money. 'What'd you guys do, rob a bank or something?' they say. We hadn't told them what we did. Turns out we had nearly five hundred bucks! Five hundred bucks! We didn't know *how* much we had, really. We'd lost track of the towns and the races. C. B. had just been stuffing the money in his pockets since Texas. That was more than a year's wages back then. I'd had a job where I was making fifteen dollars a week and that was considered big money. We felt like kings! Nearly bought another motor-sickle. At that time you could get a good Knucklehead for a hundred and fifty bucks!"

"When I got out of the service I worked for a guy who had a lawn mower business. A lot of the guys I knew at the time would come by and see me there at that shop. 'Hey,' they'd ask me, 'will you give my bike a tune-up?' I told them that I'd have to ask the guy who owned the business if that'd be OK. I told 'em that I was supposed to be repairing lawn mowers, not working on motorcycles, and I don't think this guy is really into bikes. So I went in to talk to the boss. I told him that this guy wanted me to tune up his bike and it would only take me a half-hour or so—it was an old VL—and he could make fifteen bucks. 'Fifteen bucks!' he said. 'That's more than I could make overhauling a whole lawn mower engine! Gil, can you do it?' I said, 'Sure, that's no big deal.' So he says, 'Go ahead.' Twenty minutes later I had checked it all out, put new points in it, tuned it, set the carburetion, and the guy was real happy, paid right up. Right outta the service, a lot of guys had money, you know. So the boss starts thinking about it. 'That was quick money,' he says. I said, 'Yeah, you oughta go into this. You can get used parts for nearly nothing, and there's a lot of guys who can't afford new parts. You could make some money on this.' 'Oh no,' he says, 'I don't want to invest any real money in stuff like that.' 'Look, everybody's got parts in their garage,' I told him, 'and they'd be glad to get rid of them for a couple of bucks.' Well, he thought about it but he didn't say anything.

"Then this guy comes in on a full-dress knucklehead. He said he had to get back to Texas, had some kind of emergency, and he asks me what can I give him for the bike? I'm out there talkin' to him, the boss, he's inside, and I said, 'Well, what do you have to get for it?' And he says, 'Anything!' So I figured we really had something here. I said, 'Well, I don't think it's worth more than a hundred and fifty bucks.' 'I'll take it!' he says. Well now I've committed myself, so I went in to see the boss. 'That guy out there has that Harley. He wants a hundred and fifty bucks for it, needs the money real bad, needs to go back to Texas or something. I told him we'd buy it.' 'Golly, Gil, you're always getting me in trouble! I don't want to invest that kind of money in a motorcycle!' 'But you can double your money,' I told him. 'No!'

"So I went back out and talked to the guy and by now he was pleading. I went back in and talked to the boss again and I finally wore him down. 'Trust me,' I says. 'OK I'll take a chance,' he says. So we gave him a hundred and fifty bucks. While they were signing the paperwork this other guy happens by, just out of the service, has money in his pocket, and sees the bike. 'How much for the motorcycle?' he says. Well, I just threw a figure out off the top of my head. 'Oh, five hundred bucks,' I said. 'I'll take it!' he says!

"I went back in the office and the first guy was still in there so I didn't dare say anything. I got the boss off in the corner and I whispered, 'Did ya make the deal yet?' 'Yeah, he signed off the pink and everything.' 'Well, make out some more paperwork 'cause there's a guy out there who wants to give you five hundred bucks for the thing!' 'What?' he says. I says, 'Yep.' 'Aw, you're kidding me!' 'Nope!' So he looks at his wife, she took care of the books, and they both lit up. And from that time on he was in the motorcycle business! He bought every used part he could. Guys would bring him their spare parts to sell for cash, he'd even go to the dump where guys would throw away their old parts and he'd salvage them. He wound up being known as 'Jungle Jim.' He had parts for anything. People would call from all over looking for odd parts they couldn't find. But every time I asked him for a raise he'd say, 'Raise? I can't afford to give you a raise!'

"Finally I left him and went to work for another guy. He was buying motor-sickles from guys who wanted cars, trading like, you know. He wanted me as a mechanic. I told him that I had to have some reliable transportation. I lived in Bell and he was in L.A. So he says, 'Well why don't you just build yourself a bike from these parts?' He had a lot of parts, stacks of parts. I asked him what it would cost me and he said that he got most of the parts for free or near nothing so I could just go ahead and take what I needed. I got to building a little 45. And as I went on he'd look at what I was doing and say, 'Uh, well, where'd you get *that* part?' And I'd say, 'Right over there on that shelf. You said I could have it, didn't you?' 'Okay, sure,' he'd say, 'just checking.'

"I built a beautiful little 45. And about that time the Indian came out with hydraulic forks, and he had a pair there. So I got to wondering if they'd fit on this 45. It'd be different, you know. So I'm measuring everything, what d'ya know? It fits! But once I got the engine in and everything, I thought, 'Oh no, it goes down too far.' The springs ain't strong enough for this kind of setup. But I knew a spring place where the guy always said if he didn't have something, he'd make it, one of them kind of guys. So I went down there and told him what I wanted to do. I said, 'If I could get just a little more tension on these springs it'd be perfect. He looks at 'em and takes 'em in the back where they had this spring tester. He comes back and says, 'How much more do ya want on these?' I said, 'Well the bike weighs so-and-so and it went down this far and stuff. What do you think?' He says, 'Well, we'll put four more inches on 'em and make 'em a little heavier.' I says, 'OK.'

"I put the springs back in put it back on the frame and it was perfect! Just had enough spring to it, you know. I said, 'Wow! This is beautiful!' So I bring the bike to work and the boss comes out. He looks at the bike. 'I didn't know you were gonna build that good of a bike!' he says. 'You told me I could do it!' I said. 'Well, yeah, that's OK, but I didn't know you were gonna do all that.'

"I went home that night and I was really proud riding that bike. Boy, it sure handled good. Nice and springy, you know. I went back into work the next morning and the boss says, 'Why don't you park it right up here against the wall, for show. That way maybe people going by will see it and stop in and buy something.' Well, I said sure, and didn't think much more about it. Came quitting time, I walk out front and I can't find my bike. 'What the hell happened to my bike?' I'm thinking. I go into the boss and ask him, 'Hey, what happened to my bike?' I thought he might have pushed it around to another spot or something. 'Oh, I forgot to tell ya,' he says, 'I sold it.' 'What? You sold my bike?' 'Don't worry about it,' he says. 'You got lots more parts out there. Build another one.'

"Well that's what I did, but I couldn't get those forks anymore. I wound up building three more bikes and he sold every one of them! He sold a lot of other bikes, too. He had a lot of guys who'd come in with kind of messed up bikes and he'd buy 'em and just turn right around and sell 'em 'as is.' I told him, 'You know, you're losing a lot of money on this stuff. Some of these bikes run pretty good but they look bad. We should dress 'em up a little bit. Clean 'em, paint 'em, get a little chrome on 'em. You'll triple your money.' 'Oh no,' he says, 'I don't want to invest any real money in this stuff.' I thought to myself, 'Here we go again.'

"So just to prove a point, I dressed up one bike. He agreed to that. I put it all together, looking good. I just was rolling it out with the boss next to me and here comes this guy. 'Whoa, geez, that's a beautiful bike,' he says. 'How much?' The boss looks at me and I look at the boss and he tells the guy some outrageous figure and the guy says, 'I'll take it!' After that, that was all we did. Strip the bikes, get 'em painted, decorate 'em up a little bit, push 'em out there and they'd sell. A lot of people go for those fancy paint jobs. Some didn't care how they'd run, just so they looked nice!"

As he began to describe the birth of the stroker motor, Gil's smile never left his face. Did he and C. B. Clausen realize that they were revolutionizing an entire industry? Not really. What they did realize was that there was a machine that they loved. The motor-*sickle*. They loved the lifestyle that went with it. And, like in every love affair, there are ups and downs. But the absolute intimacy—the experience of knowing every inch in and out—of the object of your love, that's the stuff that drives passion. That's real love.

"Well, there I was, working in my garage. I had my flathead motor all apart in one corner, repairing the pistons I collapsed on my last big ride, and I had my Knucklehead apart in another corner. In comes C. B.

" 'What are you doing?' he asks. I tell him I'm fixing the pistons and I see him eyeing the flywheels that were out of both motors. Now C. B. had this way of lookin' at things, a 'vision' that most of us don't have. I knew something was up, something was going on in that brain of his.

" 'Do you have a ruler?' he asks. 'Here we go again,' I thought. Yeah, I gave him a ruler. He measures the two flywheels and realizes that the flathead flywheel is bigger than the Knuck and starts to get excited and starts to put it into the Knucklehead. I had two thoughts: First, this is *my* engine. If we blow the thing up, *I'm* the one who's out a motor! C. B. ain't gonna lose a damn thing! And second, there must be a reason that no one has ever done this before! But C. B. is all excited and starts putting stuff together, the bigger flathead parts into the Knuck, and it all starts to fit! So we put the cases together, and I had some 61 barrels, we put those on and the piston sticks way out.

" 'Uh, C. B., this just ain't gonna work!' I says. 'Yeah, I guess you're right,' he says, but then starts to eye some 74 barrels I had in another corner—that 'vision' again. So we slip the 74 barrels on and the piston comes up dead even. But when we put it together and hand turned it, we heard this 'clunk.' I knew there was a reason that no one has ever tried this before!

"But C. B. had his 'vision.' We take the barrel off and look at the piston and notice that the piston was hitting the flywheel, and if we took off enough to clear the flywheel then there wouldn't be anything left 'cause it would hit the pin.

"OK, this just ain't gonna work, but . . .

"We take it all apart again and C. B. grabs some pistons from a 74 and sees that the pins are higher. Well, we hadn't thought about that, so we put the 74 pistons in and put it back together. We turn it and notice that all we had to do was to trim the pistons at the bottom on the sides where the flywheel came in. Well, all that was fine and dandy, but I didn't want to do that to my pistons. Before I could say anything, C. B. is over on the grinder, cutting up my piston! He tries it back on the motor; it *almost* clears; back to the grinder!

"Now I'm yelling, 'You ruined my piston!' He's got all this same stuff over at his house, but no, he's over here experimenting with *my* stuff! 'It'll be all right, really,' he says as he keeps grinding away!

"I mean, here I was, just a while ago I had two nice motors that I was putting back together so we could go on our next ride, and now I didn't even have one! 'C. B.,' I says, 'This just ain't gonna work! There *must* be a reason that no one has ever done this before!'

" 'It'll be all right, really . . . '

"So after all the grinding. C. B. gets the thing all back together, gets it to clear real nice, and I get to thinking that maybe we have something here! 'Yeah,' says C. B. 'There's no plates or anything under the barrels, nothing to make anyone wise that we've done anything to this motor.'

"Well, we get it all back together, but we didn't put the push rods on 'cause we wanted to time it with the lift, so we marked it and found out where the pistons come up at and where the mark is on the flywheel. So far everything's good. *So far . . .*

"Then we put it in the frame, try to kick it over and I go flying over the bars.

" 'C.B, there's something wrong here! There must be a reason that no one has tried this before!'

"OK, what we weren't doing was that in order to time it right we had to have the valves lifted. So we fixed that and tried again . . . and I went over the bars again.

" 'C.B, there's something wrong here.'

"We monkeyed around with it some more and it got to the point where it would almost start. Almost start. *Almost . . .*

"Then, by accident, we moved the distributor forward, advancing it quite a bit, just as C. B. says, 'I'm gonna try this one more time.'

"He kicks it and she fires up! We were dancing and jumping around! That distributor had been retarded, but just by luck we fixed it and she just purred!"

The stroker motor wasn't the only thing that was born within the garages, minds, and personalities of the original wild ones. A *lot* of embryonic journeys were starting to seed. The stroker was just a part of it. It was pure two-wheeled chemistry. The formula was blending and swirling, but these particular scientists didn't have white smocks, thick, horned-rimmed glasses, and test tubes. They wore old, worn leather, military-issue boots, and their laboratories were tarred over with rough asphalt. Route 66, Highway 101, the Pacific Coast Highway . . .

But the mix was perfect.

The American biker didn't emerge from some clinical social experiment; the American biker was lovingly fathered by men like Gil Armas and C. B. Clausen. By their need to simply enjoy the freedom that this country has bled for. By their need to never be walled in by anything that leaves the wilder side of life out.

We all should be thankful that Gil kept saying, "Well, here we go again . . ."

CHAPTER 7

The Tale of the Biker's Code of Life & Death

He was a club officer. His patch, the brotherhood that began in 1946, the bond was seamless. These people were family.

But now he was making his way from one hospital room to another, visiting them out of duty, out of love. He fought back tears as he saw the vacant darkness of one member's coma. He prayed that another would walk again. He held his head in his hands as he learned that another might not make it.

"Why is all this crap happening?" he asked the club chaplain, Irish Ed. It was a plea, a somber question of cosmic proportions. Divine intervention was needed for this one. There are some answers that dust-level mortals just can't come up with. Like, why the sudden rash of wrecks? Why are we having to buy "get well" cards by the box lately? He hoped that Irish Ed could be the conduit for some heavenly wisdom. He needed it.

The Boozefighters are definitely not saints, but neither have they lost the spiritual roots that were as important to the founding of this country as were the bloody, in-the-trench sacrifices of their World War II ancestors. The spirit of this crew dawned in the generation of Dagwood and Blondie, bathtub gin, and Harry James, not Ron Jeremy, Cristy Cannon, ecstasy, and Eminem, and it shows. The line between Saturday night at the clubhouse and Sunday morning may be pretty thin, but it *does* exist nonetheless. It's just up to street-pious men like Irish Ed to fill it in now and then, and to be there when things go wrong.

Bikers adorn themselves with things like skulls, dice, booze bottles, and shooting flames for a reason. A gamble with death occurs every time that bike is kicked over. We *know* that. That's just how it is. Coin collectors don't face much of a risk of hitting the asphalt at 70 miles per hour. Fly fishermen seldom get T-boned by ignorant left turners in the trout stream. Oil slicks in the road don't mean much to folks who sit around the house painting still-life watercolors of bowls of pears.

Bikers, on the other hand, shun the Muzak version of life. Most also shun the me generation, pointy-headed intellectualism of today's cyber-society, which has replaced a healthy fear and respect of "the man upstairs" with an *enlightened* reliance on stuff like maximum gigabyte hard drives and stock portfolios. The closer you travel with death, the closer you are to your chosen maker. That has something to do with it. And it's probably true that there are no real atheists when the deal finally goes down, when the walls close in, when you realize that the last of the sand is about to drop. That's when it becomes brutally apparent that we (and our computers and things) really don't have *all* the answers.

And that's when most of us really need some.

When you live much of your life on two fast wheels, just inches above the pavement, questions about mortality—and the eventual answers—are always very close. And that tends to activate the adrenaline.

That's the kind of stormy edgework that energized the original wild ones. They whetted their worldly appetites by racing against the grains in God's own hourglass. They pioneered an unbridled lifestyle that doesn't rely on the shackles of crybaby margins of safety or legislative cushions that protect your average soft-sedan citizen from anything harsh, bad, or unacceptable to pedestal-elevated manners.

Wino Willie lying in the middle of the road in downtown Hollister, swilling some hard stuff out of a giant bottle, Gil Armas spinning donuts along San Benito Street, Red Dog riding down the sidewalk: this kind of set a *tone*.

The originals *weren't* your average soft-sedan citizens. They blasted into wartime manhood by staring down the barrel of the Third Reich and the Kamikaze crazies of Hirohito's Imperial Japan. The breakneck bikes, booze, and rough roads that they embraced when they returned home were simply the stuff of relaxation, games, and good clean fun. They still are to those who have followed in their bootprints.

Occasionally, however, the game is lost. Sometimes the odds catch up and the sand in the hourglass wins. For the bikers left behind, that is always a time of reassessment, of regrouping, of wondering if it might be better to turn loose life's tail and settle into a serene pattern of Thursday night bingo, bird watching, and internet chat rooms about daytime soaps.

No. Those thoughts don't last long. The usual response is to quickly raise a collective brotherhood glass to robust and electric remembrances of a life that was never afraid to twist the throttle just that much more. Even if that meant cashing in early. The spirit of a lost brother or sister is toasted and the tales go 'round, memories of being with them in the Buffalo Chip mud of Sturgis, fighting to stay on the road with them in the bone-cracking winds of West Texas, drinking with them at Johnny's in Hollister, ridin' next to them in the traffic-snarled heat of Daytona, tappin' another keg at the clubhouse.

The tears shed for a vibrant life are sad enough; the tears shed for a nonlife are tragic. The tears that fall during the annual "Whisky Jim Run" are genuine 100-proof biker: pure, premium Boozefighter.

Whisky Jim's ashes were spread in the wind along the slopes of Chalk Mountain in Texas. He was killed riding home from work one 4 a.m. beneath the predawn pitch of the infinite and hollow Lone Star sky. There is deep-cut melancholy in the yearly ride out to that site. It's a time for quiet introspection, for that tough regrouping. Tears compete for smiles and other expressions tucked within personal, private, and individual emotions, gut-check emotions that range from the hardness of chrome to the softness of old leather.

And Whisky Jim's memory is not alone on that hillside. There are the thoughts and tales of other latter-day Boozefighters who have passed on, riders in the sky like Cowbell. Kenneth "Cowbell" York was sergeant-at-arms for Chapter 69. Irish Ed and Cowbell's wife, Monica, were with him when he died. He had a last request: He wanted his coffin to be pulled to his final rest on a trailer behind club Prez Big John's *Boss Hoss*. No problem. Naturally, the trailer was painted BFMC green.

And now there were other spirits, other meditations, more memories, and agonizing questions about mortality being raised by the quiet breeze there on Chalk Mountain. The sound of the wind started to become the roar of vintage motors, flatheads and Knucks. There was four-stroke thunder, the howl of old two-lane barnstormers carving an immortal legacy into the soft gravel of a backcountry road. Wild boys, wild men, wild ones . . .

But the originals weren't immune to rolling sevens, either. "Fat Boy" Nelson was killed on his bike in the late 1950s. Ernie Roccio was fatally injured while racing in England. Jim Cameron had the wrong size gas cap on his Indian Scout. The fuel leaked out and caught fire, badly burning his legs. According to legend, Cameron's pain was so intense that he tried to commit suicide by diving out of the hospital window. Someone stopped him.

But *no one* has ever been able to stop the traditions that erupted from their fierce way of life. Some tigers can't be tamed. Some broncs can't be broken.

The emotional breeze had shifted. Things became quiet again.

There were no lightning bolts, burning bushes, or even a plague of locusts, but an air of common-sense spirituality laid out an answer that, in reality, everyone already knew. *"Why is all this crap happening?"* That's easy. It's because there are some people in this world who want their lives to be more fun than anybody else's. Damn the consequences. If you don't want to fall off, then don't even think about climbing on. Don't open the bottle if you're afraid to drink the hooch.

"Life is not a journey to the grave with the intention of arriving safely in a pretty and well-preserved body, but rather to skid in broadside, thoroughly used up, totally worn out, and loudly proclaiming: 'Wow, what a ride!' "

—Unknown

Wino Willie, Fat Boy, George Manker, Johnny Davis, Bobby Kelton, Jim Hunter, and the rest of the founding fathers of the Boozefighters MC exploded out of the muzzle of this country's Great War years and never slowed down. That was the life they chose. That is the life that many of us *still* choose.

The run to Chalk Mountain ended with a barbeque and beer lunch for the whole group at a member's nearby farm. Most had already left when the phone rang. More "crap" was happening. On her way home, one of the Boozettes had swerved to avoid a dog. She and her bike went over the high side: concussion, three compound leg fractures. More trips to the hospital.

Visiting hour was over. As he left the hospital the questions became more intense than usual: more haunting, more disturbing. Maybe it *was* time to hang up the leathers. Maybe this "code of honor" thing—this *family* thing—just wasn't as important as trying to keep some of those grains in that hour-glass for as long as possible. Maybe it *was* time to slow down and buy that soft-sedan. Trade in two wheels for four.

He had an errand to run before he headed home. A young man in the store noticed his patch. "Are you really a Boozefighter?"

He didn't really feel much like talking but the kid seemed genuinely interested. "Yes, yes I am." It felt good to say that. Again, the emotional breeze began to shift.

"No kidding," the kid said. "I saw a special about you guys on TV and I've read some stuff and I thought it was really cool! You know, all the original guys were war vets and stuff and . . . "

He knew the story. He knew the history. But he let the kid talk. It was doing his damaged sensibilities some good. The leather began to feel real comfortable again. As the kid kept rambling, that ghostly sound began to rise once more from some far-off horizon, the unmistakable rumble of long-extinct V-twins, chain-driven, oil-spewing, springer-front, rigid relics. The wild ones had returned.

Willie and his boys were laughing and cutting up. Chilling voices cut through the crap. "You can hang up them leathers if you want, man. Go ahead, but just remember, *we* never did! There's two ways to look at life; from the inside where it's hot, where ya might get burned, or you can just sit out there in the cold just looking in."

The apparitions left as quickly as they came. The kid was still talking. Apparently he hadn't noticed the phantoms. The biker interrupted him without apology.

"Wait, wait. Hang on a second. What was that first thing you asked me? The first thing you said?"

"Uh, well, I think I asked you, 'are you really a Boozefighter?' "

He thought for a minute and smiled.

He could smell the rubber burning off of Gil Armas' tires as he spun those donuts. He could hear Gil laughing. He could see "Kokomo" in that goofy red admiral's outfit, along with Wino and Fuzzy, careening around Hollister in his Model-T truck, with a crazed drunk in an ancient wicker wheelchair tied behind, weaving and bouncing, hooting and hollering. He was sitting there drinking with the boys at the Big A bar, kicking around names for their new club, a club that was created to turn the intensity of war into the energy of life, a club—a *brotherhood*—that would prove to be immortal.

He looked right into the kid's eyes and answered him again.

It was the same response as before but with more pride this time, with a new resolve.

Are you really a Boozefighter?

"Yes! Yes, I am!"

CHAPTER 8

The Tale of Jack Jordan, the "Twilight of the Immortals," and the Rusted Nuts

A club's patch is sacred. Sometimes it's a target. Sometimes it's a flag. But it's always a *statement*. That's why it's worn. And, like all statements, some are shallow and pointless; others have an impact like suddenly being face-to-face with a Great White in deep water.

The patches of the old, long-established clubs command respect. Seniority always carries weight. Anyone—any group—can come up with a clever, cute, or ominous sounding name and get some cloth sewn into the idea. But history and decades of riding within a brotherhood can't be created by a seamstress. The patch is an outward sign of an inner spirit, one that just gets richer and stronger with time.

BFMC Chapter 21 President R. J. "Cowboy" Carter was drinking in a local Northern California bar when he was approached by a 77-year-old man. The man had an envelope of treasured, but long-forgotten photos. He had memories and a life that, many years ago, had revolved around men who wore a patch like Carter's.

The man's handshake and his words proved to be a living link to a past that is so very vital to the present. His name was Jack Jordan. Nearing 80, Carter's patch must have been like a hazy beacon to Jack, beckoning him back into the social baptism of his youth, back to a time that apparently

Former Shark, present Boozefighter, Jack Jordan.

wasn't dead and buried after all, back to the beginnings of something that was definitely and completely timeless. There had to have been a smile on Jordan's face and tears in Carter's eyes when they realized that their handshake encircled more than a half-century bringing each of them into the other's time.

What follows is "The Twilight of the Immortals," Cowboy Carter's story of Jack Jordan, first published in the national biker magazine, *Thunder Press*:

The year was 1946. As gallant members of America's armed forces returned home from the fiery skies and bloody battlefields of World War II, who might have thought that an insatiable love of motorcycling, combined with their newfound spirit of adventure, would soon lead them to become the founding fathers and quintessential cornerstones of what would be considered today as some of our nation's oldest and most respected motorcycle clubs. Clubs with names like the Boozefighters, Hells Angels, Top Hatters, and Sharks. Today the founding fathers of these clubs and clubs like them are rightly immortalized in the annals of motorcycling history as pioneers and deemed—for all time—to be the taproot of a very special breed of man, the American biker.

It's a brisk Saturday morning, and yet another great day for a ride as a silent dawn breaks over the Sierras. The day's first rays of sunlight have begun to gently transcend the snowcapped peaks on their way to warm the towering oaks that stand guard adjacent to a sleepy little hamlet that the miners of the gold rush referred to as Mud Springs. Known today as El Dorado, California, the burg itself—while unceremoniously transformed by time and grounded in history—is surrounded by well-paved roads and gorgeous mountain scenery, making it a considerably traveled hub for any and all bikers wishing to squeeze the ultimate rush from their great American escape machines. Undoubtedly the most renowned structure of El Dorado is that of the world famous biker bar and restaurant, Poor Red's, where one of the original members of the Sharks Motorcycle Club, Mr. Jack Jordan, inconspicuously works. Migrating to El Dorado from the mean streets of L.A. in 1964, Jack didn't waste much time finding the perfect job as part-time bartender in the quaint little biker bar.

I first met 77-year-old Jack Jordan as I was bellied up to the bar in Poor Red's, tossing back a couple beers. I was proudly flaunting my club's green and white colors at the time, while sitting amidst a veritable potpourri of weekend bikers including of course, the ever-present Brando wannabe types trying hard to look, well . . . *hard*. So anyway, there I was, nursing my drink and thinking that I must have walked into some sort of crazy-ass biker fashion show when out of nowhere I was suddenly, but gingerly, approached by an elderly gentleman dressed in the refreshing sight of some well-used leathers, bringing my attention to the fact that there was probably at least one well-ridden scooter parked outside other than my own. He extended his hand to me in what seemed, at the time, to be something much more than just a casual introduction. I knew right off the bat that Jack wasn't just another asshole tourist, curious about the somewhat strange name of my motorcycle club. It was then he took a firm grip of my hand and went on to say what a great thrill it was for him to once again shake the hand of a Boozefighter.

He recounted how in the late 1940s and early 1950s he was an original member of the Sharks motorcycle club in South L.A., recalling how close our two clubs became over those early years. Both clubs had formed within two years of each other and at exactly the same dot on the map; the All American Bar in South L.A. The older of the two clubs, the Boozefighters, formed in the summer of 1946, with the Sharks following suit two summers later on August 11, 1948, the same year as the Hells Angels. Back then the All American Bar (or "Big A" as the patrons called it) was the place to be if you rode a motorcycle. Matter of fact, if you weren't a biker or an ex-GI you were much better off just staying clear of the the the Big A. In my mind's eye I've always pictured the Big A as a sort of a mystic biker Valhalla with polished golden walls and busty beer tenders at your beck and call, so you can imagine the blow when Jack recalled how the famed All American Bar wasn't much more than a gas station with a small bar inside that only sat about 10 people at a time. Jack began frequenting the joint soon after his release from his old army unit, the 232nd Military Police. He recalled how the clubs were mostly comprised of ex-GIs and it really didn't matter which club you belonged to since all of the different clubs normally rode everywhere together anyway. Some active members of the Boozefighters were even sworn members of the Sharks and Yellow Jackets motorcycle clubs at the same time. It seems that back in those days, the clubs were so close-knit and since the American Motorcycle Association had listed the Boozefighters as an "outlaw" club (not allowing them to participate in AMA events) nobody had a problem with the Boozefighters belonging to more than one club at the same time.

Jack Jordan (far left) with a mix of Boozefighters, 13 Rebels, and Sharks.

He then took me on a once-in-a lifetime stroll down his own personal memory lane, recalling how clubs like the 13 Rebels, Boozefighters, and Sharks would often get together on weekends to stage races (that they called "field meets") between themselves and other area clubs. Jack went on to say that usually a field meet consisted of three or more clubs just getting together on a Saturday afternoon, finding a vacant lot, and letting 'er rip . . . that is, until the property owner eventually showed up to toss 'em all out. Standard practice was to draw straws before the event, the loser having to be the flagman (which was a really crappy job, but was necessary to start each event). The meets usually consisted of a variety of different events, including things like slow races, weenie bite competitions, fast racing around a designated course, and, of course, drag racing. He even recalled one time when the clubs all threw a wooden plank over a fallen tree to see who could ride over it the furthest without falling off. "Ohhhh, the memories . . . Those were the days," Jack sighed.

It was at that very moment his eyes teared over and his trembling hand once again rose, this time clutching pictures in a large manila envelope, suddenly making it obvious that our encounter wasn't by chance. He said they were of the old days and since I was a Boozefighter he wanted me to have them. He went on to say that Patricia, his wife of almost 50 years, had passed away not long ago and it was while in the attic sifting through a large steamer trunk containing her belongings that he came across two pictures taken of the three clubs together before a field meet.

"How long has it been since anybody has seen these pictures?" I asked.

"Fifty years, maybe never," Jack replied. It must have been the writer in me but those four words alone left me dazed and shaking like a Frenchman in a thunderstorm. As I carefully turned and scrutinized each of the faded black-and-white photos, they slowly began to weave an intriguing historical tapestry, chronicling the bygone days of motorcycling and club life in its truest form. An unbridled black-and-white look, reminding me how once upon a time in America something so innocent and so simple eventually grew into the billion-dollar pastime that so many of us readily enjoy today.

Still desperately trying to recover from an immense state of shock, it took all I could muster just to gracefully thank this now misty-eyed monarch of motorcycling and offer him a cocktail. Jack just shook his head and politely replied that he had, for more than one reason, sworn off the demon alcohol years ago. He then politely nodded, slowly turned, retreated from the bar and rode off, leaving all the other bikers in attendance (except for myself) unaware that they were, for a few brief moment in time, graced by one of the very few remaining legends left from motorcycling's glorious yesteryears.

Of course, being the president of a newly formed charter of the Boozefighters MC, there was simply no way I was going to let Jack's wealth of historical knowledge concerning my club simply slip through my fingers and fade quietly away into oblivion. As luck would have it, the Boozefighters were planning a huge birthday bash down in L.A. for their oldest living member, Les Haserot. Along with Les there would be several other immortals of the Green and White such as Jack Lilly, Jim Cameron, Gil Armas— who is considered the grandfather of speedway racing—and "Dago," an original Boozette, all together again in one place at one time for the sake of a good party. Well, I've got to say that it didn't take much prodding to get that "Ol' Shark" Jack Jordan up and ready to ride down with a pack of Boozefighters to party hearty with all his longlost buds.

Upon arriving in Orange County just south of Los Angeles, and motoring into the mansionlike estate of original wild one Gil Armas, Jack was immediately recognized and tearfully welcomed by several of the remaining immortals. First to approach Jack was his old friend Jim Cameron, a man made famous for his mischievous exploits, like the time he rode his bike into Johnny's bar during the world-famous Hollister dust-up of 1947. Jim's infamous ride was later depicted in the 1954 cult classic movie *The Wild One*.

At 77 years of age, Jack Jordan was "rediscovered" by the BFMC, prospected, and became a member of the club.

Back in those days, Jim Cameron and Jack were real close friends, with Jim even living for six years or so of his life in Jack's parents' house across the street from the old Mustang motorcycle factory on 103rd street in South L.A.

As I quietly approached, the two bros were busy sharing a story. Jim was remembering how he once grabbed a policeman's arm and he and the Boozefighters' first president, C. B. Clausen, got thrown into the pokey for the heinous deed. Pooling their money, they went before a judge the next day but unfortunately for the two wild ones, the judge wasn't in the best of moods and certainly wasn't interested in their pocket change. "It's going to be 15 days for the man that grabbed the policeman's arm," the judge roared. With that C. B. stood up and said, "I'm the man you want, Your Honor." Jim, bowled over by what C. B. had just done, looked up and said, "What the hell do ya think your doing, C. B.? I was the one that grabbed that cop's arm!" C. B. just quietly turned and said, "Hush Jim, you got a job and a family at home, and besides, I wasn't planning on doing much for the next 15 days anyway."

Now that's brotherhood!

Great story, but I wasn't willing to let Jim Cameron off the hook that easy. I still needed to hear the story about that famous ride into Johnny's Bar 57 years ago. Man-o-man, can you imagine hearing it straight from the guy who pulled it off? So with recorder rolling I said, "Jim here's your chance to set history straight. How did you get in that front door of Johnny's since I noticed it swings outward?" Jim said, "Well it happened like this. I was sitting on my bike outside Johnny's when some dummy in front of the door opens it up for me. Then he hollers at me, 'Come on in!' so I did." "How many beers did ya have that day?" I asked laughingly. "Well, I didn't have any beers, but I had some straight brown liquor. It was just some cheap Goddamn stuff we bought at the last stop earlier in the morning. But getting back to the ride, I popped up over the curbing and, well, I didn't think that Goddamn chopped Indian had that much clearance, but it did. The bar came all the way to the door so once inside I just finally parked it over in the corner, walked over, and ordered another whiskey, only because I didn't want to mix my alcohol."

Nowadays Jim still races in senior class events around California and, get this, he's still winning.

Just then Jim turned the conversation back to Jack.

"Jack, it's been fifty years since the Big Bear Run, so where ya been? Jack, are ya still riding C. B. Clausen's old bike? You must remember that

41/61 stroked to an 80 inch that C. B. built for Fat Boy Nelson before Fat Boy ran out of money and sold it to the 13 Rebels. If I remember right, you ended up trading something to one of the 13 Rebels for it didn't you? So where ya living now Jack?"

All of this was just driving me crazy. I wanted to document every shred of this primeval history of motorcycling, yet it almost felt sacrilegious for me to intrude on them like some sort of asshole paparazzi raining down on their conversations with a camera and a recorder. But, of course, I did anyway. On and on the questions poured and the answers sounded, as a flood of golden memories, hugs, and tears rushed back and forth between these two remaining living legends of motorcycling. After leaving Jim and walking Jack back inside the mansion, Jack told me yet another story about how a Boozefighter he once knew had always left his bike out in the rain on purpose, even going as far as to douse his machine with water and then just walk away. Jack said, "The bike was always sparking clean, but it was always wet. He never dried it off." Jack never bothered to ask him why but always wished that he had. Jack said that he got a big kick out of watching the Boozefighters and their antics, like that mysterious wet bike thing. Besides it also kind of eased the pain of the Boozefighters winning most of the field meets.

Next stop for Jack was as the guest of honor of BFMC birthday boy, Les Haserot. Along with being the oldest member of the Green and White at 86, Les is also known to history buffs as "the Baja King." Les made his mark in the history books as being the first person to race from Ensenada to Cabo San Lucas, Mexico, on a motorcycle, a 1937 45-inch flat-head to be exact. Even today's most accomplished bikers on far superior machines find this feat nearly impossible. Imagine, if you will, racing over 900 hard-fought miles of dirt, snakes, and prairie dog holes, with it being 120 degrees in the shade. Not only was Les the first to race the Baja on a motorcycle, he amazingly accomplished this feat 20 times between 1950 and 1954.

As Jack and I approached Les, a strange look came over Jack's face. He turned to me and said in nothing more than a whisper, "That's the guy."

"Guy? What guy?" I replied.

Just then Jack yells at the top of his voice, "You know the guy, the guy with the wet bike all the time. It's Les, he's the guy!"

"Oh *that* guy," I replied. Reluctantly deciding to leave Les and Jack alone with their memories for the time being, I headed off to the bar downstairs. An hour or so passed before I hooked up with Jack once again out by the barbeque. I just couldn't help it. I had to ask Jack if he found out anything about Les' wet scooter.

He smiled and replied, "Rust."

"Rust?" I asked. "What the hell do you mean rust?"

Jack replied, "Les kept his bike wet so that all his nuts and bolts would rust."

"This is some sort of joke, right Jack?"

"Nope," Jack said laughing. "It's simple, the Baja King said he didn't need his bike flying apart somewhere out in the Baja desert, so he kept his bike wet so his nuts and bolts would rust tight." We laughed and agreed that the mystery had finally been solved.

Just then the word trickled out that Dennis Sanfilippo and his film crew from Big 7 Productions had arrived and were ready to begin documenting this historic reunion. That's when the call went out that they now needed all the original wild ones, still scattered about the party, to regroup at the top of the hill for the photo op. With the sun beginning to set in the background, the already large and raucous crowd of Boozefighters and club supporters began to repeatedly chant: "Boozefighters-up," as the living legends began to emerge from the house and take their respective seats on the film crew's set. A sudden hush fell over the crowd, silenced not only by the amazing sight of the last remaining immortals of motorcycling all in the same place at the same time, but also by the horrible realization that it would probably be for the last time.

As the last few original wild ones were now finally all seated, I noticed still one empty chair. But why would they have put out a chair for no reason I asked myself? That's when, almost in unison, these few remaining heroes of yesteryear turned, then pointed to Jack, who was standing in the back of the crowd and yelled, "Hey you! Shark! What the hell ya waiting for? Get over here and sit your butt down." With a smile that beamed from ear to ear, Jack proudly made his way through the crowd and sat down with the rest of the pack, immediately wrapping his arms around his old racing buddy, Jim Cameron. The two bros now relived an incredible scene of brotherhood for all to see, one that I'll never forget as long as I live. Little did the "Ol' Shark" know that he would soon be officially pronounced an honorary Boozefighter. With that, the colors of the two clubs were now once again blending harmoniously together, back into the only two colors that ever really mattered: that of the faded black and white of pictures portraying a generation of heroes.

As the sun slowly disappeared beyond the horizon, it suddenly occurred to me that with this reunion, Jack's life had now come full circle. As for myself, I now realize there is no twilight for these immortals. Their lives will continue to live on, burning bright for all eternity deep within our hearts, remembered for all time. Not as elderly gentlemen in the December of their lives, but rather as they once were; the young, strong, clean-shaven immortals of yesteryear dressed in rolled-up blue jeans and button down shirts, racing their fenderless motorcycles through the streets of Hollister. These are—and will forever be—the pioneers that founded America's first clubs, the clubs that first and foremost taught us the most valuable lessons of trust, loyalty, respect, and brotherhood. For them there will be no twilight; the handing down of their legacy for generations to come will ensure their immortality.

CHAPTER 9

The Tale of Irish Ed, a Dedication to the Era of the Original Wild Ones, a Closet Preacher, Pawnshop Julie, Flying Colors Alone

The dedication at the beginning of this book lists the names of the individuals who were members and associates of the original wild ones, but there is also an unspoken reverence and respect written between those lines. This book is equally dedicated to the *era* of the original wild ones, a time when freedom didn't quite have so many asterisks next to the word. It was a time when politicians were elected to keep the peace, hire a good sheriff, and fill potholes, not to worry about motorcycle helmets and throaty exhaust pipes.

It was also a more innocent time, and, arguably, a more God-fearing time. During the 1940s, the term "family values" was more of a day-to-day basis for living than just another concept to be used as a modern day political football. Apart from any specific religious belief or affiliation, the testimony of BFMC National Chaplain Irish Ed Mahan reflects a love of humanity and a genuine caring for the brotherhood that has been a part of this club for over 50 years. His inner conflicts and the strength that he absorbed from this brotherhood helped him to survive.

When you're a true biker, you're never alone.

"When I was young I went through a conversion experience and was definitely called to the ministry. I came from a Southern Baptist background, and to me there was only one kind of ministry and that was in a suit and tie.

"Well, I got into it and I was licensed by the church in 1972 to preach, graduating from college with a degree in sociology and a minor in religion. Upon graduating, I was called to pastor a First Baptist church in a small Louisiana town. Like I say, I was totally into it, I didn't know that there was more than one route beyond the traditional pastor route, but I had always felt weird around straighter-laced folks. I just didn't feel right around them because I had a pretty wild and wooly background when I was young. I got deep into it in terms of going to state conventions and such. I'd hear stuff at the state conventions and I'd think, 'What's up with that?' I remember going to these different seminars at the conventions and I went to one on increasing offerings, and this guy was saying, 'All you pastors who are using *white* offering envelopes need to change to pink. It has been statistically proven that you can increase your church's giving by eight percent just by switching from white to pink envelopes!'

"So I'm thinking to myself, 'What's this all about?' As time went on and I heard and saw more and more things like that, I became more and more disillusioned. Well, after two years my church was a success in terms of growth, offerings, baptisms, and so on, but I felt like I needed more education, so I moved from Louisiana to Fort Worth to attend Southwestern Baptist Theological Seminary, the largest seminary in the country.

"Now there were some good professors there but I kept getting more and more disillusioned with the whole deal, because I saw too much manipulation. I was 100 percent into it spiritually. I had no thoughts of getting rich or using people to get what I wanted. It was strictly a heavenly calling. But as I saw more of the *organization* of religion, the more it bothered me. Then I started to party a bit. Then a little bit more. After a while I got my real estate license and began to party a *lot* more! In order to keep up my reputation with my family and friends, I continued to go to church and I continued to do the things that I felt I should be doing, but meanwhile my heart started to get harder and harder.

"I had actually tried to quit preaching. After my heart was totally away from the ministry I was asked by a church in Burleson, where I live now, to come and preach. That was the hardest thing I ever did. I threw up before I got up there. It was cool in there but I was pouring sweat, and everything I was saying was just an old message; my heart wasn't into it at all. I was just doing it to keep up appearances. So when I finished that night, I told myself that was it. I didn't care what, I was never preaching again. And at that point I decided that if I wasn't going to preach anymore, I was going to get rich!

"And I did. Got into the real estate game. Became a broker. Began to buy repossessed houses on the courthouse steps on every first Tuesday for five years. I did well. Then the real estate crash of 1987 came along and the bottom fell out. I wound up owing the bank about five hundred thousand so I got into the used car business. I didn't know anything about used cars but I had a friend who was into it and he said it was easy so I rented some space from him. I was in the used car business.

"That's when I really sacrificed my family for my work. I cut myself off from all the people I knew back when I was a preacher. And I made my immediate family swear that they wouldn't tell anyone that I had even *been* a preacher. All I did was go after the dollar. I didn't have any friends, I didn't want any friends. The only thing I wanted was to be rich. I wanted to be a millionaire by the time I was forty. Friends take time, and time is money, so unless you could put a buck in my pocket why would I talk to you? That's the kind of mentality I had. I went on like that and built a very successful car business which I sold in August of 1999 and I haven't worked a day since. I made a lot of money and paid the bank off everything I owed them. But I became more and more miserable and I began to lead a double life. I was one guy to my family and another guy to the world. I was always covering my tracks so that this life didn't get exposed to the life I wanted to maintain.

"I dropped out of the ministry in 1981. Quit going to church completely. My wife would beg me to go to church with her and the kids. I'd tell her, 'I'm through with church. I'll never be a preacher or a Christian again never.'

"It went like that for many years. Working harder and harder, neglecting my family more and more. I became a very angry person. When I came in the driveway at night my wife would tell the kids, 'Dad's home,' and they'd all run to their rooms because they didn't want anything to do with me. And my wife hated to see me come home, too. And I hated to come home, so . . . well, I wasn't home much.

"Then I ran into the Boozefighters.

"I found out about the Boozefighters from my son. As things went on, my son became a great guitarist, learned from listening to Jimi Hendrix over and over. He told me one day back in 1997 that he had this gig at a biker club. In the late 1960s I had become familiar with the motorcycle club scene but I had always ridden as an independent. I asked him what biker club he was playing for? He says, 'the Boozefighters.' I asked him, 'What are they, an

AA club or something?' 'No I don't think so,' he says. 'Their clubhouse is like a bar and stuff.'

"I tell my wife, 'You know, Matt could get himself in a lot of trouble at that biker place tonight. He's just 19 years old. I'm gonna go up there. I'd like to hear him play and I can get him outta there if any trouble breaks out or anything.'

"I went to the Boozefighters club for the first time that night in 1997. Man, I loved every minute of it! I'd had a wreck thirteen years before, a hit and run, and I'd quit riding. I hadn't been on a bike in all those years. My kids were all little and I thought, I'm not gonna check out while my kids were small like that. But I went to the club and just loved the whole scene, hearing the Harleys again, seeing the party. I said, 'Oh man, this is for me.' So two weeks later I had a bike.

"I hung around for a couple of months, just keeping my eyes open and my mouth shut, you know, just to make sure that there wasn't stuff going on like I experienced in the early days that you don't know about 'til you're in and then you can't get out. I was up there every Friday and Saturday night, but I wasn't committing to anything. Finally I came home and told my wife that I was going to prospect for the Boozefighters. Well, unbeknownst to me she told my mother, whom she's very close to. She told my mother, 'Ed told me last night that he's going to prospect for the Boozefighters. I've put up with a lot of stuff, I've gone through a lot of changes, but this is the beginning of the end. We're not going to survive this. He's going to be out at the titty joints and running crazy. I can take him working all the time but I can't take him coming home drunk and hollering and perfume all over him and stuff like that. This is it.'

"Well, my dad, who's 81 years old now, has been a Baptist preacher since 1951, so he calls me. Now I didn't know my wife had made this call, you understand, but my dad calls and says, 'Son, are you gonna join them Boozefighters?' I said, 'Yes sir, I believe I am.' 'Why?' he asks, 'cause he hates drinking, he hates bars, hasn't been in a bar since 1949 or 1950. I said, 'Dad, there's two reasons, neither of which are you going to understand, and one of 'em I don't understand.' He said, 'Try me.' I said, 'Well, you know I've dedicated the last 18, 20 years to getting rich and I've had no friends and I'm tired of it. I want camaraderie, and these guys really care about one another. It's like a brotherhood like I never experienced, even in the church. They hug one another, they're available 24-7 if someone has a problem. I've just never seen anything like it. Secondly,

BFMC National Chaplain, "Irish Ed" Mahan.

the one that *I* don't understand, I feel really deep, deep down to a place that I even forgot I had that God's gonna use me again . . . in the Boozefighters.' And Dad says, 'In what way?' I said, 'I don't know. Maybe I'll be a chaplain some-day.' And he goes, 'Do they have chaplains?' 'No,' I said, 'I asked but they said they never have had 'em.' Then Dad asked me if I was right with God. I had to tell him, no, I wasn't. Then he says, 'Do you want to be?' I said, 'No sir, I don't. Pure and simple. I've walked away from that part of my life. That's it.'

"So, I joined the Boozefighters. I went along for about a year doing what the Boozefighters do. After that I became friends with JQ. He and I would go to the Waffle House after every monthly meeting and he would teach me the history of the Boozefighters. Sometimes we'd be there for three or four hours, 'til two or three in the morning.

"But he asked me one night, 'Have you ever been to prison?' 'No, I never been to prison,' I said. 'Why would you ask me somethin' like that?' 'Well, I'm kind of a student of the human condition,' he says, 'and there's something that you're hiding in your life—in your past—that you're not let-ting anybody know about.' Of course, like Peter in the Bible, I came off with anger, told him he was wrong. 'I'm no different than anybody else,' I told him. 'Yeah, you are,' he said. 'You're different.'

"The very next month, after the meeting at the Waffle House, here comes the same question 'You're bugging the hell outta me,' he says. 'You're hiding something.' Again, like Peter, I denied it a second time.

"On the third month he brings it up again. He was wearing me down. I said, 'Okay, JQ, I'll satisfy your curiosity but you've got to swear to me that you won't tell anybody.' After I told him my whole story I asked him if he was surprised. 'No, I'm not,' he says. 'Now it all makes sense. You have a dif-ferent *heart* than all the rest of us. As much as you try to act *hard* it doesn't work. You're really a peacemaker. I've seen it in the meetings and such. When two brothers get into it or whatever, you're the one who's always trying to calm things down. You're a peacemaker.' I said, 'Yeah, I guess that's true.'

" 'So why don't you want me to tell anybody?' 'Here's the way it is, JQ. I'm a dropout. I'm not proud of that. I am proud of men like my old daddy and many others who labor in hard-nose, stiff-necked little churches all their lives, starving to death, disrespected, just because of *the call*. But they hang in there. I didn't hang. I quit. I'm ashamed of myself. If you were to let it out that I'd been a preacher, you know what would happen? Immediately I'd get a new nickname: 'Preacher.' Every biker would be calling me 'Preacher.' That would be a disrespect to the real ones, and I ain't going there.' He says, 'Okay, alright.'

"A few days after that, after I had sworn him to secrecy, he calls me. 'Irish Ed,' he says, 'we got a problem.' 'What's the problem?' I said. 'I was at the clubhouse last night and you know Bob and Patty? Well, they want to get married on New Year's Eve but Bob don't go to church. He don't have a preacher. He's asked a couple of other preachers but they don't want to come to a biker bar or clubhouse. A couple of 'em flat-out told him that they sure didn't want to spend their New Year's Eve with biker trash. So I was thinking if any of us had any ideas.

" 'You didn't!' I said.

" 'No I didn't, but you need to!'

"I said, 'No way, JQ! You can ask me to pay for the wedding, anything, but not that!' So JQ, like only JQ would, says to me, 'You wouldn't *come outta the closet* for a brother just one time?' I said, 'You dog!' He says, 'This is your brother, man, and you can help him. You still got your legal papers and all that stuff don't you?' I said, 'Yeah, they never caught up with me to take 'em away.' 'Well, think about it,' he says.

"So I thought about it for two or three days, then I called up Bob. 'Bob,' I says, 'I understand you and Patty want to get married New Year's Eve.' 'Yeah,' he says. 'You know anybody who'd do it for us? Any ideas?' I said, 'Yeah, *I* can do it.' 'YOU!' he says. 'How can *you* do it!?' 'Oh geez, Bob, I'm an ordained preacher.' 'YOU ARE?' I quietly said, 'Yes. JQ told me about you needing somebody and I been feeling bad, but, please, don't say anything to anyone. This is just November; at least let me stay incognito 'til New Year's. Just tell 'em that you're gonna get married at the clubhouse, don't tell 'em who or what. Please do it that way. Give me a couple more months of peace.' 'OK,' he says.

"Everything was cool. Nobody called me preacher, nobody asked me anything. This is going all right, I figured. But in December we had our big annual toy run. And we always have this big party afterward for the Boozefighters and those we invite from the toy run to our clubhouse. Starts at five. At about seven they had the first band break, and Harpoon, the chapter president at the time, gets up onstage, gets the microphone, gets everyone's attention. My wife was sitting there beside me. He starts off, 'We've got people from all walks of life in this club. We've got truck drivers, we've got an airline pilot, we've got this and that, but what none of us knew 'til real recently, and only two or three of us know presently, is that we have a real, bona fide, ordained Southern Baptist preacher as a Boozefighter!' You could hear the whole room go, '*What?*'

"My wife looked at me and I just covered my face and slumped down in my chair. 'You know who you are, Irish Ed, C'mon, get up here!' I walked up there and he goes, 'A few of us found out you were a preacher. You know, we've never had a chaplain but we really need our own guy. To hitch 'em and plant 'em, and a little prayer every once in a while wouldn't hurt either. We talked about it and we want you to be our chaplain.'

"I was floored! He gave me the chaplain patches. Then everyone yelled, 'Speech!' So I told everyone, 'You people know me. I'm not a godly man. All I can say is the message is perfect; this messenger is very, very flawed. Please don't ever judge the message by this messenger.' And I sat down.

"When I got home the first thing I did was to call my old daddy. I said, 'Dad, it happened.' He said, '*What* happened?' I said, 'I'm chaplain of the Boozefighters.' He asked me, 'How'd that happen?' I said, 'I don't know!' Then he asked me again, 'Son, are you right with God?' I said what I said before, 'No sir.' He said it again, 'Son, do you want to be?' 'No sir!' He said, 'Oh man, I'll pray for you.'

"So I went until the following August. Never really changed my lifestyle. Never prayed, never read the Bible. Hadn't touched the Bible in fifteen years. It was up on a shelf, all covered with dust. But then we had a brother killed on his bike. It was my duty to do his funeral. I finally reached up to get that Bible down off the shelf, dusted it off. Opened it up to the gospel of John and I started to read. But I also started to cry. But I got through it, still *without* repenting. After that, though, God started to speak to my heart again, after my not hearing from him for many years. He'd just say, 'I love you.' I would literally cover my ears, not wanting to hear.

"That didn't last long. I got to the point where I really wanted to come back to the service and fellowship of the Lord, but I had a fear that I couldn't, that I'd gone too far back. It was so traumatic. Then I had a heart attack. I told my son goodbye on my way to the hospital, but they saved me.

"After that I shut my business down and spent six months, every day alone. I prayed and I read the word of God. But I didn't go to church. And I needed a couple of assurances—from the Lord, not from any man—that I could be a free man—freedom is very important to me—that I could be a free man but still be in the heart-felt service of God. During that six months God gave me that assurance by reading his word.

"I came back to the Lord not really expecting to be used in the ministry, but more like the Prodigal Son, coming back as one of the hired help. That's the attitude I came back with, but God had a different plan.

"Spring was starting to arrive, and one weekend day as we rode into the clubhouse I leaned back and said to my wife, 'You know Easter is coming up. I bet that one of those Christian clubs will have a sunrise service. I'd kind a like to go to one this year, been twenty years since I've been to something like that.' Well, we get to the clubhouse and there's Big John laying outside sunning himself like a big beached whale, but he yells over to me, 'Chaplain! Come here! Me and Connie's been talkin' about it. Easter's comin' up. How about we have something here at the clubhouse, a little Easter *thing* or something.' 'An Easter *thing*,' I said. 'What are we talkin' about, John, an Easter egg hunt for the kids, what?' 'No, hell no. Why don't you get some of those people you know to come and sing and you can preach and we can have a sunrise service right here at the Boozefighters' clubhouse!' 'You serious!?' It had just been a minute before and I was tellin' my wife I'd like to go to one. 'Can you do something like that?' he says. 'We never done anything like that. I think it'd be good. Can you do it?' 'Uh, yeah,' I said.

"That Easter morning I preached for the first time in twenty years. Okay, first of all I told the Boozefighters that we had to start at *6 a.m. on a Sunday morning*! Now that's not exactly a biker schedule on the weekends! I didn't think anybody would show up. But I joined up with Big John and a couple of others and we rode in. Now we had put up a few posters and stuff in some biker bars around the area, said 'Easter sunrise at the Boozefighters clubhouse, Irish Ed's gonna preach and stuff.' We rounded the corner near the clubhouse and it was packed, bikes everywhere. I went, 'Wow!' It was still dark! It was early! And the place was packed! Bikers! I was figuring on a dozen at most. Well, I preached, said I wanted to tell 'em a love story, about how God never gives up on you no matter what. I was honest, told 'em that this was the first time I had preached in twenty years.

"For three days after that I got a lot of complimentary phone calls. Stuff like, 'Man, that was great, let's do it again next year. If you ever start a church I just might start to go again.' Stuff like that. Well, I told my wife after the three days, 'I think I was ineffective.' She says, 'Why do you say that?' 'All I'm getting are compliments; if this was really effective I'd get some opposition.'

"I didn't have to wait too long for *that* to happen. That night I get a call from JQ. 'Brother, I hate to be the one to tell ya this, but we got some guys in the club who are real upset. They're gonna have a special meeting called this coming Wednesday night—and they want you there—concerning the *direction* the club is taking, 'cause some are real upset that we had religion in the clubhouse.' I said, 'Well, okay.'

"The complaints went in different ways, mostly about the fact that sometimes the parties and such in the clubhouse get a little wild and crazy. Now some are feelin' like they can't do what they used to do, that it just doesn't feel right any more. I told them, 'Have I ever said that you couldn't do *anything*?' But they still said, 'No, you haven't said that, but still it just doesn't feel right having religion in the clubhouse!' I told them again, 'I've never said anything about not doing anything. Do what you want. I don't intend to try and turn all of this into a Sunday school. In time I might start a biker Bible study but it ain't gonna be here at the clubhouse. Everyone will be welcome, but it'll be somewhere else. I'm not a threat to you or to this way of life. If you want to put me out, that's your prerogative and I understand, because when I first came to the Boozefighters if there'd been a guy who was all of a sudden a preacher, I'd have hated him. I'd have been his worst enemy, because that's not what I wanted to hear. I was going the other way, and I sure didn't want to be reminded of that fact.'

"Turned out that the biggest complaints came from people like me. One used to be a deacon in his church a long time ago; another was from the same sort of thing. The ones that had the strongest spiritual backgrounds and had left it were the angriest. I had a pretty strong weapon, though: love. After that, when I came into the clubhouse some of those guys who were so angry would literally turn their backs on me. But I always made it a point to hug them first. It took a while, but we all worked things out through this brotherhood. Some of those who were the angriest are now some of my biggest supporters, but they don't necessarily believe the message and they haven't changed their lives in any way. But love and this brotherhood brought them around.

"That Easter sunrise service really did bring a lot of reactions. There was this one woman in particular, 'Pawnshop Julie,' a really rough woman—been involved in a lot of things, ridden with other clubs, an ex-old lady of the president of a one percenter club—well, she had been there at the sunrise. She came to me and said, 'Ed, that message really done something to me. I want God in my heart but I don't know how to go about it. Can you help me?' 'Sure,' I said. We went downstairs at the clubhouse and I shared some Scripture with her, prayed with her, about six weeks later I baptized her. I had to 'borrow' a church because I obviously didn't have one! I invited all the Boozefighters to the service and the pastor let me preach. Julie had been to jail, been involved in violent crimes, dealt drugs. We videotaped this baptism. She started handing out copies of this video to people she met who were in trouble, people who would come into her pawnshop selling what they could to survive. She'd have them see the video, and then she'd call me. 'Brother!' that's what she called me, 'Brother,' she'd say, 'how fast can you come over here? I got somebody in bad trouble!' 'It'll be an hour,' I might tell her, 'Okay, I'll hold 'em,' she'd say. Then I'd get there and counsel with them.

"She's given out about 500 of those videos. People all over the country have seen those videos. I was in her shop one day when this well-dressed, distinguished-looking couple came in. I noticed them staring at me. I was in my colors. They kept staring at me. Finally they asked, 'Are you a preacher?' 'Yeah,' I said. 'Oh, okay,' they nodded. 'Why?' I asked. 'We live in Phoenix but we have a daughter here in Texas and we come to see her a couple of times a year and we always stop by this shop while we're here to buy jewelry and such. Last time we were here, Julie gave us this video. Well, we brought it back to Phoenix. We showed it in our church, home Bible studies, Sunday school. It got passed around to everyone.'

"I walked into a Waffle House in Fort Worth one time and the waitress says, 'You're the preacher on the video!'

"Bottom line is that life has been very, very good since I totally made the commitment in my heart to live for the Lord. Now I *do* go to church. I belong to a Southern Baptist church, and a lot of the people there whisper behind my back, I know that. But I told the preacher when I came in his church that on a lot of Sunday mornings I'm not gonna be here, because I'm with my brothers on Saturday night and sometimes our stuff don't end 'til two or three o'clock in the morning. The preacher said, 'No problem. I believe in you. Just keep doing what you're doing.'

"The first month I was there—it's a church of 500 people—the preacher was giving a message. He says, 'Take Irish Ed out there, for example—Ed Mahan. I don't want even *one* of you coming to me and saying that you saw Ed, our new church member, going in and out of that biker bar down the street. Because if you watch him much you *will* see him going in and out of there 'cause that's one of his favorite places. He spreads the word of God in more places like that than all of the rest of you put together!'

"One of my sons was there that morning. When we got home he says, 'That's way cool, Dad.' 'What's that,' I said. 'I bet you're the only Baptist in Texas that has a hall pass to go to the bar!'"

"More people are driven insane through religious hysteria than by drinking alcohol."

—W. C. Fields

"It did finally get to the point where bikers were pushing me to start a church. That's scary, though, not because of the spirituality involved or the *heart* it takes, but because of that *structure* of a formal church. There are often *rules* involved in a church. But I tell people in my Bible study, 'I'll never give you *rules*. I'll give you *no* rules because you might be strong-willed enough of *your own self* to keep these rules. Then you're more lost than ever because then you've got spiritual pride on top of a lost soul. And you'll never be reached. And if you need a drink before Bible study, well, our favorite joint is just down the street. Stop off before you get here. Just check your watch and don't have so many that you lose track of time and miss Bible study altogether!' And that's how it works. They'll leave Cooter Brown's bar, tell everyone, 'Well, gotta go, gotta get to Irish Ed's Bible study.' And a lot of times someone else in the bar will say, 'Hell, that sounds interesting. I'll ride over there with ya.'

"When we started the Bible study every Tuesday I had an important criteria. I'd ask people, 'Do you go to church?' 'Naw,' they say, 'I ain't been to church in twenty years.' 'Good,' I'd tell 'em. 'You're invited.' I didn't want a bunch of *church people* in here. I wanted to get real people, most of whom had had some kind of spiritual experience at one time in their lives. But because of the established church and their little old unbending attitudes, these people got very disillusioned and said, 'Screw it all, I'm going to hell. All my friends are there anyway!'

"My ministry is aimed at those who have faced the firing squad of the established church and left their faith, not because of anything *God* had done to them, but because of those who claimed to be godly, with the fish on the back of their car, giving them the finger while they run their bikes off the road. My watchwords are: 'Keep it real.' You don't have to put on one face when you come to my Bible study and put on another face outside. Just be yourself and *we'll* love you and accept you just like you are because, I guarantee, you're not involved in any kind of problems that one of the rest of us hasn't had, too.

"There's a young man who came to my Bible study named Steven Noble. Every time I saw him at Cooter Brown's he was drunk. And not a happy drunk—a *mean* drunk. I befriended him. When we started the Bible study I said to him, 'I'm gonna have a Bible study. Do you go to church?' 'Hell no!' he says. 'Good, you fit,' I said. 'I got a Bible study on Tuesday night and I want you to come.'

"After a few weeks he actually did show up. Came back a second week, third week, and a fourth week. He had just been listening. On that fourth week he says, 'My dad wants to meet you.' I said, 'Yeah?' He said, 'Yeah. Anybody that could get me to go to any kind of church, my daddy wants to meet. But I gotta tell ya something about my daddy. The best way to describe it is that I'm *no longer in his book*.' Turns out that his dad is a writer, wrote this book called *Tabernacle of Hate*. Well, I read the book. His dad, Kerry Noble, was second in command of the second worst paramilitary religious cult ever in America as categorized by the FBI. This kid was raised in this cult. They had a showdown with the FBI and the ATF. After a week's stand-off they surrendered and his dad went to prison for two or three years. The main leader did ten.

"This kid hated his dad, hated religion, hated anything that even *smacked* of religion. He'd seen the whole deal. His dad had taken a second wife in the cult. Nobody could have any access to outside information—newspapers, magazines, TV—except the cult leader. He had everything, but the rest got no information and they were limited to this 'compound.' They had antiaircraft guns, bazookas, submachine guns, armed to the teeth. This kid knew Timothy McVeigh and Terry Nichols, saw them with their maps and plans about Oklahoma City. He knew David Koresh. For his sixth birthday he was given his first machine gun and was taught how to use it.

"He was filled with paranoia. Big Brother is coming to get you, the only ones to be saved will be those who stick with and listen to the leaders, and God's gonna open up the Earth when they come after us just like he parted the Red Sea, and he'll swallow up the enemy, doesn't matter how many come against us! All this crap. But I did read his dad's book. Two weeks later I asked the kid, 'Okay where's your dad?' He was nearby so I told the kid I'd like to meet his dad.

"We got on the phone and set up a time and I wound up having supper with him and his wife. We talked for about three hours. Turns out that he's been on thirteen different major TV shows because he's the only guy who was a paramilitary religious cult leader who now works for the FBI. He addresses every graduating class of the FBI on how to handle cults. They also have him help in sensitive negotiations with these groups. He's done a complete turn-around. He's still kind of a weird guy, but he's a good citizen now. We had a real good visit. That kid still comes to our study—I'm gonna do the wedding for him and his gal—and he still has a drink or two at Cooter Brown's—I never told him *not* to drink—but he sure controls it a lot better now."

"Getting back into the ministry was frightening to me on two levels. One was that I would lose my freedom—I simply *had* to remain a free man. The second was the fact that I really, really loved the Boozefighters and I feared that if I *came out* I would be rejected and put out, with people condemning me for being a *holy roller.* But after the initial little problem, the exact opposite has happened. These guys love me like I can't believe. A few months ago, the pastor of the church I go to asked me, 'Ed, I can't imagine how difficult it must be to be in the ministry you're in.' I said, 'What do you mean?' He said, 'Well, you know, with all those guys, wild guys, people getting naked and drinking and all.' I said, 'Are you kiddin'! With bikers you could have the holiness of Balaam and they think you walk on water, but in *your* position you could have the holiness of Jesus Christ and fifty percent of your people will be opposin' you. You can't ever be right because half of 'em are upset and the other half are happy. The next week it's the other way around. *You* can't ever please all of *your* people. My guys, if they just think I'm pretty well in touch, that's okay. They *know* I'm no saint, but I'm trying."

"A year and a half ago I began to have prostrate problems. My PSA level shot way up. I went to the doctor. He treated me with different drugs. I went through 21 days of high doses of some powerful stuff. It made me feel miserable. I went back to the doctor after the 21 days and the level had actually gone *up* a point. The doctor gave me another test that also came back with some pretty bad results. 'Ed,' he says, 'I'm pretty sure you've got cancer. I'll set you up in a couple of weeks for a biopsy, but all of the tests so far are indicating cancer.' Well, you know, I always thought that if the big 'C' word was ever said over me I'd fall apart, but I had absolutely no fear, no sleepless nights. It was like, okay, praise God, I've got a whole new ministry. If I've got cancer I'm sure that there's a whole lot of cancer folks out there who need to be ministered to and I can't really do it effectively unless I've got it, too, so praise God. And nobody was more surprised with that attitude than I was. Even my wife said, 'Ed, aren't you worried?' I said, 'I don't know why but I'm not. Since I really put my life totally in God's hands, what's to be afraid of? Worst you could do is die, then you'll go to heaven. What's the problem?'

"Things got pretty strange after the next exam at the doctor. He said, 'I don't know what happened but you're totally clear. I don't know what happened! You're released. Come back in a year and we'll check you again, but you're OK.' I was stunned, but all through that time I really had no fear, no problems. Plus I've got the best of both worlds. I can be a biker *and* I've got the peace of God inside. What could be better?"

"Though I am free and belong to no man, I make myself a slave to everyone, to win as many as possible."

—The Apostle Paul

"Now this trip I'm taking . . . As we all know, in some states, in some regions of the country, there are problems among clubs. Big John asked me if I was gonna wear my colors the whole time. I said, 'Yeah, probably.' 'By yourself?' he asks. 'Yeah.' 'Now what are you gonna do if you get yourself in a jam somewhere? What if someone, some group gets upset about you being in their territory?' 'Well,' I said, 'I'll ask their permission to reach in my saddlebags, and I'll pull out my Bible. I'll explain that I'm on a spiritual journey spreading the word to bikers. I'm so glad y'all asked! I been needing a congregation! They'll escort me outta town so fast! They won't take me to their clubhouse or beat me up or anything; they'll just want me gone!' "

Ed and I were having a couple of beers as we talked alone, surrounded by Northern California pines, listening to the sounds of big bikes on a road off in the distance. Shortly after our discussion he was setting out on his black 1995 Electra Glide Classic for a three-month trek—a *pilgrimage* of sorts—no map, no itinerary. Just his bike, his little camp trailer, a willing spirit, and his BFMC colors. The only plan was to meet people and spread the brotherhood.

"I believe that God will have people in my path, people in need, desperate people, lost people. He'll have it all 'set up' so when I get there, wherever *there* may be, it won't be a struggle. They'll just *be there*, and I'll be *there* for them."

Some journeys in the past have definitely been hard for Irish Ed. This one should be easy.

CHAPTER 10

The Tale of the Oldest Living Boozefighter

Living history is always a whole lot more impressive than inanimate please-do-not-touch antiques behind a velvet rope, priceless "collectibles" in a locked glass museum curio cabinet, or brittle, decaying snapshots and newspaper clippings.

And, sure, those huge old trees that have the giant historical slice taken out of them are interesting, but, well, they're *dead*, even though someone with an extraordinary amount of time at their disposal has counted all those insanely small rings and has been able to strategically place little yellow arrows at important landmarks in human development as the tree stood stately by: *1200 B.C., Moses dies; 44 B.C., Julius Caesar is killed; 1903, Harley-Davidson is born; 1958, Muddy Waters electrifies the blues; 1996, the Spice Girls record their first CD.* But come on, it's a tree! It never actually talked with—or even *saw*—Moses, Julius, Bill Harley and the Davidson boys, Muddy, or even "Scary" Spice.

But Les Haserot is another story. He may not have seen Brutus fouling the first Dr. J but he sure as hell saw something a lot more important: the birth of the American biker. His 86th birthday party was an event of remembrance and of reverence. Motorcycle journalist Panhead Jimmy helped us all to see that Les was still—at least in biker spirit—*forever young*.

His article, "A Real Wild One," was published in the March 2004 issue of *Thunder Press* magazine. It was a great way of saying "Happy Birthday" to Les Haserot, the oldest living Boozefighter:

That's what the patch said: "We're the real Wild Ones." Nobody doubted it after hearing the exploits of the oldest living member of the Boozefighters, Les Haserot. Friends and brothers from as far away as Texas, in addition to the California cities of Grass Valley, Sacramento, Hollister, San Diego, and Redondo Beach, gathered to honor Les' 86th birthday. My goal was to document some of the history he has stored away in that sharp mind of his.

Hosted by his old friend, Gil Armas, at his hilltop home in the City of Orange, over 60 people enjoyed seeing and listening to Les and his riding buddies, Jack Lilly (who is two months younger than Les), Jim Cameron, and Gil. The conversation focused on being a biker in the old days in Los Angeles.

There were many clubs at that time, and for the most part they all got along. The common meeting place always seemed to be the All American Café, which was located near Firestone and Hooper in South Gate. Old photos from that location showed the Yellow Jackets, 13 Rebels (of which many members split and became Boozefighters), and other clubs standing elbow to elbow and having a gut laugh together. All of the faces have names written underneath, but one face stands out. Her name is Marie. She is about the most beautiful woman I've ever seen. I mean she is stunning! "Oh, that was Les' wife," I was told. He's been blessed.

The reminiscing lasted throughout the day. Les recalled Hollister in 1936, where the CHP would actually close down Main Street to automobile traffic and let the bikers drag race. Then they would have a big Fourth of July parade. Another big event was the Cactus Derby, sponsored by Skip Fordyce in Riverside. Starting time was at midnight and it would last for 18 hours. Heading toward the Mexican border, the race route required riding off-road in the desert, averaging a certain speed, and ending back at Skip's. Les was on the return leg of the ride when he hit a cow, and while flying off the bike, his handlebar ripped his jeans and exposing his "business" for all to see. He continued on to Julian and was immediately stopped by the local cops. They explained that he couldn't continue riding with his package hanging out, and about that time a friend came along who offered Les an extra pair of Levi's. Only problem was that Les is about 5 feet 7 and the buddy was 6 feet 5. Les hiked the britches up as best he could and continued home.

Longtime BFMC member, Huck (left), and Les Haserot.

While on a ride back in 1938, Les came over a hill and found a car stopped in the middle of the road. Not being able to stop, he hit the car and flew over it. Still somewhat dazed, he tried to pick the bike up and accidentally stuck his hand in the rear spokes which were still rotating. He remembers waking up in a field after passing out for a short time and getting a ride to his brother's house. His sister-in-law had seen enough of the Haserot clan bleeding all over her house, so she made him sit on the porch with a towel wrapped on his wounds until the bleeding stopped.

The custom was that on each Saturday night, riders would bring a bottle of their favorite liquor to the All American Café and pour it into a common container. This made for some interesting drinks. After one of these evenings, one of the boys needed a place to sleep it off, so he went across the street to a gas station where he climbed into the back seat of a car that was parked on the hoist. The following morning he awoke to a very long step down to the ground. Someone had raised the hoist. Another time, Dink, who had two wooden legs below the knee and a death wish, left the All American with his pipes roaring. They heard him hit second gear, then no sound at all. When they went outside to check on Dink, they found he had run his bike up a huge mound of dirt and landed on the roof of the gas station. The cops came and arrested Dink and put him in the back of the squad car, but he wouldn't put his legs inside. The cop told him to put them inside or he was going to shut the door on them. After a few minutes of this the cop did slam the door on his legs and Dink just burst out laughing.

Another legendary member, Jim Hunter, owned many motorcycles in his time. One day he bought a brand new VL and went to the All American to show it off. Nobody ever locked up their bikes back then, but Jim chained his front wheel to a pole at the café. While he was not looking, his buddies

The 13 Rebels MC was among the other clubs that hung out at the All American, promoting "field meets" and other events along with the Boozefighters.

removed the front axle and wheel-barrowed the bike around to the back of the building, leaving his front wheel securely attached to the pole. Boys will be boys.

Jim Hunter was no slouch on a motorcycle. He held the Land Speed Record of 225 miles per hour in 1958, and was a National TT Champ in 1966 and 1967.

Racing came naturally to riders back then. Gil once got into a drag race while riding Jack Lilly's Crocker. A Crocker was as fast as it was stylish. A good Indian Chief or Scout might do 85 miles per hour, and Harleys would break into the 90s, but a Crocker was an honest 105-miles-per-hour rocket ship. During the race, Gil found himself fishtailing from curb to curb. Les asked him if he ever thought of backing off the throttle. "Hell no," Gil replied. "I was racing."

Back in those days you could go to most any vacant lot and put on a field meet or just ride down a river bottom. Les' brother-in-law was riding a JD across a river bottom one day and hit quicksand. They managed to pull him out but the bike was gone forever.

Les rode with the famous Victor McLaglen Motor Corps for two years, doing feats of skill for audiences. One such show was put on for some prisoners at a facility in Utah. The riders wore uniforms that looked much like those police officers might wear, and the prisoners booed their performance. One of Les' stunts required him to ride through a wooden structure that was set on fire. Soon after that, he found racing on flat tracks safer and left the Corps.

Les worked as the paint shop foreman for 15 years for Rich Budelier's Harley-Davidson on South Main Street in L.A., where he bought one of the early 1936 Knuckleheads for $425. The early Knuckles didn't have any covers for the valves, so valve oiling was kind of a hit-and-miss proposition. Being an off-road rider, you naturally removed the front fender before heading to the dirt. This didn't make for a very long valve life, so he sold it and later bought a 1938 model ($525). He told us that the '38 Knuckle was the best bike he ever owned. He bought the second Triumph brought into California, a 1939 Tiger. The engine blew up twice and transmission three times in only 6,000 miles. Of course, many of those miles were riding at Ascot and other flat tracks in the area. Every weekend in the L.A. area you would find field meets, hare and hound races, scrambles, or speed trials so "street" bikes were really the first dual purpose bikes.

Quoting from the 1954 Budelier H-D publication "Motorcyclists in Action," Editor Dick Hutchins described Les and wrote the following: "Our paint foreman has spent so much time in Lower California that the Mexican government has just about granted him citizenship. So, if you want to know anything about Mexico, just come in and ask for Les Haserot."

For a few years, Les just knew he could take a Harley-Davidson from Los Angeles to La Paz, located at the tip of Lower California; over 1,000 miles of bad roads, trails, washes, deep sand, and mud.

"Just think," Les said, "one minute your road is a sea of sand, dirt and dust, then you hit a tropical storm blowing in from the Gulf of California or the Pacific Ocean and before you know it, you're up to your thorax in mud!

"And petrol becomes a pressing problem. South of Santa Rosalia, its quality drops drastically. Octane rating falls to as low as 58; your motor should be set up to operate on 'subregular' fuel, and the timing retarded two degrees or more."

The 1937 45 that Les used on those trips was on display at his party, still painted in the colors of the Mexican flag. The paint scheme got him in a little jam in La Paz. While in a beer joint, a local cop waited for him to

A young Les Haserot at home.

return to the bike. He wouldn't let Les start the bike because it had a Mexican flag painted on the tank, so he had to push it back to the motel and wait for the heat to leave. The first few times he tried the trip, the springer forks cracked during the 250 miles of washboard road. Then a customer of Budelier's wrecked his new Hydra Glide, and Les installed the FL front end from the wreck onto the Flathead and smoothed out the ride for the next 54 years . . . and counting.

Les was a man among men. He, and the other originals like him, walked the walk and talked the talk. They rode the hell out of their machinery, sometimes broke it, and then fixed it. They made them go fast, they innovated and—thankfully—they lived to tell about it.

CHAPTER 11

The Tale of "Snowman's" Quest for the Originals, the Funeral of Bobby Kelton, the "Eight-Valve," Wino's Busted Tooth and the Dremel Tool Dentist, Willie and Teri Joined Together Again in the Sea, More Truth About Hollister, Goldie, Lap Dancin' for Willie

Brian "Snowman" Trum represents a bridge, the closing of an archival gap, the baby boom-Vietnam link between the original Boozefighters of World War II and the newest generation of Boozefighters. Many of the current gray-beard BFMC members fall into this middle, neo-Jurassic age period. But back in the mid-1970s Snowman was one of the first to begin to crawl through a small jagged hole in history's fence, searching in the tall grass for some CSI-sized clues about something that had begun to become his obsession. This obsession still needs to be fed virtually every day by someone else "out there" who has heard about, read about, or in some other way has come in contact with the legend of the Boozefighters and needs to know more.

There are, however, big differences.

Today's seekers fire up their computers and hyper-scan the cyber history books, eventually winding up in contact with one of us who can explain things like what *really* happened at Hollister, who Wino Willie was, the saga of Brando, Marvin and The Movie, and that, no, we don't have a chapter in the Cayman Islands or Botswana . . . yet.

But in the mid-1970s, Snowman had a biker's curiosity and a bike, and that was enough to get the wheels rolling:

"I had a connection to Hollister before I ever moved to California. I remembered *The Wild One* movie. I remembered my brother's friend, Steve, and how his Uncle Lawrence would come into town on his Harley—I don't remember if it was a Knuckle or a Pan—but he'd come into town. I was small enough where I'd sit on the gas tank and go for a ride. That was my 'thrill ride!' I'd always look forward to him coming into town. And I probably burned up more decks of cards in the spokes of my bicycle wheels than the average kid on my block.

"Later on—I was probably thirteen or fourteen—I'd walk quite a ways just so I could hang around and see all the bikers on Friday nights when they went to the White Castle hamburger place. I was like a little prospect or something. I'd offer to go in and get their sodas and hamburgers and everything because I knew that one of these guys was eventually gonna give me a ride around the block, and that's why I went there. That went on for a pretty long time. It was like, 'Here comes the kid. He wants his Harley ride,' and that's the way that went.

"Then I moved to California. I started riding heavy but I didn't know anybody. But I always wanted to go to Hollister. I had always known about it. I got a bike and the first time I had enough money to go anywhere I went to Hollister, alone, somewhere around 1976. I paid this guy ten dollars to come out to the road sign with me and take a picture so I'd have proof that I'd been there!

"I don't know what I expected when I pulled into Hollister, but nobody around there that I talked to knew anything about it. So I rode on into Monterrey and all that. When the opportunity came up for a resurgence of the club, I was more than interested. The word was that Wino Willie was interested

Snowman on John "J. D." Cameron's 1917 Harley "8-Valve."

SAN BENITO COUNTY
SHERIFF
CORONER
DIRECTOR OF EMERGENCY MEDICAL SERVICES
DIRECTOR OF COUNTY COMMUNICATIONS

HARVEY S. NYLAND
SHERIFF - CORONER

CURTIS J. HILL
UNDER SHERIFF

PATROL / ADMIN. / CIVIL	(408) 636-4080
FAX	(408) 636-1416
EMERGENCY MED. SERV.	(408) 636-4086
FAX	(408) 636-4087

BUSINESS ADDRESS:
  451 Fourth Street, Hollister, CA 95023
MAIL ALL CORRESPONDENCE:
  P.O. Box 700, Hollister, CA 95024-0700

CORRECTIONS	(408) 636-406
FAX	(408) 636-408

BUSINESS ADDRESS:
  710 Flynn Road, Hollister, CA 9502

COMMUNICATIONS	(408) 636-410
FAX	(408) 636-410

BUSINESS ADDRESS:
  420 Hill Street, Hollister, CA 9502

June 11, 1996

President
Boozefighters Motorcycle Club
Post Office Box 501946
San Diego, CA., 92150-1946

Dear Sir,

I read with interest the article about your organization in the June edition of Thunder Press Magazine. The article had a different perspective on the motorcycle event in Hollister in 1947.

The residents of Hollister and San Benito County who were at the event tell a different story and they are very worried about what will happen in Hollister on the July 4th weekend in 1996 and 1997 when the motorcycle clubs return to celebrate these events.

The article in Thunder Press states that your club will celebrate your 50th anniversary in the bars and on the streets of Hollister. As the Chief Law Enforcement Officer in San Benito County I welcome your club to Hollister and San Benito County. I hope that your members will come and enjoy themselves. There are no planned events taking place in Hollister or San Benito County on the July 4th weekend.

I hope that the Boozefighters will set an example for all San Benito County residents to see that motorcycle clubs are made up of members who are respected and productive members of the motorcycle owners throughout California, the nation and the world.

Very truly yours,

Harvey S. Nyland
Sheriff-Coroner

Law enforcement "concern" about the BFMC's return to Hollister in 1996 and 1997.

in starting the club back up. Now I had met him up at the El Camino College motorcycle swap meet. He wasn't my buddy or anything—it was like another thousand people had met him, too, nice to meet a legend kind of thing, you know—but I'd see him up there and kind a listen to the stories and do my hour and leave. But I wrote him a letter and then I went over to La Mirada to meet John Cameron and Jim Cameron, two of the other originals. Then I started to go up to Fort Bragg for Wino's annual fish fry on Memorial Day weekends at 'the Acre,' as they called it. Even had some guy land in the yard in a helicopter once, to the dismay of the neighbors. It was a Bell Ranger, and these people get out, the 'copter takes off, and they say, 'We're here for the barbecue.' Willie looks at 'em, 'Well, I have to say, that's probably the best entrance anyone's ever made to one of my barbecues!' And I got to stay in the *guest cottage*, which was a tin shed with a light bulb hanging in it. When it rained it was like being in a drum. I'd help out with the barbecuing and all that. Basically, all the young guys who would go up there would sit and listen to the history of the club, all the different stories.

"When John Cameron was starting to fail in health, Willie was staying with him down here, a lot nearer to where I live, so I got to see him a lot more. We'd go up to John's on a lot of weekends, hang out a few hours, and then ride home. But it was always about listening to them, their stories, and the kind of people they were—*are*—and all the ways in which the world was a different place back then.

"When the Camerons first came to California, for example, they converted their Model T car into a truck and started to haul lumber, which was the start of the Three C Trucking Company. John and Jim Cameron were just some of many great characters I've had the opportunity to meet. Many have passed on now but we were lucky enough to be able to hear their stories.

"One time we went to the funeral of Bobby Kelton, who was an early member of the club. The family had no idea we were coming. Jeannine Roccio had called me up to let me know about Bobby's death. She thought that we might like to pay our respects. So there was fifteen or twenty of us on bikes, and we all ride up to L.A.

"Jeannine had told the family that we might come up there, one or two guys, they didn't know. The family lived in a nice quiet neighborhood, and here we all come, riding up. Well, there were people out on the front lawn all dressed up and stuff. And here we come. They were totally shocked. I kind a took a quick look inside the house and they had a few finger foods and stuff like that, and here I've got fifteen guys. So I gathered up the guys, took 'em aside, told them that we are going to have a little meeting here before we go inside the house. 'Don't drink all their beer and *don't* eat all the food 'cause it looks like they just have enough for the family. Just be sociable and then we'll get the hell outta here.'

"So we stayed an hour-and-a-half, two hours, took a bunch of pictures. The kids got to reminisce about their granddad and all that. Then we ride off into the sunset. Then, after that, I get a really nice letter from Bobby's wife. She said what a thrill it was for the family that our guys, who didn't really know anyone there, come in outta the blue and wind up going to his wake. She said that it really was a special moment for the family. They had his old Boozefighters jersey hanging up over the fireplace. It really meant something for us to show up like that.

"The story of the 'eight-valve' is really about something very rare in the history of Harley-Davidson. When I saw this particular bike—the 'eight-valve'—for the first time, I really didn't know much about antique motor-cycles. The story is that there were only ten of them made in 1917. They were factory race bikes, and the one that John Cameron had was the only one that survived. He'd ride it around the neighborhood and stuff, and it looked like any other 1917 Harley except that it was the 'eight-valve.'

"Everything at John's revolved around the garage. They had a lot of comfortable chairs and stuff, and you could sit around and look at all the bikes that were there. And listen and share a peek into history. We'd get up there as many weekends as we could, drink a few beers, and talk with them. It was always a lot of fun. There was always a bike under construction and they'd be piddling around with it. All the old famous racing guys from the L.A. area would stop by—this was in about 1988 or 1989. We started going up there in late 1987, actually.

"When we started this chapter it was all about continuing in the foot-steps of the originals. We treaded lightly at first but we made a reputation for ourselves of being straight-up with anybody that was out there. We'd stop and pick you up on the road, take care of you, take you back home if you had a problem. Kind a that old days' ethic, the type of camaraderie that the old guys had. If anybody talks about the Boozefighters we wanted it to always be in a good light.

"Coming back from the Yuma Prison Run one time, there was this guy and his son on this little Sporty, stopped with some kind of problem. So we stopped to help. It was a father-and-son weekend, and they weren't sure what was wrong with the bike or how to fix it. So we took the battery out, checked the charging system, we did this and we did that, got 'em on the road again. I believe we bought him a new battery. We didn't know who the guy was but whenever the name of the Boozefighters comes up, this guy's gonna remember us. And I feel that all the goodwill that we've been putting out for so many years now shows in the respect that the club has gained.

"We were up there in John Cameron's garage, a Saturday or Sunday, and Wino Willie had chipped a tooth. You know how your tongue moves around on somethin' like that? He was getting irritated. There were the usual dozen or so folks there in the garage, some of us, some of the old timers, all standing around talking and stuff. Well, Willie keeps complaining about the tooth every five minutes or so about how his tongue is getting sore. And John would tell him, 'Willie, quit yer bitchin'!' They'd go back and forth like that all day.

"Willie keeps bitchin' about the tooth, so John goes into his tool cabinet and pulls out this Dremel tool—25,000 rpm or some crazy thing. Anyway, he plugs it in and it makes this loud, whirring sound, just screaming, really. Willie had been sitting in this chair so John leans on him in the classic dentist fashion of the Old West. 'This won't hurt,' he says to Willie, and Willie puts his head back and opens his mouth. At that point there were a dozen or so guys in that garage. John had put this kind of deburring tip on the end of the Dremel tool and when it hit the tooth you could hear the sound change into this sickening kind of dull screaming grind and you could see the smoke comin' out of his mouth. Willie would jump every time the tooth was ground on.

" 'I think I need another drink,' Willie would say, and now everyone is doing shots. Well, by now you've already lost two or three guys, the first ones with the queasy stomachs that just couldn't take the brutality of this spectacle! This went on another five times at least, grinding on the tooth, the sound, that horrible burning smell, the smoke coming out of Willie's mouth! And John would check the tooth each time to see if it was smoothing out. And each time there were fewer and fewer guys in the garage. By the time it was all over, the only ones in the garage were Willie and Cameron, but we could still hear it and smell it from outside!

"On Mount Soledad there is the veterans' memorial, highlighted by a huge cross and marble plaques honoring many of the veterans who served our country, including Wino. We ride up there on all the special occasions

(Left to right) Jim Cameron, Dago, Snowman, and Gil Armas.

Wino Willie presenting Snowman with his club charter.

to celebrate his life. And we always sneak up there with a picture of Wino that we hang on the fence while we're there. When Teri came down here and saw Wino's memorial, she told me that her life was complete after seeing this memorial to Wino. Two weeks later she passed away.

"Both Wino's and Teri's ashes were scattered into the sea at this little cove maybe six to ten miles north of Fort Bragg. This was the family's request. But the surreal thing about that was there was also a third person's ashes being scattered at the same time. After all of the ashes went into the ocean there were three pelicans that flew by. Two of the big birds stayed close together and flew off into the direction of where Willie and Teri were scattered, the other one went off alone."

In 1996, the thought of bringing a motorcycle run back to Hollister in 1997 for the 50th anniversary of the birth of the American biker was becoming a reality. A trial run was planned for 1996, gearing up for a truly serious gathering in 1997. But the image and drunken ghosts, a half-century old, wrapped in cracked and decaying leather, were also beginning to rise up from shallow paranoid graves.

"There was a lot of *speculation* as to just what might occur in Hollister in '96," said Snowman. "*Thunder Press* had interviewed Wino about the whole 'return to Hollister' thing. He said that he was 'anxious to go back there' and just that kind of stuff. Well, after the magazine hit the stands I get a letter from the San Benito County Sheriff, and he says: 'I read with interest about your *return* to Hollister and I certainly hope that it's not a fiasco like it was in 1947, and that you guys won't tear up the town,' and all this other crap. I'm reading this damn thing thinking this guy must be a complete moron! Now I don't add so good, but in doing the math I figure out that all the originals at that time are at least eighty years old, so I guess that if no one trips over their walker or smokes around the oxygen tanks we probably won't have any trouble.

"So we get there and it was a total bust of a run. Also going on that weekend was a big charity run out of Seaside. Maybe a thousand bikes hit Hollister for lunch and then went home. We had all the Sheriffs in riot gear, fatigues, and all this kind of stuff. When it was all said and done, by eight o'clock that night we were pretty much all that was in town. There were the Top Hatters, us, and some townsfolk sitting in Johnny's Bar. And because Wino was with us we had a couple of vehicles running around, kind a like a carpool thing. So we go around the corner to the other bar, Whiskey Creek. By now it's about eleven o'clock at night and I'm half in the bag and either a captain or a lieutenant from the Hollister Police Department comes in and asks who was in charge. Somebody points me out. I ask him, 'What's up?' He says, 'Well, things *seem* to be under control here.' I kind of chuckle and say, 'Yeah, I can imagine. There's nobody here!' Then he says, 'But we just have one question.' And no sooner does he start to ask me this question and this pickup truck pulls up out front with about five or six guys in the back, and they pile out. The cop continues with his question, 'We want to know why you're running around town with guys in the back of pick-up trucks.'

"I look at him, then I look at the pickup out front, and I tell him, 'Oh, ya mean *that*? That's our designated driver. I don't want anyone running around your town drunk!' He just looks at me and was stunned. He goes, 'Oh, thank you,' and turns around and walks out. I think about that and the letter I got, then I look at the bunch who was up there, and I laugh because literally, a lot of us *were* up there with aluminum walkers and wheelchairs with the little oxygen bottles and stuff! That made that letter I got from the sheriff even more priceless, absolutely priceless. So priceless, in fact, that I made a digital copy of it for everybody who was there!"

Over and over again it has been proven that there's magic in the Boozefighters patch—magic that continually bends time, a recurring green and white voodoo that conjures up memories and stories, and even brings people from out of ancient and forgotten shadows into a present that they never knew even existed.

Snowman lifted his eyes upward and stroked his long beard. Another Boozefighter from the distant past was about to be introduced. "We met Goldie in the usual Boozefighters' 'out of the blue' fashion. What I knew about her was that she used to race bikes and was *one of the girls*. And one of our members was in Escondido eating and a young woman who had noticed his patch walks up to him and says, 'My mom used to ride with the Boozefighters.' So the member naturally gets her number and we make contact with Goldie. And here we go again with the 'Lord works in mysterious ways' kind a thing. Just so happens that on that weekend Wino was here in San Diego. So we make arrangements to have a barbecue. When she walked through that door they had not seen each other for fifty years! It was definitely old home week! Wino and Goldie sat on that bench over there and talked about old times all day. Then we were also able to get Goldie reunited with Teri.

"Same thing basically happened with 'Red Dog' Dahlgren. He was the first of the old-timers that we came in contact with. His wife, Virginia, saw one of our members at the Yuma Prison Run. She said to him, 'You know, my husband's a Boozefighter. Red Dahlgren.' Well, the member was one of the newer guys who didn't know the history that well. Turns out that Red was there. He'd been going to that run for twenty-something years. So he came on over to our camp, introduces himself to us, asks how Wino is, and goes through the whole list. He and Virginia partied with us the whole time. We gave him one of our shirts. He says, 'Oh man! I haven't worn one of these in a while.' He had a great time and stayed in touch until he passed away.

"At first, everything we did was kind of hit and miss trying to get them here. But our ability to keep trying worked real well. It was like, well if you can't make it here to see so-and-so, well here's their phone number, give them a call. After a few years it really became something they *wanted* to do and we would do our best to make it happen.

"New York Myke, the owner of San Diego Harley-Davidson, was genuinely touched when me and Willie went down to his shop. I had Willie riding around in my side hack, hitting all the bars and stuff. We took him to a strip club down here. We had them open a few hours early just for us, had the girls come in early, got Willie some lap dances and all that. The joint was all ours, it was all for him. 'Course I'm glad he didn't *die there*!

"One of our 'self-inflicted' obligations from the very beginning was to get as many of these old-timers together prior to their passing away as we could. And I think we've been pretty successful doing that. We do our best to keep it going *like it was*. Getting all these guys together in one place has been our mission since we started the charter. All the work and effort that we've done is a testament to the brotherhood that we have to make this stuff happen. A lot of people will go out of their way to pick some of our guests up—hundreds of miles in some cases—to make sure that they're there at some given time so that they all can see each other for a couple of hours. We've paid their gas or their air fare, hotel room, whatever it would take to get them to come down here and be comfortable, and to make sure they get home safely. Now some of the originals were pretty well off, but some weren't, so we always made it a point to say that, 'You're coming here and we're paying for it.' Like the Del Mar Mile. We hotel 'em, but a couple of the ol' boys just wanted a sleeping bag and to be able to stay here in the back yard. They figured they'd be drunk lying out there anyway! Nothing's changed after fifty years, ya know!

"We've had 'em all here at the house: Jim Hicks, Red Dahlgren, Wino, J. D., Jim Cameron, Johnny and Jeannine Roccio, Gil, Dago, Les Haserot, countless others have all been here partying. And we've all been on the road together, going to Hollister, coming back from Hollister. 'Course a lot of 'em had to trailer their bikes and just run 'em around town maybe, but we have a great time with these guys. We ride the old roads like they did, too, like taking Route 33 coming up the middle of California, where there ain't nothing but oil derricks and nothing else. You can go for miles and miles and never see another vehicle, just like it was back then."

And that seems to be the essence of the entire legacy that was left by the original wild ones, trying to keep all of the important stuff—the traditions, the striving for fun, the freedom, the independent attitude—*just like it was back then.*

CHAPTER 12

The Tale of the Mysterious Lost Boozefighters' Stories

"You're not drunk if you can lie on the floor without holding on."
—Dean Martin

The state of Kansas has brought many things to American society (besides Dorothy and Toto, of course). The "Happy Cracker," for example, described as "the world's strongest and fastest hand pecan cracker," was invented by Kansas alfalfa farmer Kermit Murphy. Ethel on *I Love Lucy*—Vivian Vance—was born there. So was *Easy Rider*'s Dennis Hopper. Ike, our country's 34th president, is buried there, as are James Naismith, the guy who invented basketball, and Lucy Hobbs Taylor, the first woman dentist in America.

And, yes, those three *are* dead.

But that's OK, because there *is* a lot that is alive and seriously well in Kansas. The Boozefighters Chapter 49, for example. And that's where you'll find "Grump."

And Grump himself found something, something far more valuable than the ruby slippers or the Tin Woodsman's oil can. He found the *Mysterious Lost Boozefighters Stories*!

Somewhere, at some point, Grump acquired a jolting handful of first-person accounts of the day-to-day, green-and-white existence from the summer of 1946 into 1948. It appears that it was finally written around 1993, when, if you follow the clues in the text, the writer would've been about 64 years old. His stuff contains legendary names and places, and even the cool-cat slang of someone who had come up in the 1940s. These stories were penned by an unknown hand (he's just referred to as "Jim" at one point in the stories), a hand that obviously twisted the throttle with other club brothers, a hand that never signed his full name at the bottom of his work.

Maybe he was just as happy that way. Maybe he was just content to live the life, enjoy the brotherhood, and jot down what he saw, knowing that someday he'd put all of his notes together, knowing that someday, someone just might want to look into the heart and soul of the original wild ones.

He was right.

Now it's time to pour a cold one and raise a glass to an unknown wild one, brother Jim, wherever he may be. And how about a chaser for Grump, for unearthing the *Mysterious Lost Boozefighters Stories*.

THE BIG A

It was summer 1946. My family had just moved from Montebello to Los Angeles. We rented a small house at 101st Street and Central Avenue in the section of South Central Los Angeles known as Watts. Seeing that it was summer holiday, I had taken a job with Friction Materials Corp. on South Main Street, near Slauson Avenue. Each day on my way to work I would ride up Central, continuing on Hooper Avenue to Slauson. As I crossed Firestone Boulevard I would notice this old run-down Flying A service station on the southwest corner. There was one two-pump island, a wood-frame (8x10-foot) office, and out back a two-car lube bay-repair stall. It was a prefab steel structure, all adorned in very weathered yellow and white paint. Night and day there always seemed to be a group of motorcycles parked there. English and American bikes, choppers, cafe, and desert racers mostly. So, on one Saturday morning "The Kid" wheeled his bronze-head AJS 500 "Lunger" into that assemblage of esoteric iron, parked, and entered the Big A, the domain of the Boozefighters.

Now you must realize, that was 45 years ago, and although my first love was/is motorcycles, my father being an ex-Indian factory rider, and later, curator/manager of a Class A speedway racing group, there were always motorcycles around my digs. So, my association with the Boozefighters, although a milestone in the maturing process of a 17-year-old jitterbug, as a memory seems to be a bit jaded and faded now. I only hope there is still enough electrolyte to sustain the surge of electron activity necessary to separate fact from fiction, myth from reality, and alas, truth from fantasy.

The Big A! A beer bar in back of a run-down gas station in South Central Los Angeles. Meeting place and hangout for the postwar, so-called "outlaw" prototype motorcycle club. The club was the people. Cats with names like Wino Willie, Jumpin' Joe, Yoyo, J. D. Jones, Fat Boy and his ol' lady, Dago, Igor, Curly Cantlon, Louie Thomas, Stinebalm the Swede, and then-bartender/owner, Fat John. There were more. Some riders that tasted fame, like Arch Johnson, Don Hawley, Chuck "Feets" Minert, and Long Beach Triumph race bike builder, A. J. Lewis. They removed the lube rack platform, covered the ram post with a homemade wooden bar, and assembled a bunch of stools. The wings were sawed off of the sign on the roof, leaving just the big letter "A," hence the name, "Big A," the focal point of Boozefighters' activities.

There were other clubs of contemporary stature, but none remains in the annals of serendipitous mayhem with the verve and mystique of the Boozefighters. I guess the oldest of the motorcycle clubs still in operation at that time was the 13 Rebels, a group founded by movie stunt men back in the 1920s. The Yellow Jackets and the Orange County M/C also predate the Boozefighters. Sister organizations were the Rams, Checkers, the North Hollywood Crotch Cannibals, and the Gallopin' Gooses M/C. Hells Angels back then were a group of young cats in San Bernardino. How time changes things.

Day-to-day routine activities were cruising the bars, partying and checking out the weekly races around the L.A. area: the speedway at the Lincoln Park (located on the south turn of the long-time abandoned Legion Ascot Speedway, i.e., the original Ascot), the quarter-mile at Rosecrans and Western Avenues, the Box Springs Grade TT in Riverside, Nail Flats (nicknamed "Rusty Nails") near San Pedro, and Corriganville, a Western movie set and racetrack up near the town of Newhall.

BAGGING YOYO

I remember one Sunday evening. We were returning from a TT race at Corriganville. Each of us brought a gallon jug of wine to suck on all afternoon, while sitting in the hot summer sunshine. We were gaggling home, with pit stops at several bars along the way, when someone suggested we fall into DeMay's drive-in, a local hot rodder hangout, for supper. We were pretty well wasted, tired and dirty—dirty? No, filthy! Vile! Repugnant! Yoyo sat at the counter and ordered first a bowl of chili, then hogged down an order of spaghetti with meatballs, finishing up with a milk shake. Now Yoyo, looking his best, resembled a cross between Dr. Frankenstein's monster and Charlie Chaplin, let alone sweating all day at a dusty racecourse. He was one of those tall, skinny red-necked cats. When he starts to walk, first his head starts nodding like he means yes, then his shoulders pick up the movement, followed by his hips and pelvis undulating in the exact opposite cadence of what his upper body is doing. Next he swings each leg forward, dragging his toes, and then drops his foot down in what you might call a "clop step." He was wall-eyed with a cue-ball haircut. Well, it was warm and steamy in the restaurant, and with the mixture of red wine, pasta, chili, tomatoes, beans, hamburger, onions, milk, ice cream, chocolate, digestive enzymes, stomach acids, and assorted herbs and spices it wasn't long before the laws of physical science and chemistry sprung into action. Yoyo had a problem. He dropped like a dead buffalo. There he was, sprawled on the floor, eyes rolled back, lids half closed in a slack-jawed coma. His face bore the jaundiced pallor of a night nurse's pantyhose. We could have just left the cat crapped out on the floor, but Wino Willie thought it would be best to remove him. Wino grabbed his feet and drug him out into the parking lot. There weren't many patrons in the place and I could see only two carhops working, only five or six cars—I guess Sunday nights are slow. Now most of us were all for leaving this "Mother" there in the lot. But Wino was loyal to a fault and declared we should take him home. But how? He never would have made it on the pillion post. If we tried to drag him some sober judge would have called it premeditated murder. So the only thing to do was to commandeer a motorcar and drive him home. Now I'm not clairvoyant or psychic or anything like that, but I figured it was time to start my bike and wait by the driveway.

There was a young man and his date sitting in this real clean, dark blue 1934 Ford coupe, eating their dinner. It was probably fate, or maybe just not this kid's day. Wino walked up to them and asked, real nicely, if he could use their Ford to take Yoyo home. I guess Wino didn't care for his response to his inquiry, 'cause the next thing I saw was Wino pulling this young fellow out of his car and putting him flat on his back! The girlfriend seemed to be losing her composure. Wide-eyed, screaming, she sat frozen, petrified with fear. She wasn't about to leave a car that was surrounded by wild and drunken bikers, and there just wasn't room for Yoyo to sit inside. Wino slipped into the driver's seat and started the engine. Meanwhile, three or four of the other cats picked Yoyo up and sprawled him over the hood. There he was, on his back, head on the cowling vent, arms stretched out to either side, his legs dangling down over the headlamps. I was beginning to think in a short while this scene might somehow get a bit out of control! So I pulled the clutch and slipped the AJ into first screw. I did hear the little voice deep down in my conscience tell me I should do something about this. I thought the only heroic thing I could do, at this point in time, was to get my little white innocent 17-year-old ass out o' there! The last I saw of Yoyo for the next 30 days or so was him riding around DeMay's parking lot on the hood of this '34 five-window, regurgitating a four-inch fountain of red vomit about a foot-and-a-half straight in the air, and this hardened blonde professional car-hop, wide-eyed, face blanched, fist clenched, screaming, "Call the cops, Goddamn it. Somebody call the cops!"

JOHNNY'S JUKEBOX

There was this bar on South Main Street (about 185th Street) in an old Airstream trailer, called "Johnny's Crash Inn." No connection to Fat John at the Big A. The Crash Inn was common meeting ground for the Boozefighters and the Gallopin' Goose M/Cs. John opened about six each morning—some of these cats couldn't make it if they had to go more than four hours without a drink. One morning this old cat shows up in a three-quarter-ton pickup truck with two or three jukeboxes in the bed. He asks John how business was and if he could put one of his jukes in the bar. John told him right up front that he didn't think that was such a good idea, but this cat was real insistent and told John he could keep 50 percent of the profit. Five cents a tune wouldn't pay the rent, but this was most likely the only gig the geezer had going for him, so John said, "What the hell . . . If you want to take the chance, knock yourself out." The old man brought the thing in, loaded it up with records, and plugged it in. It was truly a thing of beauty! Round top, convex front, a lot of glass tubes with lava-lamp stuff bubbling up the front, and soft lights that would change color.

Well, this electric wonder sat there a week or two with hardly a play. If it wasn't that it was all enclosed, I'm sure the big stack of 78-rpm records would have been covered with dust. These cats just weren't interested. It wasn't that they didn't like the music—they just didn't appreciate Dinah Shore, Vaughn Monroe, or "Doggy in the Window." Maybe you could have got them to go to the Bach Festival if you could convince them they were giving away some "Bach Beer!"

Then one night the inevitable happened. During the course of a somewhat intemperate discussion, centering on the subject of one fellow's inability to substantiate the exact origin or even the identification of his father, he implied that the other gentleman's mother was performing sexual exhibitions in a socially unacceptable manner. Civil decorum waned, and an altercation ensued. The glass front of the music machine was smashed, broken bits and lava crap spread all over the floor, and the soft lights no longer changed color. A shame really, but as with most catastrophes, there was one redeeming asset. One now had access to the inner workings of the musical marvel. So it wasn't long before Bing Crosby's "White Christmas" was replaced by Big J. McNeally's "Good Rockin' at Midnight." "Stardust" gave way to "Drinkin' Wine Spodie-Odie," and "Little Doggie in the Window" became "Sneaky Pete Beat Your Heat." Next to go was the coin box, then a rewire job that made it possible to play the thing by just plugging it into the wall. When the old man came back for his collection he just stood there staring at the machine. After a while he turned, eyes watering, to look at John. Then he just went away. From then on the main attraction at the Crash Inn was the free jukebox. "I told the cat I didn't think leaving that thing here was a good idea," was all John could say.

FAT BOY, MACK DADDY

Every Friday night all the cats would go to Lincoln Park for the Speedway races. The Boozefighters came to own this old Pierce-Arrow limousine. They painted it bright green, wrote "Boozefighters" on the sides, adorned it with the club logo, an old drunk's head, eyes half shut, and flies buzzing around. Friday nights we would meet at the Big A, pile into the "Greenhouse," and motor to Lincoln Park. We would share a couple gallons of wine at the racetrack, then return to the Big A and drink until 2 a.m. It was one of those Friday nights that found Fat Boy and Yoyo drinking beer together after the race. Fat Boy was a kind a short, stocky cat, not really fat at all. He worked construction jobs all his life and had a hard, well-tanned body. He looked much like, and had mannerisms similar to, Burt Reynolds, who was a movie star years later. Dago was Fat Boy's old lady, an olive-skinned Italian girl who rode a Harley-Davidson with Drake wheels and rods and Texas Machine Shop cylinders and spacers. That sucker must have been out to 90-plus cubic inches. She could stand on the pedal and kick that sucker through like a lumberjack. She made a living shagging for Rapid Blueprint Co. When you shag for a living you just show up every morning, get in line, and they call you as needed. Every day is payday, and you can collect in cash if you wish. Such was the reputation of the

Boozefighters that when she wore her club sweater to work, she just rode to the head of the line and no one would dare say a thing.

Now I was sitting in the bar with Curly Cantlon. Yoyo was sitting with Fat Boy, and Dago had crashed in the back seat of the Greenhouse. Yoyo was carrying on about how horny he was after 30 days in Lincoln Heights (L.A. County Jail). He kept talking about how he was going to take his last $10 and see if he could score a streetwalker up on the Avenue. Fat Boy says, "Why do that and take a chance on getting the clap or something worse? You could give me the $10 and crawl in the back seat with Dago! She's so wasted that she'll probably think it's me anyway."

"You really don't mind?"

"Hell no! What are friends for?" So Yoyo hands Fat Boy the $10, and slips out to the parking lot. Curley and I are right behind him—this was something not to be missed. Fat Boy put the money away and ordered another beer. Outside it was darker than King Kong's armpit. You could just make out Yoyo quietly opening the car door and pulling himself in, pants and skivvies around his ankles.

All was dead quiet for a few moments. Then "What the hell do you think you're doing, you sonofabitch? Get the hell out of here!" Yoyo didn't even get the door closed before he hit the ground like he was blown out of a cannon. Dago, her blouse open and belt unfastened, on top of him kicking, scratching, biting, slugging, and yelling at the top of her lungs. She sat on his chest with her knees dug into his shoulders, punching him in the face with both fists. Yoyo was able to crawl away, after Dago wore herself out hitting him.

He drug himself back into the Big A, pulling up his drawers, bleeding from the mouth, lips and cheeks swollen, and plopped down next to Fat Boy. "That didn't take long, how was it?"

"How was it? How was it? I want my money back!" retorted Yoyo.

"What do you mean, you want your money back?" Fat Boy smiled. "A deal's a deal! Didn't I set the whole thing up for you? If you're not romantic enough to win her over, or man enough to subdue her, that's not my fault! Just to prove I'm your friend I'll buy you a beer—hey John, set one up for my friend, will ya?" Yoyo wiped his mouth with his sleeve, and drank the beer.

Curly turned to me and said, "Fat Boy was right, you know."

I said, "Yeah, but what about Yoyo, he let her get on top. Now there's a gentleman!"

I could tell you more, but I think you've got an idea of what life was like with the Boozefighters, how it was and all.

JOHNNY THE JUG AND MEATBALL

Victorville was jumping, bikes everywhere, cats wearing colors from all the western states. The bars were overflowing, all the restaurants had lines of folks waiting to scarf. We cruised around for a while and soon ran into this cat from the Jackrabbits M/C who knew Wino Willie. He told us about this Mexican cafe just east of town on Highway 18. I'm not sure I remember the name—Mama Lupe's or Sister Lupe's—anyway, the beer was cold and the food good. We checked it out. Seemed to be a hangout for the local sodbusters, an old day-coach railroad car with a Quonset hut attached to the rear. As we pulled into the parking lot, you could hear the jukebox wailing, "Out in Petersburg everything's fine, all them cats are drinking that wine, smashing out windows and kicking down doors, they'll drink a half-gallon and scream for more!" Sounds like a class place to me! Once inside we sat down, ordered a round of "Red X" (Lucky Lager) and schemed on supper.

There were four girls waiting tables. Our waitress was a tall, slim twist with dishwater blonde hair, and just about enough good stuff wiggling to stop conversation. We were on separate checks so she moved from one to the other taking orders. I sat at the end of the table so she took mine first. When she got to Johnny the Jug she broke out in a big grin (his "Lady Magnet" seemed to be working). When she left us and moved between tables, chairs, and people on her way to the kitchen, I couldn't help but think she moved like a snake with hips. The Jug caught me pinning her, and gave me a wink. I just closed my eyes, nodded my head, and smiled. She brought us another round of beer, said our dinner would be here soon. She wore Levis that looked painted on and a kind of peasant blouse, loose, low-cut, and made out of an old Japanese World War II flag. It had a big, round, red spot on the front, with Japanese writing down the sides, under her arms.

Our dinner arrived, and as she set the plate down in front of the Jug he asked, "When do you get off work?"

"Anytime I feel like it. I don't work here. Eddy, the owner, lets me fill in for tips on crowded nights."

After supper we all had one more Red X, all except Yoyo. He was drinking Delaware Punch, being in training for the big race and all, getting ready to practice his art on the course.

"Grump" (left), discovered "The Mysterious Lost Boozefighters' Stories."

We paid our bill, left a tip, and started toward the door. The Jug turned around and called back, "Hey, Meatball, you coming with us?" Her smile grew into a wide grin as she pulled the pencil from in back of her ear, and tossed the order pad on the counter. Yoyo was in the truck and out to the road by the time we got our bikes started. Jug tickled the carburetor, and before he could crank it through, Meatball was on the Tiger's pillion and groping for the pegs. Fat Boy turned to Dago, "Looks like the Jug got him a pillion fairy." Dago just looked bored and kicked her big stroker Harley to life. Yoyo and Swede led the way and we were on the road again.

Even though it was biting cold, the high desert air was crystal clear and sweet and dry. When it's 80 degrees in Los Angeles and 110 in Victorville, the high desert always seems more comfortable. But, the air is thin, and it was far from 110 degrees. I have no idea just how cold it was, but it hurt to take a deep breath. I couldn't feel my hands or feet, and the cold even cut through my thermal knockers. Damn, I was colder than a Klondike sewer rat!

We had been going east; now we turned north, off the pavement. The dirt road turned into a sand wash. It was near the old Sidewinder mine in a place they called "Crash Canyon." As we rode north on the creek bed, you could smell the smoke of fires, and we soon saw other riders camped out on the sand. We pulled up and I rode over to the side of the canyon where the earth was a bit more solid. I pulled the AJS onto the stand and J. D. pulled in beside me, along with Wino, a cat named Curley Cantlon, and a couple of the Yellow Jackets. This is where we were to meet our racers in the morning.

J. D. started to scrape away the brush so we could bed down. Fat Boy and Wino started a little fire with dry brush and twigs. I walked across the creek and picked our sleeping bags out of the truck bed. A tiny sliver of moon broke through the overcast and as far as you could see up the canyon folks were camped. I walked back and threw J. D. his bag and we rolled them out. I stripped to my knickers and crawled in. Johnny the Jug and Meatball were already in the sack, their clothes tossed all over. I don't somehow think their minds were focused on neatness. They were about 10 or 12 feet from J. D. and me. The sleeping bag was left unzipped. It was cold, but not as cold as when we were riding, so leaving the bag open gave more room to move around inside. I didn't think their minds were focused so much on sleeping either! There was about 4 or 5 inches of Mission Bell left in the jug, so J. D. and I passed it back and forth while we watched the skin show. J. D. was thinkin' out loud, "Man, if Fat John could get a floor show like that, he could have a cover charges down at the Big A."

"If he could keep his license, it would be more like an uncover charge," I added.

All at once Meatball sat straight up and in a loud whisper said, "Don't they call this place the Sidewinder Mine? What would we do if a snake slithered into our sleeping bag?" Johnny the Jug grabbed her shoulders, pulled her back into the bag, and rolled over on top of her, "The only snake you have to worry about is already in the sleeping bag." Fat Boy broke up and gave out a raucous "Haw, haw, haw!" Dago gave out with, "Shut up! If you're going to fantasize, beat your meat and go to sleep."

The sky had cleared some. I could even see a few stars, now and then as the clouds were passing. The wine was gone, J. D. was comatose, and the fire had become an ashtray of embers. At last the day's hype was mute, once in the arms of Morpheus.

Too soon the visions of sugar plums were blown out of my wee little head by a God-awful racket coming up the canyon. It was this old flathead, orange Dodge pickup, weaving through sleeping bags and around motorcycles. From behind the wheel came this honkey nasal whine, "Joanne? Joanne? I know you're here somewhere. Where are you honey? Joanne?" Meatball jumped out of the bag and started pulling on her Levis. By now John the Jug was out of the bag too.

"What's happening?"

"It's that Goddamn Eddy. He owns the restaurant, remember? He's my landlord—he owns this lousy house trailer I've been living in." She told Jug, "We get it on sometimes, ya know, just for the rent. He doesn't own me, though! Nobody owns me, nobody!"

Eddy's truck had stopped and the headlights were shining on Jug and the Meatball. She crossed her arms in front of her. They were really cold, her in the Levis and the Jug buck-ass naked. Eddy walked toward them, stopped and picked up the blouse, looked at it, then threw it down again. This Eddy was something else. He stood about 5 feet 10, a stocky redneck farm boy. He walked up to Meatball, reached out with his fat left hand and grabbed her by the hair. His face was flushed, and in the headlamp's glare you could see tiny red and blue veins that turned his puffy cheeks into road maps. He held his right hand up, palm open as if he were going to cuff her. He looked like he was in pain.

"What are you doing here? Why are you here with him and not home with me?" His eyes were welling up.

"Why am I here with him?" she quipped. "Why am I here with him and not with you? Drop your pants and everyone will know why I'm with him and not with you!"

That did it. The dam burst. Tears rolled down his fat, puffy cheeks. He tried to say something. His mouth moved a little but nothing came out. He slapped and backhanded her three or four times across her face. By now Fat Boy, Jumpin' Joe, the Swede, and myself were just standing around the principals, closing in and ready to throw dukes. The Jug said, "Just let it be; let them work it out. It's not our business. Besides, the point spread is too wide." The code governing such things is clear: Never fight over a woman or money. They come and they go. You just wait a while and they'll be back. Eddy dragged her by her hair, with her scratching and kicking, to the truck, threw her in, and drove away. By the time I looked back to the Jug he was in his sleeping bag, with Meatball's blouse rolled up under his head like a pillow. No honor lost here, I reasoned.

Yoyo yelled out from the truck where he was nesting, "Will you cats knock it off? I've got to get some sleep if I'm going to practice my art in the morning." The clouds had moved back in; it was overcast. The morning sky was once again covered with gray. We were camped on the west side of the canyon and between the east canyon rim and the cloud cover was a shaft of bright sunlight that struck my eyes like a dagger. J. D. was up, dressed, and grinning like an ape. "Come on, Jim, get up! Me 'n' the Jug got the fire goin' again."

"How the hell can you do it?" I ask.

"Do what?"

"Do what?!" I replied. "Drink Port wine all day, have five or six beers with a double order of chili verde for your supper, drink some more wine, stay up half the night watching people screw, sleep in a frozen food locker on a bed of sand, and be so wide awake and so *Goddamned ugly* at the crack of dawn?" The daggers that were my eyes suddenly leaped to the small of my back when that crazy bald-headed asshole grabbed the foot of my sleeping bag and poured me out on the canyon floor

I rolled up the bag and looked for the truck. It was gone! I guessed Yoyo couldn't wait to go practice his art. Up front of where the truck was parked set a new dark-blue Ford station wagon. "What's that?" I ask J. D.

"That's Don Hawley's girlfriend's new car. She and four of her coed pals from Compton College drove Hawley up here this morning." I turned my head, ever so slowly, to see Dangerous Don sitting on his haunches by the fire. He was holding a paper cup of coffee.

I walked over. "Where did you get the coffee?"

"I brought it with me, and there's some buns and stuff in the wagon. Knock yourself out!"

"Where's your rib?" I ask.

"She and her friends took a hike up to the bushes on the rim, they had to take a leak, it was a long drive, we drank a lot of coffee. It's getting late. We better slip," he added. You could hear bike engines starting up and down the canyon. I took the last hit on my coffee, watched as the little campfire jumped to life, and finished the bun.

Don Hawley and I went back a long way. We went to different schools together. We used to hang out at the Clock Drive-In on Atlantic Avenue, and see each other at the midnight drag races on South Avalon, the old divided highway. If ever there was a natural racer it was "Dangerous Don" Hawley.

J. D. walked over to the fire, unbuttoned his Levis, and started pissin' it out. Soon he was joined by Jumpin' Joe, Fat Boy, next by Wino Willie and Curly Cantlon. White steam rose in a great billowing cloud. The coeds had come back and one of them snapped a picture. The last time I ever was in the Big A, I remember that snapshot taped to an old yellow steel wall. Five of my boyhood heroes pissing out a fire in Crash Canyon on January 4, 1948.

RIDING "THE BEAR"
THE BIG BEAR HARE & HOUND RACE

We gaggled up Highway 247 and turned right on this dirt road that was the starting line. It was one of those roads that had been scraped out of the desert with a bulldozer blade. There was a rise on the shoulders where the earth ended up after the scraping. Just east of this rise was the starting line. Over on the other side of the road, to the west, was a big parking area. The Los Gatos M/C was there in force with a big banner on poles that was stretched across one end of the parking lot. These cats came down from Northern California every year, from the very early days of the Bear, with a gang of expert riders. Groups from other clubs, too, established their pits at the west side of the road, in front of the parking lot.

There were bikes everywhere. Most every make and vintage. Mostly AJS, Matchless, BSA, and Ariel 500 Singles. The 500 Singles were the most popular. They were light (by 1948 standards), torquey, and fast and would pull the side of a mountain like a tractor. Other makes in abundance were Zundapp, Norton, Velocette, BMW, NSU, and Jawas. Of the twins, the

Wino Willie and J. D. Cameron at the Big Bear race, 1949, in Yellow Jackets club jerseys.

most abundant were Triumph Speed Twins, Tigers, and Trophies; AJS; Matchless (Bud Hare was on a Clay Smith 600 Matchless from his cam shop in Long Beach); and BSA. Other bikes were Panther, Royal Enfield, Douglas, Harley-Davidson, Indian, and a 61-inch Crocker ridden by Ed Johnson, the famed L.A. flat-tracker. Of course there were a bunch of "corn popper" two-cycles: BSA Bantams, Dots, Villers, James, DKW, Francis-Barnetts, and Jawas, ridden mostly by young, novice riders. Many two-strokes started—in fact they would fly off the start. Few finished, however, and those that did always finished late, too late to be scored. Most blew up or crashed in the first 50 miles or so. How things have changed in the last 45 years!

We spotted Don's truck about the middle of the pits. Yoyo had the bikes unloaded and was tinkering with the Enfield. Ross Bernstein, the Shell Motors tuner, had the Scout on a rear-wheel stand. He had already run it, had the plugs out, and was making a carburetor mixture adjustment. The "cheerleaders" drove the station wagon back into the parking lot. J. D., Wino Willie, and I followed them. I could use some more coffee, and the buns looked good, too. One by one, the rest joined us and we established Boozefighters' headquarters around the Compton College delegation.

There must have been a hundred or so bikes running around us, racing out into the desert, checking out their scoots. Carburetor and spark plug checks. Tire style and pressure checks. Chassis adjustments and last-minute sprocket selections. Some of the Indian and Harley riders had stretched frames and chains on their rear wheels. There were a few pits that had blankets stretched out on the ground, feverishly trying to put engines or gearboxes back together. The air was thick with exotic fuel and castor-oil smells. "Nine o'clock, one hour to go," someone said. I walked to Don's pit. There were a few flakes of snow in the air, a few tiny bits of crystal jewels delicately held in the fingers of the dry brush.

I've never ceased to be overwhelmed by the Big Bear Hare & Hound. In 1948 there were 377 official entries, times five crewmen, add 1,500 spectators, equals 3,385 people. In 1954 there were 986 official entries!

The snow was falling steadily now, a light snow but enough to cover the desert. Don and Yoyo had taken their bikes to the starting line and the hare was getting ready to take off. The starting line was about 100 feet east of the road and ran parallel. More riders filled the starting line as the hare took off. I don't recall who the hare was—a member of the Hollywood Three Pointers M/C, AJS mounted and cooking! He carried lime sacks in a newspaper-boy's bag draped over his shoulders. We watched as he sped up the desert incline, past the Big Rock hill, where the starting bomb would soon go off, and disappeared over a ridge that lay about a quarter-mile due east.

I ask Don, "How do you follow lime markers in the snow?"

"You don't have to. He'll leave a big mud trail, and unless you're leading, there will be no doubt where the course runs."

I gave Don and Yoyo a pat on the back and walked down to the starting line to check out the other racers. Everyone had been running their engines to keep them warm. I saw our Triumph-mounted man, Arch Johnson, and two movie stars, Keenan Wynn on an AJS, and Larry Parks on a brand-new Goldstar BSA that his wife, screen star Betty Garrett, had given him as a Christmas gift the week before. The riders with sponsors or some club affiliation wore vests or silken "bibs" (like Class "A" speedway riders) proclaiming their benefactors. There was half-mile ace Bert Brundage, on a Frank Cooper AJS; Aub LeBard on a LeBard and Underwood Matchless; and auto racer and speedway star Mack Bellings on a Milne Brothers Ariel Red Hunter. One by one, the engines were shutting down, with the start approaching. You have to start with a dead engine, then when that starting bomb goes off, kick your bike to life, and bug out. The riders were getting antsy; every eye was trained on the Big Rock hill.

It's the waiting, you know. It's the waiting that seems so hard. You know you're good. You've proven that to yourself over and over again. You've proven it to others, your sponsors, the people that have come here to help you, and to the fans who have come to watch you. It's become dead quiet now. The more focused you become, the quieter it seems. You wait and wait.

Steve McQueen summed it up in the 1971 movie *LeMans*: "A lot of people go through life doing things badly. Racing is important to men who do it well. When you're racing, it—it's life. Anything that happens before or after is just waiting." When I look back at the memory of it, the mind's eye picture of the Big Bear, of *that* Big Bear, I remember the waiting. It seems hours ago that the hare left. "Will ten o'clock ever come? God, it's quiet, this waiting."

The bomb burst! Engines started, clutches engaged, and a square mile of California's high desert turned into a plowed field. Clouds of snow and dirt rose in a plume from each machine as they sped off toward the horizon. I strained to see who was leading as they crested the quarter-mile knoll. I looked for Hawley who was wearing a Shell Motors sweater over his leathers, but with 300 riders moving at 80 miles per hour over rough country . . . I walked back to the truck, is what I did.

Ross Bernstein was sorting out tools and spares, setting up for our first pit stop. We were servicing Don Hawley, Arch Johnson, and, oh yeah, Yoyo. We split up into two groups. Group A was Bernstein, Fat Boy, and Johnny the Jug. Group B: Curly Cantlin, J. D. Jones, and myself. Swede Kertzenbalm and Jumpin' Joe would drive the truck, see to all the gear, and be the official "go fetch it" gang. Group A would work the first stop, when the riders would come through the starting line on the first pass. Then they were to bug out for the Holcomb Creek Crossing and gas stop No. 3. Our group, Group B, would see to the second gas stop, when they passed through again. Then we would toss our gas cans and stuff into the station wagon and bag ass for the finish line at Fawnskin. There, Group A would meet us.

Bernstein set out two sets of gas cans; the first for Hawley, the second for Johnson and Yoyo. He "hipped" me to the scam. The Scout had been tuned to run on a special Don Francisco gas mix, the red and yellow cans. The solid red cans held Flying A 100 plus. Don Francisco was a local fuel mixer who was playing with nitro blends and such even back then!

The snow had stopped. The clouds were beginning to break up. The sun was poking its rays through the overcast here and there. Jumpin' Joe was snoozing in the truck cab. I ask Swede if he would like a cup of coffee, and we walked over to the wagon. The coeds had covered the windows with blankets. I lifted the tailgate to the sounds of giggles and shrieks! The girls were changing their clothes, getting ready for the pit stops. It was Don Hawley's idea. If there were a bunch of chicks dressed in tight sweaters, white short shorts, and Li'l Abner boots, standing in the pit, jumping up and

Original wild one, Jim Hunter, on the L.A. scene in the late 1940s.

down, wiggling all over, and screaming their lungs out, there was no way he could not see where his pit was! I closed the tailgate and they handed us cups of coffee through the window.

We walked back to find the truck backed into the pit. Ross Bernstein had all the tools and spares we might need laid out in the bed like an operating room table.

Everyone was in his or her pit area, all ready and once again, waiting. There was a quiet that comes with the snow, a stillness that slows the adrenaline flow. Everyone's eyes were turned toward the road. If you can picture this dirt road, scraped out of the desert floor by a bulldozer's blade, with great mounds of earth lining either side, where curbs would be if this were a city street, then you can see that crossing the road meant having to navigate two big old jumps! The riders would return from the east, crossing the road to the west, and into the pits.

At first it was a buzz. Like a bee, getting louder, sounding like an angry bee. Louder still, like a hornet. A lone rider, flat out and cooking. His engine raced as he hit the first jump, shifting gears in the air. He cleared the second jump and came into our midst. It was the hare, sliding the AJS scrambler into the Hollywood Three Pointers M/C pit. Refueling took about 10 to 15 seconds. He grabbed a drink of water(?), clean goggles, and split like a scalded dog. Due west. The coeds came running from the station wagon in ski caps and coats. There was no rush. The hare had a 45-minute head start on the field. That head start proved to be closer to 30 minutes in reality. The hounds were closing in.

The time passed more quickly now than it did waiting for the start. It didn't seem long before the first riders were arriving. The girls had their coats off and were lined up, ready to do their stuff!

First rider over the jump was Matchless-mounted Aub LeBard, followed a few seconds later by Dutch Sterner on an AJS. About a minute later came Nick Nicholson on a Branch Motors Velocette. A couple of moments later a gaggle of 10 or 15 riders were coming over the jump into the pits. Looked like ducks popping up in a shooting gallery. Next rider to "pop" over was number 88, Don Hawley, followed by 40 or 50 more. Upon pinning Hawley, the coed chorus line went into action, like football cheerleaders, high kicking, screaming, and just plain jumping up and down! Man, did it work! Don pinned the pit right off. Not only that, it confused the competition something fierce. All these cats were checking out the girls! Riders were running into each other, falling down, missing their pits, and even their pit crews were smitten in slack-jawed wonder. Fat Boy had the funnel in Don's tank and Johnny the Jug was pouring in fuel. Bernstein asked Don if everything was OK, he nodded and said that he could blow off these cats at will. He was laying back to let the eager beavers beat down the brush. It was easier to get lost by missing lime if you were up front, plus "cooling it" now saved the machine for when times got tough. Arch Johnson had pulled up in back of Hawley and the "A" Group rushed to service him.

More riders were pouring over the pit jump now. It wasn't long before Yoyo came on the scene. The gals went into their act once again, with a repeat of the first chaotic rapture of the lost demeanor. He was serviced in and out like a pro! The Enfield sounded great. I was amazed! Swede said he was counting and figured Yoyo was 78th out of 337 starters!

The hare led the field by 22 minutes on this second pass. The girls were once again on stage to welcome Don Hawley, who by now had worked his way to 9th overall!

Arch Johnson was in 22nd place when he rode in. He had gone down hard jumping out of a rock wash, tweaked the handlebar, and put a big dent in the Tiger's tank. The knees of his leathers were worn through and blood-soaked long-johns were peeking through. He climbed off and grimaced as he did a couple of deep knee bends. All the while I was pouring gas, J. D. and

Curly were yanking on the handlebar. I must admit, they got it pretty straight. The engine had died; I climbed on and after five or six tries, it lit off. Arch was back on and set sail with vengeance. Yoyo was next. Curly said that he had practiced his art all the way up to 64th. I was flabbergasted! J. D. gassed him up. One of the showgirls handed him clean goggles and gave him a kiss on the cheek. That must have worked like a shot of nitro! Yoyo was standing on the pegs and spinning the wheel clear out of sight.

Hawley's main squeeze drove the station wagon up to where the truck had been parked, and while the coeds were getting into warmer garb, "B" crew was stowing the gear in the back. The sun was out now and it was getting a bit warmer. We drank some more coffee and polished off the buns. It was a little after 1 p.m. when the girls pulled out and J. D., Curly, and I mounted up and took off for Fawnskin and the finish.

Dago and the Amazon and some of the others had split from the desert early and were already in Fawnskin when we arrived. They had parked their bikes within a block of the finish and made sure the rest of the crew had a parking space. It wasn't a hard thing to do when you were wearing Boozefighters or Gallopin' Goose colors. Those coeds weren't so lucky, though. They had to park the station wagon a mile away, so J. D., Curly and I ran a shuttle and packed 'em to the finish line. It was almost 3 p.m. and long shadows and about 2 feet of snow on the flat meant that the temperature was descending rapidly. J. D. had bugged out and come back with a half-gallon of the Red Staple of Life and we passed it around.

It wasn't long before the hare came sliding in. His buddies from the Hollywood Three Pointers M/C lifted him off a very tired AJS scrambler and carried him around on their shoulders. The officials had the sign-in sheet ready and the finish judges were at their stations.

The first rider in was Dutch Sterner at 3:22—five hours and 22 minutes—on the Cooper Motors AJS.

The official finish "window" lasted one hour from the time Dutch arrived. Ninety riders were officially credited with finishing. That didn't mean more riders weren't going to make it to the finish. Cats would be straggling in 'til midnight and after. Some riding, some riding two up, hell, some would even be walking to the finish! Arch Johnson had finished 31st and had to have help getting off his bike. He said that Hawley had gone down and slid into a snowdrift. "I couldn't stop. If I had, I wouldn't have been able to help him anyway." Don dug himself out and finally finished 51st.

After a while, Bernstein and Kertzenbalm drove up in the truck. J. D. asked about Yoyo. "He came walking into the Holcomb Creek gas stop holding his shoulder, said he had crashed and wiped out the front wheel and forks. Johnny and Fat Boy are staying with him until we get back."

I packed Hawley to where the station wagon was parked. The coeds had no trouble at all getting a ride. The basic crew decided we were going home via Skyline Drive. I ask Dago if she was going back to the creek and ride home with Fat Boy. "That sumbitch can find his way back without me holding his hand," was her reply.

The ride back down the mountain was much more carefree on the southern side. There was no ice and very little snow and, although the temperature was falling, at the moment it was warmer than it had been all weekend. We rode through San Bernardino, Pomona, and stopped in Covina for gas. By the time we hit Pasadena we had run out of adrenaline and Mission Bell to drink. It was a bit warmer in Los Angeles than when we left. The coed that was driving pulled into the closed gas station and parked the wagon by the pumps. Don was asleep in the back with the other young ladies. We rode past them and parked in front of the Big A. Fat John hadn't returned yet, so we sat on the asphalt and kicked back against the building. Dago and Amazon had dropped out when we rode through South Gate, where she and Fat Boy lived. J. D. Jones was nodding off. Curly Cantlon and I were shuckin' when Jumpin' Joe and Fat John rode in. John unlocked the padlock and swung open the door. On went the lights and radio. "You cats want a beer?"

Now that was a silly question!

Headlamps shown through the door. It was Bernstein driving Don's truck. Yoyo was sprawled in the passenger's seat. We left the bar and gathered around. Yoyo was passed out drunk. Still in his leathers, unzipped and open to the waist. He clutched a plastic bag full of ice to his shoulder. "I think he's got a busted shoulder," said Bernstein. "We've kept him drunk so as to keep him quiet." Don Hawley walked up and tossed me our sleeping bags. "I hope that Okie didn't barf in the truck!" The plastic bag was leaking a stream of ice water straight over his belly and down to his huevos. If he couldn't feel that, he was anesthetized! Hawley and Bernstein got into the "Harem Hawler" and drove off.

"Where's the Enfield?" I ask.

Swede shook his head, "Still in the desert, man. The whole front end is crashed. Forks, wheel, triple clamp, the whole damn thing, wasted!"

(Left to right) Jim Hunter, Dick Caroll, and Bobby Kelton at one of the many races the BFMC participated in.

"And you didn't bring it back?" I added.

Well, as the tale did unfold, it seems Yoyo's silent partner, his sponsor, the benefactor with complete faith in his riding skills, was truly a silent partner, seeing as he didn't know Yoyo had his bike! On the Friday night before he took the week off, Yoyo pinched the Enfield. It seems he was helping the salesmen push the used bikes off the lot and into the service shop at closing time. Yoyo made sure the Enfield went into the gunk rack instead of being locked inside. When everybody cut out, Yoyo just rode that sucker home.

About this time some of the other cats started riding in. The radio was kicking, the beer was flowing, and the party was starting, serious like. Kertzenbalm slipped behind the wheel and started the truck.

"Where ya going?" asked J. D.

"I've got to get Yoyo home and cleaned up. I'm going to take him into work in the morning."

"Take him to work?" I questioned. "Hell! This cat needs to be in a hospital not a motorcycle shop!"

"That's the whole idea. Now, Yoyo ain't got no insurance plan, so he's going to punch in, then tell Louie that he slipped and fell down in the gunk rack! That way he can get fixed up and his workman's comp will pay for it!"

"Don't you think it's a little funny, a Royal Enfield scrambler is pinched off the lot the day before Yoyo takes a week off. He comes back to work the day after the Big Bear all beat up and hung over and then breaks his shoulder before he even starts work?"

Swede looked at me with his mouth open, and before he could say anything else I added, "When you get him home look in the garage. You'll find a mudguard, lights and a license plate. You better get rid of them because if Louie Thomas' mind works like mine there's going to be cops out there looking around before noon!"

Swede shook his head, smiled, and said, "Man, do you think anyone would ever believe Yoyo would ever ride the Bear?" As the truck drove away, I thought, "Some day they're going to put a plaque on a cell at Lincoln Heights jail with Yoyo's name on it." Hell, I wonder what Yoyo's name *is*?

Four or five riders from the Gallopin' Gooses came riding in and filled up where the truck pulled out. One of them was Johnny the Jug. Sitting on the pillion, hanging onto one of those cheap suitcases, the kind you can buy in the five-and-dime that's made out of pasteboard, sat Meatball. God, she looked bad, like someone pushed her face into a garbage disposal. She turned her head away. Both eyes were blackened; she had a cut on her forehead, and another on her upper lip. Her jaw was swollen on the right side, black and blue, from her cheek to her chin. I'm sure she was crying, but how could you tell with her eyes swollen shut? The Jug helped her down and held her up, walking her to the can. She left her suitcase on the Triumph's seat. It slid off and broke open on the ground. Some of her stuff spilled out. There was a chalk "Cupie" doll holding a feather like a fan in front of her; three or four pair of knickers, the pastel kind with the days of the week on them; a cigar box with old letters inside; and one of those hydrometers with a "go/no-go" gauge on it.

I didn't feel much like a party anymore. I tied my sleeping bag to the AJS and pumped her to life. J. D. was by the door, sucking on a Red X. We waved to each other. I kicked into first screw and engaged the clutch.

The Los Angeles cold was back, damp, and slick, but the air was a bit refreshing on my face and in my hair. Yoyo came around a few days later and everyone signed his cast. He never demanded it, but he gained some respect after his ride. Oh yeah, he bailed out this time; he didn't go to jail. Lucky this time!

Two years later I saw Meatball, still playing house with the Jug, pretty as a picture, still with all that good stuff wigglin'!

CHAPTER 13

The Tale of Faces From the Past, The Three-Week Party, the Old Farmer in the Model A

I was sitting next to one of the original wild ones, Jim Cameron, at the Boozefighters' Fall National Meeting in Fort Worth, near Chapter 69's legendary clubhouse down on Bessie Street.

We were in the sweaty convention hall of a hotel that was beginning to reel a bit with age. Just for added effect a workman had left a hose running on the roof in an attempt to thaw out the frozen main air conditioner. Water and soggy chunks of plaster began to fall from the ornate, 1950s-style high ceiling onto the once-lavish carpeting. That giant rug that must have seen the footprints of thousands since it was new, the centerpiece of the vast room. Now it was just worn wool in a final stage of faded elegance, still softening the steps of a mix of gatherings that included massive conventions of elementary school teachers, wrapped up in serious round table discussions about stuff like the best ways to head off paste-eating; loud, shout-lined self-awareness seminars, complete with frozen toothy grins, bad hair, and the kind of screwed-tight enthusiasm that would rival hot dice tossing on a big-boy 'Vegas table; and hooded, solemn prayer gatherings that would invariably evolve into weird orgies of tongue-talking and bodies collapsing into quivering fetal positions, all in the name of "signs from the Holy Spirit."

But not today.

Faces and images of the Boozefighters' youth.

This time the footprints belonged to bikers. Three-piece patch-holders taking steps that were especially long—striding all the way back to 1946—in boots that were continuing a loving march and never missing a beat.

R. J. "Cowboy" Carter handed Jim two pictures, old black and white photographs that he had received from 77-year-old Jack Jordan while the two were drinking in a bar in Northern California. Jordan had seen Cowboy's patch. He remembered the Boozefighters. He had known them, ridden with them. He wanted these pictures in hands that would appreciate them, honor them. The shots were of rows of bikes and their riders outside of the old Mustang Motorcycle Factory in Los Angeles. Your eyes would immediately go to the faces of the boys—the men—in the picture, and then to their bikes.

No true biker could look at pictures like these without drifting straight into those pages. They pulled your own heart right out of your body and put it smack into the soul of one of those guys, feeling the hard beat as you fired up one of those fenderless screaming Knucks or Flatheads for a cannon-quick run through the still-wild west streets of L.A. That too-hip Clark Gable-style hair flew helmetless in the wind. After maybe a short stop at the All American for a cold one—or two—you could imagine heading on down Coast Highway for a cannon-quick run along the ocean, decades before storm-troopers in cities like Huntington Beach and Newport added things like exhaust pipe decibel-level meters to their list of equipment necessary to "protect and serve."

I looked over Jim's shoulder as he looked at the pictures. His finger was running slowly along the once-glossy 8x10s, near the faces, then behind the faces, to the men he had shared rides with, shared drinks with, that he had shared his life with. He was caught up in the vortex of an almost blown-out tornado, one that seemed to regain steam and wind every time someone infused this kind of love for the brotherhood back into it, picking Jim up and dropping him right back into the middle of his youth, into the knowing eye of a beloved storm.

His finger trembled slightly but his mind and memory were pure and calm as he dug deep for names to go with the faces. Some of the handles may have disappeared but the brotherhood did not.

I had tears in my eyes that I was not ashamed of. Jim had images in *his* eyes, images of his youth and the entire life that he has led.

As I watched, a part of me wished that I had been there, in those pictures, on my way to the Big A to drink with Jim and the rest of the boys. But

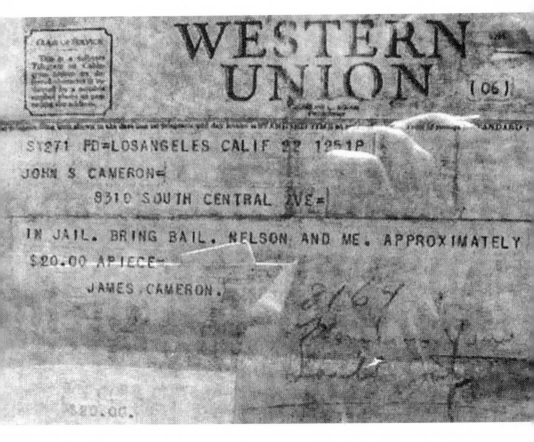

Jim Cameron's appeal to his brother, J. D., to bail him out. "We'd get thrown in jail from time to time," said Vern Autrey. "Usually for speeding or being drunk, nothing worse than that."

I was also very grateful that I was here now, in a position to be, as Hank Williams Jr. says, *"carryin' on an old family tradition."*

I had recently been given a copy of a telegram that Jim had sent to his brother John—"J. D."—another of the original wild ones, so many years ago. The text of the wire read: "IN JAIL. BRING BAIL. NELSON AND ME. APPROXIMATELY $20.00 APIECE. JAMES CAMERON."

Jim Cameron and Fat Boy Nelson in jail together . . . and it would take 20 bucks to clear up their debt to society. Boozefighters, through and through. Like Vern Autrey had told me, "We'd get thrown in jail from time to time, usually for speeding or being drunk, nothing worse than that."

I looked at the faces in those photos again. None were ever destined for grim mug shots in one of today's modern county lock-ups. This was the portrait of a different time, a different set of standards, a different attitude. Today's hypersensitive, .001 BAC paranoia tends to turn the fun-police loose like sharp-spurred Dobermans on anything resembling a good time.

Bay Area blues man Tommy Castro often sings a great little tune called "Nasty Habits." "Everything I do is bad for me," he laments. "I like to drink, I like to smoke, they say it's gonna kill me, and that ain't no joke. "

So? Seems to me that there was a certain degree of innocent charm in the fact that back then a beer too many or a friendly scuffle could get you a free night at the gray bar hotel and a 20-buck "get out of jail" card instead of a federal indictment.

"We had a party one night that lasted three weeks," Gil Armas once told me. "We all went to a friend's house near the All American, but after a while we realized that none of us had any money and we were runnin' out of

Jim Cameron, 2004.

booze. So Wino came up with an idea. 'I know,' he said. 'I'll go quit my job. They'll have to pay me everything right away, back pay and all that, and we'll be okay!' Well, we thought that sounded great so we all did it. We had all kinds of money for booze. We didn't have jobs after that but at least we were having this great party!

"After three weeks the cops finally showed up. 'Boys,' they said, 'the neighbors feel that a three-week party is long enough.' So that was pretty much it for that one, but it was okay; we just looked forward to the next one!"

Fifty-plus years later, Gil was still riding. But one weekend he was out in a very rural area of the Southern California desert—alone—and an electrical problem killed his bike. Time pretty much stops when you're stranded far from even downtown BFE. No one came by for hours, until an old farmer seemed to just "beam in" from the heart of the plains . . . in a Model A pickup! Gil wasn't sure if his senses were vapor locking or if this was real. Was this 2000-somethin' or was this still 1946?

The farmer was a big guy, and he managed to muscle Gil's bike up a makeshift ramp and into the ancient Ford, taking him to where the bike could be repaired. The old fashioned kindness, the vintage iron the farmer was driving, this was all pure Boozefighter. Just another high-level dose of green and white karma.

Maybe the longevity of the BFMC doesn't really rely on going *back* in time to study and emulate the history and heritage. Maybe it's really a case of pulling the truth and attitudes of that time through the socially locked keyhole of *now*—the *present*—and shotgunning them between the eyes of the modern citizenry. Maybe we *all* really are the faces in those pictures, poised to ride forever, dedicated to life's simple pleasures—20-buck bail, three-week parties, a helping hand on the road—and the genuine biker spirit of men like Jim Cameron, Jack Jordan, Gil Armas, and the rest of the original wild ones.

CHAPTER 14

The Tale of Big Jim, Three Hundred and Eighteen Bikes, a True Biker's Last Will & Testament

It's not about living in the past. It's about respect. It's about understanding that the most valuable wisdom usually comes with age. And the bottom line is always brotherhood. And it appears that—within *these* circles at least—there is little room to move when it comes down to modernizing, changing, updating, or streamlining the concept. It seems damn good just the way it is. The way it was. The way it's always been. Like the wheel, fire, sex, and American lager, some inventions and concepts came right out of the chute just as God had intended. Don't mess with 'em. The type of brotherhood that was handed down by the original wild ones is immortal, as any true biker will attest.

But how about the bikes? Every one of the originals that I know still has bikes. Les Haserot still has the bike that he took the legendary Baja trips on. Gil Armas has a garage full of his racers. Jack Lilly has bikes in his airplane hangar next to his ultralight.

So here, well into the twenty-first century, in a two-wheeled fantasyland that now defines itself more in terms of centimeters rather than cubic inches, a world filled with belt drives, rubber mounts, fuel injection, computer-driven idles, alarm systems, and billet logo-stamped high heeled boots for your old lady, BFMC member "Big Jim" Pierce needed an actual piece of a sanctified relic. He needed a dip in the bona fide Holy Water that the originals were baptized in.

"Big Jim" Pierce and his two-wheeled tribute to the originals.

To begin with, Big Jim understands the soul of metal. He created the yellow Deuce and the lead-sled Merc for the classic flick *American Graffiti*. But his latest project, his orange Harley flathead, was different. Not only was this to be a monument to the memory of the BFMC "originals," it was also going to be a rolling *last will and testament*.

"I built this bike to look just like a bike from the era when the originals were riding, starting out as a club. I did all the work myself, just gathering parts from all over the place. When it was all said and done I had used the parts from three hundred and eighteen other bikes to make this *one*. And, all total, I have fifteen hundred dollars in her."

That's fifteen *hundred*, not *thousand*!

Big Jim was practicing another lost art—parts scroungin'—and he was turning the wrenches himself. And Big Jim also wanted the bike to have the same immortality as the brotherhood it was spawned from. "I've willed the bike to my chapter of the Boozefighters on one condition: that they never change a thing on her. Nothing. It's to remain just as it is, a tribute to the originals."

That shouldn't be a problem.

This entire brotherhood—the focus, love, and dedication of guys like Big Jim—is in itself a living, breathing tribute to the originals.

CHAPTER 15

The Tale of McWino Burgers, Showtime at the All American, Shiny Tambourines and Wild Monkeys, The Studebaker and the Forklift, The Drunk in the Sawdust, Hot Water Heater Racing, No 'CLOSED' Sign, No Locks

Nothing produces a warm, loving, cuddly, caring, and comfortable feeling in a classic movie like a great bar scene. The space-cowboy honky-tonk in the first *Star Wars*, every scene inside Rick's in *Casablanca*, the spooky isolation of the creaking, dusty tavern in *High Plains Drifter*: just ain't nothing like a *drinking establishment* with character. A good bar is simply the ultimate "clean, well-lighted place." It's where friends are made, friends are lost, deals are done, pool is hustled, cards are cut, bluffs are called, eyes are met, hands are shaken, backs are stabbed, lips are kissed, tongues are tied, the weak are eaten, and the strong survive.

This kind of thing—this *comfortable* warmth—just gets in your blood.

Every year in Durango, for example, at the Four-Corners Run, we head straight for the old Diamond Belle Saloon in the Strater Hotel, where Louis L'Amour wrote much of his Sacketts series of books. Each year at Sturgis we can't get to Deadwood fast enough to hit every one of the Old West dives along the main drag. Thirty-eight miles north of Harley's head-quarters in Milwaukee is the Mineshaft, a joint that makes a point of living up to its name.

Well-worn, slightly booze-stained, but friendly welcome mats are out there if you just take the time to look.

There's a lot to be said for taking that happy, peppy, laugh-tracked *Cheers* atmosphere and bending it a bit—maybe a lot—catapulting it back over time's wall, back to the swinging doors, dirt roads, wooden sidewalks, and the sound of spurs clinking or the hammer of a Colt .45 being slowly pulled back.

But we really don't have to go that far back. Maybe we can just go back to the times when there was a different kind of horse galloping along Main Street, an antique iron horse. Maybe we can just go back far enough to kick over an old Knuck and make a sundown run along PCH, cut across to Gaffey, and drop down Fifth to Shanghai Red, then back to Long Beach for a quick one at Joe Jost's, then toward downtown and a stop at the Pullman, and then end the evening "where everybody knows your name," at the All American.

The address that became the second home—or in some cases maybe the first—for the original members of the Boozefighters MC was 1143 East Firestone Boulevard, South Gate. That area was—and *is*—a perfect fit for boots and leather, and for the occasional old bike that might just spit out a quart or two of 50-weight. Gucci and Armani probably won't be putting up any marble-lined showrooms near that magic vortex, where Manchester becomes Firestone, anytime soon. Most of the shirt collars along that stretch of Route 42 are blue-on-union-cotton; there aren't many with sequins on pastel cashmere.

But back in the mid-1940s, a few green and white jerseys were mixed in among the well-worked blue industrial denim. If the world, as a whole, was the apparent playground for the original wild ones, then the All American was the centerpiece, the extraslick slide, the merry-go-round, and the monkey bars, all rolled into one.

As Jack Lilly began to spin that slightly off-center carousel into a story about Wino making "his version" of burgers behind the counter at the All American, my mind began to drift. There were hazy images of an old *Saturday Night Live* episode, Belushi in the diner slinging cheeseburgers, served with chips and Pepsi. But there was something different, as the picture—and my imagination—cleared up. Yeah, there it is, a green-and-white three-star bottle on that big chest behind the greasy apron. And I could hear the sound of bikes outside.

"We were hanging out at the Big A, as usual," said Jack. "Business was slow and the owner said that he needed to run an errand. He asked Wino to keep an eye on things for him while he was gone.

"Well, he left, and here's Wino *in charge*! Okay, this older couple comes in, very nicely dressed. They sit down at the counter. Wino walks behind the bar and asks 'em, 'What'll you have?' The old guy says, 'We'll have a couple of burgers.'

"Wino proceeds to dig a couple of beers out of the ice box, pops the tops off, puts 'em in front of the couple, happy, smiling. 'There ya go. That'll be 40 cents.'

"They all kind a looked at each other for what seemed like a real long time. Then the old guy says, 'Burgers. I ordered a couple of hamburgers.'

" 'Yes sir,' says Wino, 'but this is the only way I know how to fix 'em! Oh, and that'll still be 40 cents.'

"The old couple kind of just looked at him again. And he was big, muscular, and grinning. They looked around at the rest of us. We were dying. We were trying so hard not to laugh. We were just dying!

"So this old guy pulls out a 50-cent piece, gives it to Wino, and says, 'Keep the change.' Then he told his wife to stop whining, drink up, and don't make a scene! The old guy downed his beer, the wife had a few sips, he grabs her by the arm and says, 'Let's go!'

"As they were leaving, Wino just couldn't leave it alone! 'How'd you like those burgers?' he asked. 'Great,' the old guy says, quickening his pace a bit, 'And you fixed them just right, too.'

"When the owner returned, Wino tells him, 'You ought to hire me as your manager. I already got you two new customers and they loved the way I poured their burgers.'

"The owner just looked at Wino—seemed to be a lot of that going on lately, people just *lookin'* at Wino—and then he starts scratching his head,

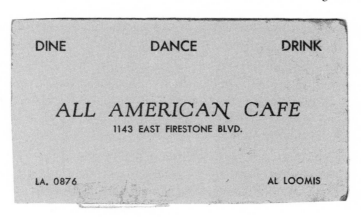

The All American Café was the gathering place for the originals.

slow kind of Oliver Hardy style. We couldn't stand it anymore. We were rolling, laughing our asses off! And, no, he didn't make Wino the manager."

It didn't really matter if it was inside the All American, or out—the circus was always in town, and under this particular brown-bottled big top it was continuously showtime.

One of the original wild ones and bike racing's iron man, Jim Hunter, rolled up in front of the Big A one time on a brand new bike. When the others saw it, it was like dangling a shiny tambourine in front of a Rhesus monkey: They just *had* to mess with it.

"I remember one night I was at the All American with my new bike," said Hunter. "Well, I was hanging around, drinking, and I got a little drunk. So I chained my front wheel to a gas pipe in front of the building and went home with a friend.

"The next morning I came back for it and it was gone! All but the front wheel and the chain! *They* were still there.

"I was going crazy! Then it turns out that some of the guys had unbolted the wheel and moved the rest of the bike behind the bar! I was madder than hell! I was ready to fight every one of them, but they were all laughing too hard. Just as well, 'cause I probably couldn't have whipped a one of them!

"Well, I got over it and learned a valuable lesson, too. Always chain your bike *through* the frame!"

"The original wild ones," as mentioned before, is a term reserved for the members *and associates* of the founding Boozefighters. The exact original, *official, bona fide* members kind of roll into those types of discussions that get a tad more intense as more tops are popped and the "Old No. 7 Brand" of that famous Tennessee sour mash pours. But through the minutes of the old meetings and other cryptic writings that required essentially the same type of analytical translation and study as, say, the Dead Sea Scrolls or Egyptian inner-pyramid hieroglyphics, the general, *arguable*, consensus is that the very first five members were "Wino" Willie Forkner, George Manker, Johnny Davis, "Fat Boy" Nelson, and Bobby Kelton.

Jack Lilly was there from the outset and *later* became a member—and it was in his Studebaker that the subject of beginning a motorcycle club was first discussed—but he was a truck driver and was often gone for periods of time, missing out on the initial formal "inebriated conception."

It was dark, a Southern California springtime evening, and Jack and some of the boys were sitting in his Stude' out behind the Big A. Wino was working nearby. Rust never sleeps, and true wild ones never rest. There was never a lack of more fun cards to deal and the ante was always a big laugh.

If Cheech and Chong had been making movies in 1946, this probably would have been the scene that made the ad trailers. Jack and the bunch were smoking, drinking wine, kicking back in the bullet-nose. Here comes Wino on a forklift, lights off, and you know he was grinning, a crazed jackal in control of some heavy-duty industrial power, sliding in behind the car.

The situation had only one answer. The Studebaker simply had to be lifted off the ground. With, of course, the wine drinkers still inside. And their panic would be hilarious, at least to Wino. It was perfect logic. Okay. Lift off.

Then, naturally, he dropped it.

The car bounced a few times. "That's some pretty good wine!" said Jack as the springs began to settle. "Then we realized what was going on, 'cause Wino gets off of the forklift, laughing his ass off. We all called him a bunch of names, but then told him to get in the car and have some wine.

"Later, as we began to run outta wine, Wino said, 'Hey, I've got this idea about starting a new club. What d'ya guys think?'

"Well, we thought that sounded good so we all went inside the Big A and talked about it. They were kicking around some possible names and that's kind a where we left it.

"I was a truck driver back then and right after that I had to be on the road for a while. Well, I get back and head down to the Big A and by then they were really getting this thing together. I guess Walt Porter had already come up with the name that everyone kind of liked and Wino says to me, 'Hey, what do you think of this new name that we thought of for the club?' 'Well, what's that?' I said, 'cause the last I'd heard they were thinking about naming it the Bats or the Henchmen. So Wino says, 'the Boozefighters.' I said, 'Well, I guess so. That's fine.'

"I actually thought it was kind of a funny name, but then I heard the story about how Walt Porter had muttered it out, so I figured it was perfect."

The rides, the events, the parties, and the field meets all brought out the group: the members, their friends, riding buddies. Within a matter of months the *official* membership grew. The famous 1947 group shot that was taken where the early meetings were held—in the back room at the All American, surrounded by cases of Old Gold beer—began to present the varsity team, the first stringers.

The early colors in the shot reflect the economic climate of the times, when priorities may have been bikes and booze before wardrobe. Not every jersey has the three-star bottle on the front. The truth was explained in excerpts from the club's early notes: "Some of the members didn't want to pay for the extra cost of the bottle embroidery."

With or without the stitched-in bottle, the riotous green and white sideshow was running at full speed right out of the gate. Jim Hunter, whose motorcycle racing trophies have gilded the walls of the BFMC museum in Fort Worth, remembered another typical day at the All American.

"John J. D. Cameron was actually more of a quiet, serious-minded businessman type than the rest of us. One day he was rolling kind of fast into the Big A. We saw him coming so we got his brother, Jim, to lie down on the sawdust floor right in front of the door. Then we piled a bunch of beer bottles all around him.

"Well, J. D. comes in through the screen door and he didn't even so much as look down. He just steps over the drunk on the floor. Seemed like he didn't even think much about it, just a normal day at the Big A.

"J. D. heads for the bar and starts discussing with Wino about getting a group of the guys together to go unload a boxcar and make a few bucks. Meanwhile, Jim hadn't moved. He was just lyin' there in the sawdust, trying not to laugh, with all those beer bottles all around him.

"On the way out, J. D. steps over the drunk once more. Then he turns around and yells to Wino, 'And, hey, don't bring this guy. Just leave him here on the floor where he belongs!'

"And we never did find out if he realized it was his own brother or not!"

As Jim Hunter rolled out even more stories about the three-ring circus that was the All American, the chaos needle was just about pegged. The brilliant innocence of the 1940s was digging in. And the fun, pure abandon: This is what *Cheers* would have been like if the Three Stooges, Jonathan Winters, and Soupy Sales had been in the cast.

"One day Walt Porter drove his new second-hand car to the Big A and parked in the next door garage's hoist area. Walt had been drinking, of course, and proceeded to pass out in his front seat. A little later C. B. shows up, notices Walt's car over the hoist, and naturally decides to have some fun. He turned the lever on the hoist and raised the car just about two feet and left it like that.

"About two hours later Walt comes hobbling into the bar. His hands were all dirty and his elbows were all skinned up. He was still kind a groggy but C. B. says, 'So, Walt, how are you liking that new car?'

"Walt says, 'Aw, it's okay, but it takes some gettin' used to. Stepping out of that sucker can be a real bitch!'

"Another time all the guys decided to have some fun by having a scavenger hunt. They made up a long list and put silly things on it that would be impossible to carry on a motorcycle. One such item was a *hot water heater*!

"Everyone jumped on their bikes with their list and took off from the Big A parking lot. Walt Porter happened to remember seeing a junked-out water heater lying near a curb a mile or so away, so he heads there on his old Harley 45. He picked up a long rope along the way.

"Time went by and a lot of the guys returned with what they had found. We were standing around in the parking lot when we heard this God-awful racket coming closer and closer. Then we saw sparks flying all along the road behind an approaching motorcycle!

"As it got closer we recognized it to be Walt Porter with a long rope attached to the back of his bike and the other end tied to a hot water heater! The water heater was skidding from side to side and banging along and bouncing as Walt was dragging it. It was horrible: the sound, the sight, the sparks were flyin' everywhere!

"Ol' Walt must have been real proud of his accomplishment because as he got right near the front of the All American he shot the gas to the bike, really turned it on!

"Then he made a sharp turn into the parking lot, slammed on his brakes, and skidded to a stop. For about a half-second he stood up, straddling his bike, his hands in the air, this big victory expression all over his face. But that changed to panic in a big hurry because that big water heater just kept going straight. The rope tightened back up, and there went Walt and his bike down the street behind the hot water heater!

"Walt picked himself up and we were just roaring with laughs. We were dyin'. Of course, Walt was the king of the one-liners. He looks at us, 'Guess I forgot water heaters don't got no brakes!' "

And this straight, no-chaser rush back in time had no brakes, either. I was definitely out in the middle of the deep end at this point. I was sitting at that long-extinct bar. But it was real. It was there again. *Here.* Jim Hunter was still talking. Others were talking. Ghosts were talking. The original wild ones were talking. I was laughing and drinking and so were they. It was a brotherhood that not only spanned years but it also crossed dimensions.

"Red was running late for a Boozefighters meeting. Now he knew that he'd

The most famous Boozefighters picture of all, meeting in the back room at the Big A.

get fined fifty cents so he had to come up with something, some kind of plan . .

"He knew that everyone was a war vet and was still a little shell-shocked. So the meeting had started, it was just getting going, and he sneaks up to the back door of the Big A and reaches in and turns off the main light switch . . . and at the same time he throws in a whole pack of lit firecrackers—big ones, boomers!

"Well, it was crazy chaos! Everybody running around, hitting the deck, smoke everywhere! By the time someone finally got the lights on and the air began to clear, there was Red sitting calmly in his chair like nothing happened!

"With all the goings on no one ever did remember that Red was late. He saved himself fifty cents! 'Course he had to have bought the firecrackers, but whatever he paid for them, it was worth it!"

Another round was served, Little Rascals never quite growing into those staid, drab, grown-up clothes with an endless supply of booze, laughs, and wildfire energy to match.

"Bobby Kelton got one of those new Triumph British bikes. He bragged about how quick it was and what good of gas mileage it got. Well, Jim Hunter and Vern Autrey, I think, came up with a plan. Every night when Kelton was busy drinking and talking they'd sneak outside the Big A and pour about a half gallon of gas into his tank.

"Over the next couple of days Bobby would brag about getting 65 miles a gallon! Then they'd sneak out and add a full gallon. Pretty soon Bobby is bragging that his new Brit bike had improved to 100 miles a gallon! 'Just can't believe how good them Brits make bikes!' he'd say.

"Then Hunter and Vern started *draining* gas from Bobby's Triumph. First a quart or so, then a half-gallon, then finally a full gallon.

"So there goes Bobby. He starts crying the blues. He said he figured it was all too good to be true. 'Them Brit bikes are great at first,' he admitted. 'But they sure wear out in no time at all!' "

"Everything is funny as long as it's happening to someone else!"
—Will Rogers

"A favorite routine at the Big A was for someone to come up with a suggestion to make a move to some other bar for a drink. And the last one there had to buy the beer. All kinds of trickery was involved.

"Everyone would jump on their bikes and hurry to kick them over. A lot of times you'd find that someone had pulled a spark plug wire or a coil wire or had clamped a piece of cardboard to a front wheel spoke so that it sounded like something was breaking up into pieces when they took off!

"One night Gil Armas was hauling ass on his scoot when suddenly he smelled something really bad! It was stinking! The further he rode the worse it got. He finally had to stop and check it out. Something was definitely burning. It was awful.

"Well, one of the guys went by Gil as he was stopped and he yelled out, 'Hey, Gil, how do ya like the cheese?'

"They had squashed a big chunk of Limburger cheese into the fins of his motor!"

Now it was last call. The lights started to dim, A wavy-haired kid in an old stained apron started to sweep the floor and put the stools up on the tables. The bartender emptied the last of the ashtrays.

But no one put up a "CLOSED" sign and the lights never went out completely, and I swear that I never did hear the sound of a door lock as I walked out into the parking lot.

And the patrons, the young guys sitting at the bar, never left. They just seemed to fade slowly away along with their laughs and their smiles. But they really weren't going anywhere; the years, the days, the nights, these men, this isn't something that is corralled by a lock or by time.

I fired up my bike. I could feel the last of the fading eyes watching me as I headed off into the night. I rode along well-lit roads and freeways that were just fields and dirt back in 1946, but it didn't matter. I hit high gear and it was all out. I knew where I *was* but I had lost any grip on *when*. I was running at about 80 along the curve that melts the 105 into the 405 near the airport. I needed the darkness of the coast. By Dana Point I was southbound on PCH, the Mother Road of the California coast. From there to San Diego it was just me, the bike, and the spirit of those boys at the Big A.

By the time the sun came up I was all alone on Mission Beach, but we were all together again. I looked at the sunrise behind me and then to the cold gray of the horizon to the west.

I grinned. I turned the bike around and headed north, back to L.A.

Maybe Wino can make me some of those special burgers for breakfast . . .

CHAPTER 16

The Tale of One More Journey Back to 1947, Hollister (Revisited), Eyewitnesses to the "Riot"

Okay, this may not be a history book—in the purest sense—but, like salt around the rim of a Margarita glass, there are a few important grains that just have to be attached to the good stuff to enhance the flavor.

You never *dilute* 80-proof gold; you simply *add* to it.

In a way, discussions of Hollister 1947 are like talks about good-looking women and bikes. Some subjects just never get old and there is always a new twist.

Hollister can't be ignored because it was, without question, the linchpin of this entire lifestyle. It was like Super Bowl I, the Packers, and the Chiefs. It was like the first pizza delivery by Mama Theresa in 1889. It was like Irene "La Belle" Woodward, the first seriously tattooed American woman, hitting the circus circuit in 1882. There are some things that have definitely changed the entire social structure of the U.S. of A.

The equation is easy: Hollister equals the American biker, and the Boozefighters MC is the sum total of both.

In 1998, Mark Gardiner, author of the book, *Classic Motorcycles*, sought out eyewitnesses to the races, Gypsy Tour, and "merriment" that rolled through this country junction corner of San Benito County on July 4, 1947. He wanted "to fully document this important event in motorcycling history."

(Left, in the shadows) C. B. Clausen and Bobby Kelton (center), Hollister, 1947.

Excerpts of the interviews were published in *Classic Bike* magazine, but the full text of the eyewitnesses' statements are the kind of thing you should read as you settle into at an end stool at Johnny's Bar, with something hard and dry in a short glass, a "bucket," a sipper, slowly absorbing the booze and the words of the people who *were there*, slowly absorbing some of the *true* history of the Birthplace of the American Biker:

BERTIS "BERT" LANNING

Bert Lanning was 37 years old when the 1947 Gypsy Tour rode into Hollister. As a mechanic in a local garage, he had direct contact with many of the bikers involved.

"I worked in Hollister, at Bernie Sevenman's Tire Shop, right on the main street. I had motorcycles myself, a Harley 45 and a Triumph. I'm eighty-eight now and my eyes aren't good enough to ride anymore, but I've still got a bike in my garage!

"There were a mess of 'em. Back then, beer always came in bottles, and there were quite a few of them broken in the streets, so the bikers were getting flat tires. They'd bring them into the shop, either to get them fixed or they'd want to fix them themselves. Eventually it got so crowded in and around the shop that guys were fixing tires out in the street, running in and out to borrow tools. Maybe a couple of tools went missing. Anyway, my boss got nervous and told me to close up the shop. I thought that was great because I wanted to get out there myself.

"Main Street was packed but it wasn't nearly as bad as the papers said. There was a bunch of guys up on the second floor of the hotel throwing water balloons. I didn't see any fighting or anything like that. I enjoyed it. Some people just don't like motorcycles, I guess."

BOB YANT

Bob Yant owned an appliance store on Hollister's main street. Back then, appliances were built to last, and so was Bob: He still works the store every day.

"In 1947, I had just bought into my Dad's electrical contracting and appliance business. We had a store right on San Benito (Street). There were motorcyclists everywhere; they were sleeping in the orchards.

"Our store was open that Saturday. Guys were riding up and down Main Street, doing wheelies. The street was full of bikes, and the sidewalks were crowded with local people that had come down to look. Actually, it was bad for my business; my customers couldn't get to the store. It was so slow that I left early and let my employee lock up.

"On Sunday, I went to the hospital to visit a friend. There were a bunch of guys injured on gurneys in the hallway but I think they were mostly racers. There must've been about fifteen of them, which was quite a sight in such a small hospital.

"There was no looting or anything; I was never afraid during the weekend. You know we had a few hassles even when the motorcyclists *weren't* in town. I think some guy rode a bike into 'Walt's Club' (a bar) or something, and somebody panicked. The Highway Patrol came *en masse* and cleared everybody out.

"The day after everyone had left, near my store, there were two guys taking a photograph. They brought a bunch of empty beer bottles out of a bar and put them all round a motorcycle and put a guy on it. I'm sure that's how it was taken because they wanted to get high up to take the shot and they borrowed a ladder from me. That photo appeared on the cover of *Life* magazine. (Note: the photo actually appeared on page 31 of *Life's* July 21, 1947, issue.)

"Not long after that they turned the little racetrack into a ballpark."

CATHERINE DABO

Catherine Dabo and her husband owned the best motel in Hollister. When bikers were being demonized in the media, she always defended them.

"My husband and I owned the hotel, which also had a restaurant and bar. It was the first big rally after the war. Our bar was forty feet long and a biker rode in the door of the bar, all along the bar, and through the doors into the hotel lobby!

"We were totally booked. Every room was full, and we had people sleeping in the halls, in the lobby, but they were great people. We had more trouble on some *regular* weekends! I was never scared; if you like people, they like you. Maybe if you try telling them what to do, then look out!

"The motorcycles were parked on the streets like sardines! I couldn't believe how pretty some of them were.

"It was great for our business. It gave us the money we needed to pay our debts and our taxes. They all paid for their rooms, their food, and their drinks.

"They (the press) blew that up more than it was. I didn't even know anything had happened until I read the San Francisco papers. The town was small enough that if there had been a riot anywhere I'd have known about it! I had three young children. We just lived a few blocks away, and I was never scared for them. I think the races were on again in 1951. My husband and I always stood up for the bikers. They were good people."

AUGUST "GUS" DESERPA

Gus Deserpa lived in Hollister. He is the smiling young man seen in the background of the famous *Life* magazine photo.

"I was a projectionist by trade. I worked at the Granada Theater, which was on the corner of Seventh and San Benito. I would have got off work around 11 p.m. My wife came to pick me up and we decided to walk up Main Street to see what was going on.

"I saw two guys scraping all these bottles together that had been lying in the street. They positioned a motorcycle in the middle of the pile. After a while this drunk guy comes staggering out of the bar and they got him to sit on the motorcycle, and started to take his picture.

"I thought, 'That isn't right,' and I got around against the wall where I'd be in the picture, thinking that they wouldn't take it if someone else was in there. But they did anyway. A few days later the papers came out and I was right there in the background.

The crowd outside of the Hollister jail, 1947.

"They weren't doing anything bad, just riding up and down, whooping and hollering, not really doing any harm at all."

MARYLOU WILLIAMS

Marylou Williams and her husband owned a drug store on Hollister's main street.

"My husband and I owned the Hollister Pharmacy, which was right next door to Johnny's Bar, on (the main street). We went upstairs in the Elks' Building to watch the goings-on in the street. I remember that the sidewalks were so crowded that we had to squeeze right along the wall of the building.

"Up on the second floor of the Elks' Building, they had some small balconies. They were too small to step out onto but you could lean out and get a good view of the street. I brought my kids along. I had two daughters. They were about eight and four at the time. It never occurred to me to be worried about their safety. We saw them riding up and down the street, but that was about all. When the rodeo was in town, the cowboys were as bad."

HARRY HILL

Harry Hill is a retired U.S. Air Force colonel. He was visiting his parents in Hollister during the 1947 "riots."

"I was in the service then, but I was home for the long weekend. Hollister was a farming community back then. The population was about 4,500 or so. Now it's a bedroom community for Silicon Valley and the population is about 20,000.

"Before the war, they had motorcycle races out at Bolado Park, about 10 miles southeast of town. I believe the big event was a 100-mile cross-country race. Back then the AMA had a thing called a Gypsy Tour. People would come from all over on motorcycles. Besides the races, there were other contests: precision riding, decorating motorcycles.

"I liked motorcycles. I started riding in about 1930, and at different times had both Harleys and Indians. I stopped riding when I enlisted in the Air Force—in about '41—so my bikes were old 'tank shift' types.

"Back then, the race weekend wasn't necessarily the biggest thing in town but it was as big as the rodeo or the saddle horse show. It seemed to me that there were always two or three people killed during those weekends, people racing and riding drunk. But things changed after the war. They got a lot rowdier.

"In 1947 I was still on active duty. I guess I was quite a bit more disciplined than the average biker that rode in that weekend. It was such a madhouse. My parents were elderly, too, and I didn't feel it was right to leave them alone so I stayed around the house. I sure heard it, though.

"On Sunday I took a look around. It was a mess but there was no real evidence of any physical damage, no fires or anything like that.

"There seemed to be a lot more drinking going on when the motorcycle boys were in town than when the cowboys were in town. When the motorcycle boys got rowdy we used to say, 'Turn the cowboys loose on 'em.'

"Years later I started riding again. Frankly, I was worried about the image we had as motorcyclists. [Motorcycling's] reputation got real bad, but I rode because I loved it."

JOHN LOMANTO

John Lomanto owned a farm a few miles from Hollister. He was an avid motorcyclist and a well-known racer.

"I worked with my father on our farm, which was just a few miles from Hollister. We grew walnuts, apricots, and prunes. I had a '41 Harley and was one of the original members of the Hollister Top Hatters Motorcycle Club. In fact, the first few meetings were held in one of our barns, but later on we rented a clubhouse in downtown Hollister. We met three times a month. We were a real club, with a president, a secretary, a treasurer, and all of that. Our wives came, too. Our uniform was a yellow sweater with red sleeves.

"There were a few races going on that weekend. I think there was a half-mile race and a TT. I didn't go to the races but I rode my bike downtown.

"It was pretty exciting. The main street was blocked off and the whole town was motorcycles all over the place. Everybody had a beer in their hand; I can't say there weren't a few drunks! But there was no real fighting, none of that Marlon Brando stuff.

"When it was over, attitudes changed a bit toward motorcycles. Most people were all for it (allowing more races and Gypsy Tours). Of course, the merchants made nothing but money that weekend. Still, some others wished they'd never come back."

Along with interviews from some of the people in the town, Mark Gardiner also discussed Hollister 1947 with two of the original wild ones, Gil Armas and Jim Cameron.

GIL ARMAS

Gil Armas still rides a 1947 Harley Knucklehead. He competed in dirt track events and later sponsored a number of speedway riders.

"Back then I was a hod carrier; I worked for a plastering outfit in L.A. I had a '36 Harley and rode with the Boozefighters. We used to hang out at the All American bar at Firestone and Central. Lots of motorcycle clubs hung out there, including the 13 Rebels and the Jackrabbits.

"Basically we just went on rides. Some of us went racing or did field meets, where there were events like relays and drags. There was an event called 'missing out,' where you'd all start in a big circle, and if you got passed, you were out.

"At first, most of our racing was 'outlaw' races (not sanctioned by the AMA) that we organized ourselves, but a few years later a lot of us went professional and raced in (AMA sanctioned) half-miles and miles. I retired (from racing) in '53.

"I just went out to Hollister for the ride. A couple of my friends were racing. My bike was all apart, and I threw it on a trailer and towed it up there. I didn't want to miss out on the fun. I ended up sleeping in the car.

"We started partying. There were so many motorcycles there that the police blocked off the road. In fact, they sort of joined in. There were four of them in a jeep. We sort of had a tug-o-war, with us pushing it one way and them pushing it the other. Tempers flared a little when somebody stole a cop's hat, but it all blew over. There was racing in the street, some stuff like that, but the cops had it under control.

"Later on, the papers were telling stories like we broke a bunch of guys out of jail but nothing like that happened at all. There were a couple of arrests, basically for drunk-and-disorderly. All we did was to go down and bail them out. In fact, a few of the clubs tried to force the papers to print a retraction. They did write a retraction, but it was so small you'd never see it.

"The bar owners were standing out front of the bars saying, 'Bring your bike in.' They put mine right up on the bar.

"On Sunday, the cops came back with riot guns and told us all to pack up and leave. At first, we just sat on the curb and laughed at them, because there was no riot going on! But we left anyway.

"In those days, if you rode a motorcycle, then anybody that rode a motorcycle was your buddy! We (the Boozefighters) were just into throwing parties!"

JIM CAMERON

Jim Cameron is still a motorcycle racer, riding a Jeff Smith–built BSA Goldstar in vintage motocross events.

"Because of my age," he laughs, "AHRMA will only let me compete in the 'Novice' class!

"I was a Boozefighter. The Boozefighters were formed a year or so earlier. Wino Willie had been a member of the Compton Roughriders. They had gone to an AMA race, a dirt track, in San Diego. In between heats, Willie—he'd been drinking, of course—started up his bike and rode a few laps around the track, just for laughs. Eventually they got him flagged off. The Roughriders sort of kicked him out of the club for that. They felt he had embarrassed them.

"Willie decided that if they couldn't see the humor in that, he'd start his own club. Back then a bunch of us hung out at a bar in south L.A. called the All American. Several clubs met there: The 13 Rebels, the Yellow Jackets. Anyway, Willie was talking to some other guy about what to name his club, and there was another drunk listening in (Walt Porter). The drunk pipes up,

A Boozette with Boozefighters outside of the Hollister jail, 1947.

'Why don't you call yourselves the Boozefighters?' Well, Willie thought that was funny as hell, so that was the name.

"The name Boozefighters was misleading. We didn't do any fighting at all. It was hard to get in. You had to come to five meetings, then there was a vote. If you got one black ball, you were out. We wore green and white sweaters with a beer bottle on the front and 'Boozefighters' on the back.

"Back then I was 23 or 24, I guess, and I had just come out of the Air Force. I'd been in the Pacific but Willie and some of the others had been paratroopers over in Europe. They had it pretty rough in the war. I had an Indian Scout and a Harley 45 that I used as a messenger.

"Back then, the AMA organized these 'gypsy tours.' One was going up to Hollister on the Independence Day weekend. That sounded good, so a bunch of us decided to ride up there.

"We left L.A. Thursday night and rode through the night. I think my Scout only went about 55 miles an hour, so it took quite awhile. I think we rode until we were exhausted and stopped to sleep for a few hours in King City. It was about 6 a.m. when I woke up. It was pretty cold and when the liquor store opened I bought a bottle, which I drank to try to get warm. Then I rode on into Hollister.

"It was about 8:30 Friday morning when I arrived there. I was riding up the street and I see this guy—another Boozefighter—come out of a bar, and he yells, 'Come on in!' So I rode my bike right into the bar. The owner was there and he didn't seem to mind at all. He could see that I was already pretty drunk so he wanted to take my keys. He didn't think I should go riding in my condition. The Indian didn't need a key to start it but I left it there in the bar the whole weekend.

"I don't think there were more than maybe seven of us from the L.A. Boozefighters there. There were some guys from the 'Frisco Boozefighters, too. One of our guys had a '36 Cadillac. He used that to tow up our trailer. We had a trailer with maybe fifteen or sixteen bunks in it, stacked three high on both sides. Basically, we'd drink and party until we crapped out, then we'd go in there and sleep it off.

"They claimed there were about 3,000 guys there. I think most of them went out to the dirt track races outside of town, but we didn't. We were having fun right there. The street was lined with motorcycles and the cops had blocked it off. Basically, guys were just showing off; drag racing, doing power circles, seeing how many people they could put on one bike, and we were just watching and laughing.

"The leader of the 'Frisco Boozefighters was a guy we called 'Kokomo.' He was up in the second or third floor window of the hotel where there was

Jim Cameron, 1947.

Vern Autrey on his way to Hollister, 1947.

a telephone wire that went out across the street. He was wearing a crazy red uniform, like a circus clown, and he was standing in the window pretending like he was going to step out onto the wire, like a tightrope walker. It was funny as hell!

"There were a couple of cops there but they were playing it cool. Basically, they didn't arrest anybody unless they did something to deserve it. The one Boozefighter I can think of that got arrested was a 'Frisco guy. Some of them had come down in a Model T Ford. It was overheating, and while they were driving down the street he was trying to piss into the radiator. Anyway, they arrested him and Wino Willie went down to try to get him out. He was pretty drunk at the time so they arrested him, too. But they let them both out after a few hours.

"Around Saturday night I started to sober up. After all, I had to ride home on Sunday. I guess I got my bike out of the bar and headed home at about 4 p.m. on Sunday. It definitely wasn't as big a deal as the papers made it out to be."

CHAPTER 17

The Tale of Cops

Bikers vs. cops, cops vs. bikers: this is the kind of downhill chat that generally needs a light hand, some degree of delicacy in the handling of the debate, the kind of subject that often gets awkward, like a bad human smell in a crowded public place.

Lots of discussions require some pretty tightly wound tact. Like when you have to tell the mean drunk with the .357 across the street that you just ran over his favorite dog, or when you need to casually mention to your best friend that you've started to date his ex-wife, the mother of his three teenage daughters, right after the judge gave her the house.

But there is nothing like rising to the occasion. Yes. Honesty first.

Biker vs. cops, cops vs. bikers—a fragile and volatile *tête-à-tête*.

Present-day members—*all* members—of the Boozefighters are brothers, but like all brothers they reserve the right to have different outlooks on things. Some chapters allow officers of the law to be members; some chapters may not express that exact same open-arms warmth.

But with cops, of course, there always has been a certain degree of de facto segregation anyway. They often tend to flock together. There are many law enforcement motorcycle clubs: The Choir Boys MC, the Iron Crew MC, Untouchables MC, the Blue Knights MC, and a bunch more.

And that's fine. Opposites really only attract if you're a magnet or a masochist.

But there are shades of gray—or blue—or black roofs and white doors as this case may be.

Original wild ones Jim Smith and Johnny Davis were members of law enforcement and they were also proud wearers of the green and white. Wino Willie never was exclusionary. "We never hated anyone. We had enough of that crap during the war. We didn't care what race or color a man was. We fought for *everyone's* liberty."

And evidently that included cops.

Smith became one of the first presidents of the club. And according to Duke, one of the modern rebuilders of the BFMC brotherhood, Wino Willie once referred to Smith as "the best damn president we ever had."

But there is, yes, a small bend in the tale about this. Jim Smith occasionally would arrive at some of the meetings at the All American driving a dump truck. The other guys just assumed that it was his job: running the thing. One day, however, one of the members was speeding on a south L.A. highway and was pulled over by a motorcycle cop. Sure. Jim Smith.

A deal was struck.

Smith wouldn't write him a ticket just as long as the secret of his *real* profession stayed between them, which it did for quite some time. Jim felt that the other guys might "feel differently about me if they knew."

Eventually the booze-flavored beans were spilled, but it didn't make for a sticky mess after all. It sure didn't bother Wino. "It got where it didn't matter. Jobs were hard to find and, Jesus, this guy had two! He was well-liked and elected as one of the club's first presidents."

But Vern Autrey and Gil Armas have both talked freely about the originals doing some offhand "vacation time" to pay the tab for a few too many brews at the All American or a few too many miles-per-hour along Firestone. But Vern and Gil each hit you with the same, coolly gracious, no-big-deal attitude that translates into simple acceptance of the sometimes high cost of fun.

Sometimes the mouse gets the cheese, sometimes the cat blocks the hole. Same game, different day.

But there was an especially ornery cat, however, who took it upon himself to sharpen his claws around the All American every chance he could. Officer Bell. And Officer Bell didn't like motorcyclists. He didn't like straight

Wino Willie Forkner, pre–World War II, pre-Boozefighters.

Life *magazine's famous staged photo from their July 21, 1947, issue that kick-started the media's image of the American biker.*

Wino Willie, On the Road, Hollister 1947

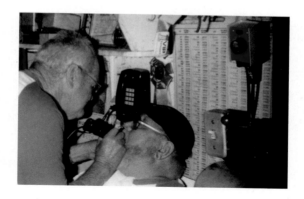

J. D. grinding on Wino's tooth with a dremer tool. "When it hit the tooth you could hear the sound change into this sickening kind of dull screaming grind," said Snowman, "and you could see the smoke coming out of his mouth!"

Les Haserot in 1938.

"Willie liked the looks of those three stars so much," said Teri, "that he put them across the barrel of the bottle [in the club patch]."

"I went to Hollister alone, somewhere around 1976," said Snowman. "I paid this guy ten dollars to come out to the road sign with me and take a picture so I'd have proof that I'd been there."

Filming the action scenes in The Wild Ones.

Original Wild Ones in their later years: (left to right) Jim Cameron, Wino Willie Forkner, John "J. D." Cameron, Johnny Roccio.

The legendary Ascot Speedway (just south of L.A.) 1949; Johnny Roccio (number 18), Ernie Roccio (number 3).

Jim Cameron won the Big Bear race in 1955.

Hunter: "I was in it to win."

The paint scheme on Les Haserot's 1937 bike got him into a little jam in La Paz. While in a beer joint, a local cop waited for him to return. He wouldn't let Les start the bike because it had a Mexican flag painted on the tank.

Modern day BFMC members side by side with some of the surviving original Wild Ones.

Jack reunited with Crocker No. 103, after over a half-century of separation.

A year before he passed away, the oldest boozefighter, Les Haserot (left) was interviewed by BFMC historian, Jim "JQ" Quattlebaum.

Those were tight-knit times. If you rode, you generally knew the others who did, too. Vern Autrey knew my uncle Bub (left). Uncle Bub rode his Knucks and Indians all over the Long Beach area.

"We got to Riverside," remembered Jack Lilly "having a good time, and I stayed too long. My wife (Lorraine, pictured on one of Jack's Indians) was waiting for me up in Idyllwich. But with no lights it took me forever to get up that hill in the dark.

There is a special term in the legends that surround BFMC members Dink Burns and Vern Autrey (pictured). They were real *tough.*

Wino Willie Forkner, 1920–1997.

Original wild one, Johnny Davis.

pipes, speed, or expired tags. He was indeed a specialist and wrote his tickets accordingly. In one day he cited Vern Autrey three different times.

Then, in what was probably a divine act of karma—or at least an example of cosmic humor—Officer Bell got whacked in a car wreck that busted his leg. It was a tender scene of the human condition. Officer Bell was visible to the Boozefighters, sitting in the front room of his home near the All American, reading, resting his casted leg, listening to the radio, framed elegantly by his large oval, Spanish-style front window.

The originals were sincerely caught up in fits of melancholy and angst. They felt *bad* for Officer Bell, theorizing "that the poor guy must be bored to death, stuck in that room, with no bikers to hustle or hate."

Vern suggested that they send Officer Bell something to let him know that they were thinking about him. The boys found a perfectly rectangular, smooth brick. They painted it, naturally, BFMC green with white around the edges. In the middle were the tender, caring words, "Get well soon." Simple, effective, direct, sensitive, quite Hallmarklike, really.

The delivery of the message became, fittingly, a club run. The entire group rode over to visit their buddy. Then-president, Johnny Davis, "exhibited true leadership" by personally delivering the *gift*, yes, right through the center of the Spanish oval.

A celebratory drag race brought the boys back to the Big A, where there were undoubtedly many glasses raised to the misty-eyed concern that they all had shown to their favorite local badge.

"I told the judge," said Jack Lilly, "that I couldn't pay the fifty dollar fine. It'll take four weeks to make that much if I don't eat or buy gas!"

But in the real world of twenty-first century motorcycle club politics, cops can present a problem. Stealth and dishonesty are not rewarded in motorcycle clubs. Stealth and dishonesty, though, are the driving wheels of undercover law enforcement. It's simply what makes their jobs work.

Books have been written, jail doors have been slammed, range wars have been ignited, short fuses have been lit, and some pretty tall enemies have been entrenched by cops and would-be authors who have wanted to unearth some real juicy bedrock and make a quick jump from amateur to pro with some scandalous scoops.

The Boozefighters MC has worked hard at having nothing to hide so— on the surface—whether a member is a cop or not only matters in a personal sense, not a professional one.

U.S. Senator and BFMC member Ben Nighthorse Campbell (R-Colorado), is direct: "Sure, like all motorcycle clubs, we've got members that are cops. The big difference is that we know who ours are!"

Most of the time.

One chapter of the BFMC began to experience more than just a few "routine" visits from the local P.D. Questioning of members and picture-taking of colors and patches became an annoying habit.

Hmmm . . .

A club official describes what happened next: "Shortly thereafter, a 'good-type' guy with a sharp-looking bike started hanging around, attending parties, going on club rides, and getting closely acquainted with the club's mode of operation. It was learned that the 'hang-around' was in fact a policeman. However, it didn't alarm us. We didn't have anything to hide. Later that policeman quit coming around and we found out that he'd got a promotion from the 'gang division' to 'internal affairs.' "

Hmmm again.

Original wild one Jack Lilly also looks back on the early encounters with the scales of justice with the same grin and sideways glance that Vern Autrey and Gil Armas had. "Back in 1940, a while after I bought my '39 Crocker, the headlight went out. I didn't have the two or three dollars to buy a new one until I got paid again.

"I was on my way home from work when I came up on a big traffic jam. Cars were backed up for a long way, but I noticed that way up ahead a lot of them were turning off on a side road. Seemed like a good idea to me.

"There was a little narrow bridge that squeezed off the right shoulder, so I whipped my bike around the left side of the cars and sped on down the center line between traffic. Well, lo and behold, I passed a cop in the process. He turned on his red light and made a U-turn to come after me.

"I got to the side road, made a right turn, and shot the gas to the Crocker. I was doing a pretty good job of getting out of there until the road came to a 'T' and the traffic was backed up even worse than before.

"The cop caught up and pulled me over. He said I was in a lot of trouble!

" 'Why were you riding down the white line?' the cop asked.

" 'I needed to get around all that traffic!' I said.

" 'Why were you running away from me? You must've been going at least forty-five or fifty miles an hour, and there's a twenty-five mile-an-hour speed limit on this road!' he said.

"I looked at him, 'Actually, I was running at about sixty until I got to this congestion, but I wasn't running from *you*.'

" 'Then why were you speeding?' he said.

" 'Well, I need to get home before dark because my lights don't work!'

" 'Young man,' he says, 'I don't believe I'd have told me that part if I were you.'

"The law back then said that anyone speeding more than twenty miles an hour over the speed limit must be hauled in to the P.D. station. The cop wrote me up for reckless driving, speeding in excess, and no headlight.

"At the station, the justice of the peace reviewed the citations and assessed a fine of fifty dollars. I didn't have enough for a headlight much less a fifty-dollar fine! 'Then it'll be three days in jail, but if you can't pay,' the justice said, 'we can let you pay it over time.' I told him, 'I make twenty-five cents an hour at my job. It'll take over four weeks to make that much if I don't eat or buy gas! And I still won't have a headlight! I'll take the three days!'

"The next morning they woke me and the other prisoners up early and fed us hash and coffee and then loaded us up on a bus. We were taken out to a road, issued 'idiot-stick-sling-blades'* and instructed to cut weeds along the side gullies.

(*Author's note: No, I had no idea of what an "idiot-stick-sling-blade" was. Because of professional credibility, I had to find out. It was necessary. My search took me into the heart of Cleburne, Texas, where such things are evidently well known, revered and actually used. Cleburne is also the home of an infamous criminal case involving a local woman and her illegal sales of

Jack Lilly: "The cop caught up and pulled me over. He said I was in a lot of trouble!"

"female stimulation devices," but I digress. I was informed, by an expert in the field, that "had I ever been a country boy or a convict in Mississippi" I would have known what an "idiot-stick-sling-blade" was.

"It's also in the family of yo-yos," I was told, "Not the string type but the weed cutting type. It's a tool for cutting weeds. You grabs the end of the long handle and swings it close to the ground like a golf club, except the other end has a blade device and slices weeds near the base of the stalks. Occasionally a few toes get sliced off, too, hence the expression, 'Idiot!'")

"At noon we were hauled back to jail and fed beans, ice tea, and a cookie. After we finished that I wandered back to my cell and piled into the bunk.

"Late that evening I noticed that the rest of the inmates—all sweaty—started to return to their cells and the jailer locked their doors one by one. When he got to my cell he yelled, 'What the hell are you doing here? We've got an APB out on you!'

"Immediately they took me back in front of the justice of the peace. 'This man escaped from the work detail!' the jailer insisted.

" 'How could I have escaped?' I asked, 'I was in my cell all along!'

" 'Why didn't you get back on the bus after you finished lunch?' the justice asked.

" 'I thought we were through for the day, so I just went back to my cell. Do I still get to eat supper?'

" 'Put this man out on the street!' the justice told the jailer. 'We're not going to waste the taxpayers' money feeding someone that won't work!' "

There was apparently just something about Jack that brought out the best in cops, even after four or five decades.

"My grandson was drag racing down in San Clemente and he snapped a chain, so he left his bike parked by the curb overnight in front of this gas station. When he came back in the morning the bike was gone.

"I always figured it was the guy in the station that did it. It was an all-night station. Anyway, it took the cops three days to find it. What was left of it was right there behind the station!"

Sometimes the personal and professional senses *do* get shackled together in kind of a conscious-driven chain gang when bringing law enforcement into the brotherhood.

"Let me tell you something ironic about this whole subject," a current chapter member related. "Some time ago, as I was serving on the membership committee, a brother gave me an application for a guy he was sponsoring.

After looking it over, I noted that the applicant was a policeman. I knew the guy looked familiar, but I couldn't place him. Suddenly, it dawned on me. I emphatically stated to the prospect, 'You're the SOB that gave me a speeding ticket about four months ago! You'll have hell to pay before you get my vote!'

"The heck of it was that six months later he had proven himself to deserve membership. It was my own fault for getting caught speeding. He had just done his job like 'we the people' had employed him to do.

"I voted 'yes.' Besides, I'll bet we motorcycle jockeys stand a better chance getting off with a warning the next time he stops one of us!

"Now we're not a 'cop club,' that's for sure, although we don't exclude them from association or even membership. We figure that you can benefit in working with them for mutual understanding, rather than against them and establishing animosity. And, like I've said before, if you don't have anything to hide, you don't have any reason to fear. And if any one does have something to hide, they don't need to be in the Boozefighters anyway."

Wino's statement about having fought for "*everyone's* liberty" probably tacks a pretty good bottom line onto this little theme. But then again, the grins of Vern, Gil, and Jack said a lot, too. Maybe the real bottom line is actually very uncomplicated, straightforward, and simple: "Occasionally you just have to pay that high cost of havin' fun."

CHAPTER 18

The Tale of the Big Bluff

Talk is genuinely cheap. The only time bluffing should ever be considered even marginally healthy is during the heavy confines of a potent poker game. Even then it requires a good chunk of skill, wide vision and a complete grip on the immediate situation. Otherwise you might as well be walking down Main Street at high noon, naked in April, singing Christmas carols through a bullhorn. You're exposed and under the gun of a microscope that will reveal truths that will permanently scar you, embarrass you, and probably worse.

Some environments, of course, provide a tougher crowd than others. Bikers come to mind. And it's not that everyone doesn't have to start somewhere. That's not the issue. Whether you're 16 or 116, if you feel that gypsy blood pumping and you have the money and the heart, buy a bike and *ease* into this lifestyle. Cool. Have at it.

But the key word is *ease*.

"Bulls in Chinese shops" (as Archie Bunker put it) break things and make asses of themselves. No one is ever going to lynch a hang-around or a prospect because, well, *he's a hang-around or a prospect*. But "bulls in Chinese shops" can get turned into prime filets pretty quick if the damage gets too ugly.

It's like the baffled look on the cute chick's face when she's sitting at a bar and Mr. Suave makes his move. Somehow she doesn't quite believe that he's a jet plane pilot and a software zillionaire, when she just happens to notice he's drinking a Lucky Lager—which he just sprung a 30-cent tip for—while sporting some spiffy pastel polyester from the days when "YMCA" and "Boogie Oogie Oogie" were still climbing the charts.

There are just some situations, some rare lifestyles, where a bluff can turn into a bust pretty quick.

The original wild ones not only laid down the basics of this way of life—they left a written history. Like hieroglyphics on the cave man's wall, ancient animal skin scrolls buried in tombs, or carvings in petrified rock, these boys have proven that they were the real deal. Clubs may come and go but there still are a few honored American biker MCs that have hung in there since the days when the Allied World beat back the bad. These guys deserve the respect that seniority always affords, and the ones who possess some ironclad, Perry Mason, airtight proof of their origins are worthy of a special toast.

This is the kind of stuff that can snatch that bullhorn away from the ass in a hurry.

The originals were the originals, and, as I've mentioned, that includes a fair amount of people. But just like when the long lost relative of a new lottery millionaire (that no one in the family seems to remember) suddenly shows up from behind the faded beige drapes with his hand out, there will always be those who try to revise history by crowding onto the bandwagon, trying to wrap some thick wool around the smart sheep's eyes in order to put themselves on a holy pedestal.

A few *tales* are one thing—the fish might keep getting bigger as the story grows longer—but the fact remains that a fish was definitely caught, reeled in, buttered up, fried and eaten. Its growing size might just be decorative color on the walls.

But there are limits . . .

"I confronted him, and I told him I knew better."

Several years ago, during a period when the club was really beginning to take a serious and accurate look at its history, a BFMC officer was suddenly introduced to one of the alleged kinfolk behind those drapes. An old guy had slipped his version of four aces past an unsuspecting member and was about to be introduced to a big BFMC gathering as one of the

founders and first members of the Boozefighters. The officer had his sus-
picions so he went directly to a couple of the genuine originals. It was time
for some knowledge, some sage wisdom from the masters, Grasshopper.

"They wouldn't talk about this guy directly at first. They're kind a
gentlemen in that way. They just won't go disputing somebody right off
the bat, but little by little I finally got it outta them. First, Jim Hunter. He
said, 'Well, go study the minutes of the meetings and see what you find
out. You got 'em, don't ya?'

"I said, 'Yeah.'

" 'Well, look at 'em!' he said.

"Well, I did, and that's when I began to learn a lot about myself, too.
I started to learn how to go about researching stuff like this.

"I found out that this old guy had indeed *applied* for membership in
the Boozefighters, asked to be a prospect around 1947. They did let him
prospect. And they had a rule that you had to make four meetings. They
had weekly meetings every Wednesday night. The minutes of the meetings
showed where this ol' boy made his first meeting. He made his second
meeting. He made his third meeting, and he made his fourth meeting and
asked to be voted on.

"Turns out that he was voted down, because nobody really knew him
all that well yet. Then you go reading on in the minutes, a few months later
this guy wants to prospect again. He makes the first meeting. He makes the
second meeting. Then the minutes stop mentioning him again.

"Then about six months go by and his name crops up again. The
minutes mention that this guy was with another club that came over to the
All American one night and they all talked about an upcoming field meet,
and that's pretty much where it all ended.

"The thing was that this old guy had met one of our members and
history began to change a little, maybe a *lot*. And this member bought the
stories hook, line and sinker. The member starts to make a big deal out of
the fact that he's discovered one of the original Boozefighters who started
the club and so forth.

"That's when I began to inquire and research and talk to Jim Hunter.

"Well, when the big night for all of this 'celebrity' stuff was about to
happen, I met this old guy. I greeted him cordially. I didn't say much to
anyone. There were only a couple of other people who knew what I had
discovered.

" 'What are you gonna do?' they asked.

" 'Well,' I told them, 'I don't want to rock any boats but I am gonna confront him, and he's gonna keep his mouth shut. He can tell some stories but I ain't gonna let him *lie!*'

"Sure enough, he gets there and it's getting to be a big deal. He's telling how he started the club and all of that.

"Finally I got him and said, 'Can I talk to you privately about something?'

" 'Yeah, sure,' he says.

"We went off to the side and I said, 'You know, I've heard a lot of BS in my life but this is starting to take the cake.'

"Then I said, 'Tell me, how long were you in that *other club*?'

" 'Oh, well, uh,' he says.

"I told him, 'I know you joined that *other club* after 1947. I was just curious. After you got turned down by the Boozefighters the first time and didn't make the meetings on your second try, is that when you joined the other guys?'

" 'Well, we were all together,' he said, 'We were all the same.'

" 'No you weren't,' I told him.

" 'Oh yeah, it was all just like one big club.'

"I said, 'Nope. Sure, there were several clubs that all hung out at the Big A, and that you all rode together a lot, but the bottom line was that Boozefighters were Boozefighters, Yellow Jackets were Yellow Jackets, Sharks were Sharks, Gallopin' Gooses were Gallopin' Gooses, 13 Rebels were 13 Rebels. Sure, you all ran together, I know *that*.'

" 'Well, that's what I mean.'

" 'No, all those clubs were different and distinctive clubs. You've been kinda leading people on here to think that you were a major part of the *founding* of *this* club. You never even applied for membership 'til 1947. The club started in 1946.'

" 'Well, I was *around* back then!'

" 'But you weren't part of the founders of the club! If you'd said that you'd like to tell us some stories about the guys who hung out at the Big A and a lot of the characters in the various clubs, that would be fine, but that's not what you're sayin'. Now, it's like I said, I've heard a lot of BSers and you're one of the best—*but*—you need to cut the BS out or I'm going to expose you here in front of this whole group. I'll go along with your basic story that you ran with a lot of these guys in the old days, great, but shut up about that *I helped to found the club* stuff! And I don't want to hear any negatives about any of the old timers, especially Wino! OK? If we can understand this we'll get along just fine.'

" 'OK, alright,' he says. 'No problem!'

"Well, the guy that brought him had no idea that we'd had that conversation or what I knew. Sure enough, when it came time for the old guy to speak he gets this big build-up and intro. The old guy just kinda says, 'Nah, it was a long time ago. I can't remember all those details. We all just kinda partied together and had a good time back in those days. Just glad to be here.' And that was all he said."

Adding spice to a campfire yarn and yes, *lies,* are two very different things, as is shoe-horning your way into the biker culture, as opposed to simply allowing the social butter to melt gracefully into that coveted, golden-brown, adventure-filled waffle. But all of these things are together, sharing the same orbit around the fiery center of the biker world, a world that guards its genuineness so very closely.

A note that I received recently from current BFMC member Mad Dog makes a damn good case that this gypsy blood we all have may already have been thickened with a strong dose of 50-weight before we even came down the chute. Maybe it's a question of *when* it starts to pump, not *if*:

It's a fact to me that one is born a biker. You can't *become* one. The stories I've heard about the originals reinforce this. I have ridden something motorized with two wheels since I was around fourteen. Before that I used to chop out my bicycles as a youngster: extend the forks, add sissy bars and ape hangers. Hell, I even put on the toy "Varoom!" engine.

My big brother was a biker and the first time I saw him on an old Sportster, I knew that someday that would be me on a bike. I have ridden as an independent for all of these years 'til I met some Boozefighters. It has changed my life. I have finally met other people who think and feel the way I do about motorcycles. They are brothers to me now, brothers I never knew I had before. I liken it to having a child. They are so much a part of your life that you can't live without. You never knew you were missing that part of *yourself.* This is what the Boozefighters MC is to me.

I had an uncle who was a World War II vet, a paratrooper in the 101st. He was also a biker back in the days when our club started after the war. One night as he was heading home from work, he was struck broadside by two asswipes who were drag racing and ran a stop sign. His body was recovered on the roof of a house some 80-odd feet away.

My mother hated motorcycles from then on.

Well, I was in the Air Force years later and wanted to buy a motorcycle. I needed my mom to send me a savings bond that I had to help me pay for it. She was so against me getting a bike that I could feel the steam coming off her over the phone.

After a long conversation, I had convinced her of how much that getting the bike meant to me and how it wasn't the motorcycle that had killed her brother; it was the jerks in the cars. After that, she opened up to me about how her and my dad had ridden on a Harley from Beeville, Texas, to Corpus Christi back in the 1940s and how much fun it had been for her.

I figured that my uncle was probably a lot like our founders, the original wild ones. Being part of this club is honoring the memory of my uncle, too.

Sure, bikers may be a tough audience to play to, but that might just be because of the loving loyalty and passion that men like Mad Dog have for this brotherhood. On one hand, there definitely isn't any patience with a complete fabrication, but there is a great deal of compassion and respect for the good ol' boys who dug our first trenches, and for the accounts and legends they bring with them.

Before this book was published, excerpts from Gil Armas' tale of the origin of the stroker were printed in other media. That generated a letter, a 'very interesting' letter, a sticky, cryptic screed from a self-proclaimed "credentialed" motorcycle expert. When I first read it I thought it was a joke. But then after I contacted the guy who had written it I began to feel some horrible pangs of evil truths, like when you stick your tongue into a light socket, or when you force yourself to watch a long segment on the news network about yet another vile mutant who was found by the cops to have corpses under his house and body parts in his fridge. Pain and goofballs are real and have to be dealt with.

This guy who wrote the letter, a Grinch with a computer and the style of a humorless Mr. Peabody (without his boy, Sherman), was very upset that Gil's tale didn't follow precise, clinical guidelines in discussing the mechanics of a bike.

At one point in his stroker story, Gil said that, "The piston comes up dead even." But no! This was, to Mr. Grinch, the slide-rule equivalent of an inquiry into whether the Monkees really played their instruments or not.

I was pretty slack-jawed that this guy had taken the time to write: " 'The piston comes up dead even.' Completely wrong. EL stroke 3.5 inches. EL cylinder height 5.405 inches. FL cylinder height 5.53 inches. UL stroke 4.28125 inches.

"The stroke difference between the two motors is 0.78125-inch, so the piston is 0.390625 inch higher up, and will stick out of the EL barrel by about that much. Substituting an FL barrel increases the barrel height by only 0.125-inch, and still come out of the FL barrel by 0.265625-inch."

Damn! And I had two full pages of this stuff. Wouldn't you like to invite that guy over for a few beers and to watch a movie? You'd probably have to sit through two hours of him explaining the fact that "apes couldn't really talk because of genetic discrepancies in their facial muscles and that the antigravitational devices on the spaceships couldn't really function because of the improper alignment of the disgronificator drive."

Eventually I became convinced that the letter wasn't a joke and that this guy was real. And I was also sure that he had many rotting cadavers under the floor of his living room, and that it was a lead-pipe cinch that he had a four-foot piece of rebar stuck up his backside to boot.

Dude, lighten up.

But these orbits all do intersect. There are the great pretenders, there are the headstrong rookies who come off as posers, there are fragile-ego liars, and there are legends that might just become a bit bigger than life, but it's the cornerstone lives they celebrate that are important, not each tiny grain of minutiae that might just fall around the campfire.

The guy with the rebar up his rear added the comment that Gil's story supplied " . . . yet more proof that old men have poor memories, but excellent imaginations."

So the hell what? Jimmy Buffett likes to write about what he calls "fictional facts and factual fictions," stuff that is all definitely derived from life's experiences one way or another. We certainly made a fine dinner outta that fish. That's a fact. Whether or not it keeps growing big enough to leave more and more leftovers really doesn't matter. In a way it just adds more juice to the stew.

Maybe my reply to the Grinch-guy can put all of this—the rookies, the pretenders, the wannabees—into a neat box, and any of us who might have occasionally stepped into that particular quicksand on our way to realizing that we were, as Mad Dog perfectly put it, "born bikers."

Thanks for your interest in our book excerpt about Gil Armas and his version of the stroker. I must admit that when I received your note I thought it was a satire, like something from an old *Saturday Night Live* sketch, or more appropriately, from a vintage *Firesign Theatre* LP skit. Then I realized that you were serious, and your opening line is *indeed* serious. And poignant. Yes, "Old men may have poor memories but excellent imaginations," but "old" isn't necessarily a negative term, at least not to me. Gil Armas, and the rest of the World War II vets who returned home to found this lifestyle may not have known that the "stroke difference between the two motors was 0.78125," but they knew enough to keep the things running. They understood that the essence of this lifestyle was in the freedom that they had just fought for, and the fact that on those open roads of the 1940s a motorcycle was the best tool for the job.

This book, *The Original Wild Ones*, is not a shop manual or a tech booklet. It is the tales of the men who kicked this whole way of life into gear and the heritage that they passed on. Did Gil miss a few of the technical details? Probably. But did he and men like C. B. Clausen get their hands dirty in cold garages just trying to keep their bikes on the road when there wasn't a Rodeo Drive boutique-style Harley dealer on every corner? Definitely. Did they have access to all of the high-priced Snap-Ons and computer-aided knowledge that you do? No. But just maybe it was their spirit that has brought us to where we all are today, a spirit that enables you to do what you do and me to do what I do. I have been riding since 1966. You, apparently, have also been around for a bit, but there is one more fact that is pertinent—Gil Armas has more miles under his belt (oh, excuse me, *chain*) than you and I put together.

And, as Colombo always said, "Just one more thing." The next time you're in a biker bar and the guy sitting next to you starts telling a story, why not just sit back and listen, and appreciate that colorful aspect of the biker culture instead of giving him a technical anal exam."

CHAPTER 19

The Tale From South of the Border

Border towns are not G rated. They usually have the same cultural ambience as a Saturday night swinger's party at Attila the Hun's place. They have the same class and upright dignity as a drunken Jerry Springer guest, a defense attorney, or a toothless Bangkok hooker that smells a lot like Friskie's Tuna Feast.

And, certainly, that's what makes 'em fun.

Tijuana, right on the California/Mexico border, is 132 miles from South Gate, California, 132 miles from where the All American served as the brown-bottled midwife to the Boozefighters MC. And 132 miles is easy access. It was a hop, skip, and a simple straight-piped jump to the Devil's Disneyland for the original wild ones.

Vern Autrey talked about how the boys would "up and head for the border just for the hell of it if things got a little slow at the All American"—or if the random mood suddenly hit, like a restless midnight alley cat leaping the back fence with no particular plan in mind other than to find *something* that would kick a normal evening's crazed adventures into an even more intense overdrive.

And Wino and Teri loved to fish along the Baja coastline.

Mexico produced a even bigger spark for original wild one Les Haserot. Les was known as the "Baja King," an oil-stained royal title that was not given or inherited; it was *earned.*

"To my knowledge," says Les, "I'm the first motorcyclist to dare the full 900-mile distance from Ensenada to Cabo San Lucas, known as the Baja Race. They didn't give out awards for that, because motorcycles were not included as a division or class. Only cars and trucks were counted because no one figured a motorcycle could make it on a 900-mile stretch of desert dirt.

"Why'd I do it? Just for the adventure, I guess, and to prove it could be done.

"I built up this old 1937 flathead 45. I kept it stock but changed and added a *few* things. I put a 6-gallon gas tank on it, removed the battery box, and put a 1.5-gallon oil reserve tank in its place. I also rigged up a magneto for juice, filled my saddlebags with spare parts and tools, strapped a bedroll and some clothes on the back, filled my canteen, and took off.

"I'd have to find these little towns or communities to get gasoline. None of them had gas stations but there were always barrels of gasoline that someone would siphon out to fill my bike. I'm kinda proud of those runs, especially since I repeated the same adventure 20 times, all the way through 1954."

Les' 20 south of the border 900-mile banzai circus acts were pure Boozefighter greatest hits material.

Another of the original wild ones, Johnny Roccio, crowns the king: "In addition to being one heck of a good guy, Les was *perfection* when it came to his bike. We could ride through mud one day and the next time you saw him his bike would shine. I mean even down to the spokes on his wheels, they'd shine like new!

"Another thing. Every spring and fall he'd make the Baja Run. No matter what was going on, he'd do the Baja. Most of us couldn't justify taking the time off from work. Les did the Baja and made allowances for work and other things around that. He was the Baja king!"

The entire southwestern borderline of the United States contains the unwritten page of pure adventure. The originals knew this. All it took was a steady hand, a fearless *caliente* soul, and a wild will. Stories will be written, pictures painted, real lives lived.

"Nothing in this club is more important than the history, attitudes, and spirit that were laid down by the originals for the rest of us to follow," says National BFMC Historian Jim "JQ" Quattlebaum. "So I figured that it was damn well time for a bunch of us to relive some of the types of adventures that Vern, Les, Wino, Teri, and the rest of them had down in Mexico. Like Vern said, they'd just 'up and head for the border just for the hell of it.' So, OK, fine, so would we!

"This trip made us feel so close to the original wild ones. This is the kind of stuff they did. These were some of the same kinds of absolute and complete messes they'd get themselves into—then out of—then laugh about later. Then do all over again! It led to a tale—'The Tale of the Community Bean Pot and Other Frijole Stops South.' This was kind a like a semester final in Boozefighter 101. This was a tribute to Wino and all the rest; after all, we *are* the result of what they all taught us.

"We had set up our tents on the banks of Lake Amistad, just above Del Rio. During the day we fished for bass and at night we went across the border to Ciudad Acuna to party. But it was back at the campsite that the 'community bean pot' was born. "It was a big, five-gallon cast-iron kettle that we set up over the open fire on Friday night. By breakfast time the next morning the *frijoles* were nice and soft and hot. But, being typical bikers, some arguing broke out about the damn beans not being 'properly seasoned.'

"The main cook really stirred everything up. 'If you're such a great cook,' he told the main complainer, 'why don't *you* just take over?' It all went south pretty fast after that. The guy who was doing most of the bitching looked at the cook and poured his whole cup of morning coffee into the bean pot. Everyone went nuts laughing.

"But then it all didn't seem like such a bad idea to let the bean pot kind of represent our 'what-the-hell' attitude. So along with the coffee, everyone started adding their own personal touch to the *Frijoles del Boozefighter*: a couple of potatoes, some onions, ham hocks, more black pepper, a glass of wine, some tequila, a whole can of stuffed jalapeno peppers, a little more tequila. Right after sunset, a couple of June bugs dove in and disappeared pretty quick. Just good protein, we figured. And, wouldn't you know it, those beans turned out to be some of the best *frijoles* any of us ever had. *Unusual*, yeah, but real tasty.

"Monday morning we broke camp. Most of the folks headed home, but a few of us headed south, across the border into Mexico. It's a whole different world down there, and the Coahuila state roads are the first clue. It really makes you respect what Les Haserot did. Highway 29 takes you through little villages like San Carlos, Zaragoza, and Villa Union, all little towns of just a few hundred people.

"By noon we pulled into a larger town called Sabinas, named after the river that runs through the middle of it. There must have been a population of a couple of thousand or so and for some reason, they all came out and were lined up along the road on both sides as we came riding in. By the time we got to the downtown square, it was packed with people looking at us.

"We parked and a crowd surrounded us. I asked a young teenager if there was going to be a parade or something? He spoke broken English but I understood him to say, 'Sí, señor. *You* are the parade!' We had noticed that a lot of people had been eyeballing our ride through the smaller towns. Later we learned that word was getting passed on ahead to come out and see those 'American bikers.' Just how the word got ahead of us is still a mystery 'cause we didn't see any telephone lines along the road and sure as hell, no one down there had a cell phone then.

"The teenager said that he would guard our 'mucho grande motor bikes' while we 'toured' the square and the wano shops. It wasn't going to cost us 'mucho dinero,' he added. We got some tacos at one place, a bottle of tequila at another, gave our 'bike guard' a couple of bucks, and headed out. Lots of spectators waved good-bye and a lot of little kids ran along side of us for a few small blocks. Man, we really felt kinda like *dignitaries*!

"From that point on, we started gaining altitude. Outside of Monclova, we gassed up before beginning our climb into the mountains, the Sierra Madres. There weren't any more little towns, and the air was refreshing. It was *cool*! We were somewhere around the 10,000-foot level as we topped the pass. The sun had gone down and our leathers felt good. We saw a lightning storm along the peaks to our right. Since it was far away, it made for a beautiful sight as we snaked our way slowly down the backside of the mountain

"But we were heading back into the heart of the desert, with all of its power, all of its unpredictability, all of its danger. The temperature went up. Way up. But we started to hear a strange *cracking* sound in the distance ahead of us. As we topped one of the rises in the foothills we saw what looked like a giant white snake stretched out across the highway below. We slowed down and eased up to it. It was literally a river of hailstones pouring downslope from the mountains, covering the road in a mass, twenty yards wide. We stopped, of course, and occasionally an 18-wheeler would plow right through it, spraying hail everywhere and making a huge crackling sound.

"There happened to be a little picnic area on the side of the road so we pulled off and parked, sat on the tables, and pulled the leathers off. The temperature was back up to around ninety. We decided to wait until the hail flood receded before we tried to push on any further. But after the second cigarette one of the guys started yelling, 'Hey! Those damn hailstones are

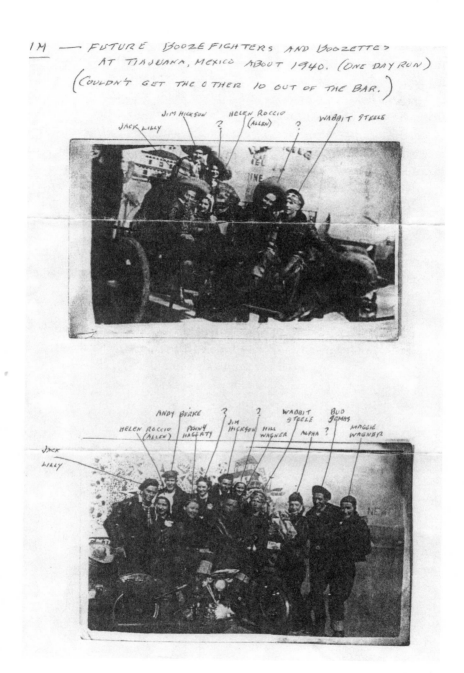

Wild bike trips to Mexico were common among the originals.

coming in behind us, too!' And, sure enough, they were flowing into the picnic area. It was kind of like a weird, icy lava flow from a frozen volcano, and we were about to be swallowed up!

"What you should never do in a case like that is to panic. What we did, naturally, was to *panic*. We jumped on the bikes and started to fly back up into the foothills from where we just came, but the road up there was now also covered with icy hail. We watched a truck make its way through it and we realized that this 'river' was in a low spot; we'd be neck deep if we tried to go through there. We were cut off in front and from behind and it was beginning to flood in the middle, too. 'We're trapped!' one of the guys yelled. I just looked at him. He was right, of course, but I couldn't help but feel that this was really a movie. Sylvester Stallone just *had* to be on his way with about thirty-six helicopters and the entire of the Navy SEALs team, or maybe Chuck Norris, Arnold, or at the very least, Spiderman. Hell, we would have settled for Big Bird or the Teletubbies, if they could have done something about these damn rivers of hail.

"We turned around and headed back toward the picnic area, but it was gone. It was under the *other* hail canal. Arnold, Chuck, and the Teletubbies were real conspicuous in their absence. But as a couple of trucks ground their way through the *Rio del Picnic Area* we noticed that the hail river was going down a bit. We could see now that it wasn't all *that* deep by how high it came up on the truck wheels.

" 'Okay, we're gonna get washed away if we stay here much longer, if we don't do *something!*' noted one of our more observant rocket scientists. There was a strong silence as we all just looked at him with that *look,* the look like we all give our TVs when we're watching football and its about the fourteenth game of the season, the playoffs are on the line, the clock is winding down, our team is four points down, it's 4th and 1 on the eight-yard line, and the commentator says something like, 'They really need to pick up this first down, Bob.' Damn! Really? The sun rises in the east, cheap apple-flavored Schnapps will make you barf, and I'm never gonna get the chance to sleep with Britney Spears. I mean, we just looked at him.

"Sure, he was right and we were all about to become seriously dead and frozen *gringos,* but, damn! Anyway, we kind of just shook that bit of insight off, and we decided that there really was only one shot: try and get through the least deep of the two road-covering hail *rios.*

"I went first, slow. We sure as hell didn't want to drop any bikes in the flow. The hail rush got deeper, then it kind of leveled out, but the hailstones were rattling against the fenders and shooting out everywhere. The only saving grace was that there wasn't as much *water* as hailstones, and that eased the possibility of being washed away.

" *'They really need to pick up this first down, Bob and, wow! They're bringing out the chains for a measurement. Looks like they've got it!'*

"We were finally cruising along the desert. It was hot but everything else seemed to be going fine. Our map and calculations showed that we should be arriving at a little town pretty soon, and 'pretty soon' wasn't a mile *too* soon. Two of the guys were riding Sportsters with 2.2-gallon tanks. At forty miles per gallon, they'd usually hit reserve at the eighty-mile mark, leaving an eight-mile cushion to make it on in to wherever we were headed. Our little conversion table showed that the next town was approximately seventy-five miles from the last gas stop. At seventy-eight miles, one of the Sportys hit reserve, and the other one did at seventy-nine. (He didn't have a windshield.) We still hadn't even seen the lights of the upcoming town. We all started sweating and it wasn't because of the hot night air. But as we topped a rise we could see the town—a big city—maybe three stores, and one of them seemed to have a light on.

"But no gas pumps. Anywhere. There was a sign that said *Meson*, meaning an inn, tavern, or motel, maybe. We pulled into the driveway and went into the main part. We saw about three or four tables with red plastic covers, a counter with a few cane chairs, and a cashier's booth kind a thing. A cowbell was attached to the front screen door, and it scared the crap out of us as it 'clanked' us into the place.

"A thin Mexican guy came out from a back room and just stared at us for what seemed like a real long time.

" 'Hola,' he said.

" 'Howdy, you got any gas?'

" 'Nada.'

" 'Do you know where we can get any?'

" 'Nada.'

" 'How far is it to the next town?'

" 'Nada.'

" 'Which movie did you like better, *True Grit* or *The Muppets Take Manhattan*?'

" 'Nada.'

" 'My brother here eats old shoelaces.'

" 'Nada.'

" 'This isn't gonna work,' said our NASA engineer. We all gave him *that look* again.

"Then we really fell down an ugly hole. Things started to shape up like a cross between an old episode of *I Love Lucy*, an ancient Bill Dana/José Jimenez bit, and the worst chunk of political *in*-correctness imaginable. And I didn't give a damn. I was tired! It was nearly 10 p.m. by this point, and we sure as hell weren't gonna get far on empty tanks so I proceeded to try and ask about renting a room using sign language. Our *innkeeper* seemed to understand, sort of. 'Sí, señor, mucho cabana aqui.'

" 'Uno cabana, poquito dinero! For the three of us,' I said.

" 'Sí, señor,' he said, taking a ring of keys off of a nail-hook on the wall. We followed him to a room. He unlocked it, turned on a light, and we could see that it kind a looked like a broom closet with a single bunk.

" 'Nada,' I said, 'We need mucho room for three—*tres hombres*—space! All three! We need mucho big room!' He showed us a bigger room with one regular bed. It even had a radio. We could use sleeping bags on the floor. *This* would work. But then we started horse-trading on price. We started holding up hands full of fingers. He *said* twenty dollars. I *said* ten. Then it was eighteen–thirteen. Finally fifteen bucks was agreed upon. But for some reason that we couldn't figure out, he started to act mad and began to unlock all of the cabana doors—*all of 'em*—pulled the master key off the ring and handed it to me. As he stormed back to his little office, we followed him, trying to tell him that we weren't going to pay fifteen bucks for each of those rooms! We got back to his desk and I gave him the fifteen and said, 'That's it just fifteen, no mas!'

"But he kept bitchin' about something in Spanish. Finally a truck driver that had come in for a cup of coffee spoke up in English, 'What he's upset about is that he normally rents his rooms out for $1.50 to $2 a night. He says you insisted on renting all of the rooms—the *whole* inn—and he's only going to average about $1.25 a room. And he doesn't understand why you Americans need twelve rooms anyway, since there are only three of you! That is, unless you have more of your biker friends coming in later?'

"That made me feel great. I was quite a horse trader. I managed to enter into some slick negotiations that scored a dollar-fifty room for only fifteen bucks! But then again, it was the first time that I ever rented out a whole motel!

"For 'security' reasons we decided to all stay in one room anyway. I got the truck driver to explain to our *host* that he could go ahead and rent out the other rooms, which he did as the night wore on. After that, our Mexican version of Conrad Hilton was pretty happy. He even made it clear that his wife would serve us all breakfast in the morning, for free.

"But this skit wasn't over. José Jimenez was still pretending to be an astronaut, and Ricky was still yelling at Lucy in Cuban. Les, Vern, Wino, and all the rest would be proud . . .

"We were trying to order our breakfast from our beloved innkeeper's *esposa*. I asked if I could get a menu. 'Sí, señor,' she said, happy, peppy. She went into the kitchen and came back with three bowls of some kind of soup.

" 'What the hell is this?' one of the guys asked.

"Our señora heard him and tried to explain that it was the *menudo* I had asked for. This wasn't a popular breakfast selection amongst our little Gringo group. 'I'm not eating guts for breakfast!' was just one of the comments. We *graciously* declined our *soup* and got our lovely waitress to bring us *frijoles* and *huevos*.

"But wait, there's more . . . And by now I shoulda known. But I didn't. I asked her for some *leche*. I didn't feel that this was a request that was especially odd or dangerous.

" 'Sí, señor,' she said, and then we could see her telling her husband *something*. We could see our guy through the window. He had gone out and pitched some cactus leaves or pods or whatever you call them on the ground. This skinny cow comes up and starts to eat them. She looked like she had bovine TB or something, but our boy here starts milking her. He got maybe a quart at the most and came right in and poured the hot milk right into a glass, no straining or anything.

" '*Leche!*' he said, smiling and pleased, like the *maitre de* at Spago's. I just stared at the glass. And I knew it wasn't going to get any colder or clearer, but I stared anyway. I could almost feel the wormlike bacteria boring into the walls of my stomach lining. I could see me trying to figure out ways of disguising the 'bag' that I would soon undoubtedly be attached to, buying books like, *Learning to Live With Catheters*. This wasn't good.

"We looked at one another. We needed a new plan, like just how to get the hell outta town. But there was the little problem of *nada petrol*—zero gasolino. I tried, once again, to have a productive bit of communication with our innkeeper-turned-dairyman. 'Hombre,' I said, pleasantly fingering my glass of stewlike *leche*, 'are you sure you don't know where we can get some gas . . . *petrol*?'

" 'Sí, señor. Petrol aqui.' We all looked at one another again. Things had obviously *changed*. We followed him out to the back of the restaurant. He takes this piece of plywood off of this old 55-gallon drum that had the word 'PETRO" hand-written on the side. It sorta smelled like gas, but I swear that I saw some *living* worms wiggling around inside of the barrel. We were desperate, so there was no use haggling over larva octane. We each began dipping into the vat and filling up our tanks.

"We only had fifty miles to go before we hit the city of Saltillo. Our Super Chief Worm Fuel got us there, but the bikes hiccupped, farted, and puked all the way. Saltillo is a college town. It's unusually modern and clean for the area. And they had another important luxury: an airport. Not that we wanted to take a plane ride or anything, but we badly needed some decent fuel. Flying machines do, too. Even in Mexico. We rolled into a flight service facility. We drained our gas and oil tanks, refilling with Aeroshell 60W and some potent 98-octane gas.

"We putted around downtown, found a decent restaurant, rested and regrouped in a wooded park, then headed east. The highway was in good shape and it took us back into the mountains.

"I was thinking of Les again as I saw my generator light come on. It was about fifty miles over the mountain pass into the city of Monterrey. And we definitely knew we were in Mexico again. Their normal traffic moved like '50s-style American demolition derbies. Our bikes were no match. But we saw a motorcycle cop waiting in the middle of some congestion at a red light. I snaked up the white line and pulled in next to him. He was on an old Police Special.

"I startled him and he didn't seem especially happy with me but I kept smiling and I pointed to my generator light. 'You got a Harley repair shop anywhere around here?' I asked, 'I need to get my generator repaired.'

" 'Sí, señor,' he said, then motioned for us to follow him. The damn cop took off like a bat, flyin' down the crowded street, weaving in and out of traffic. At several intersections he turned his siren on along with the red lights. It was like we were going to a fire, or the hospital, which is where we'd probably wind up if we kept riding like this, I figured. Me and one of the guys were staying with him pretty good but our other buddy was lagging way behind. I was getting ready to abandon the chase. I didn't want us to be separated, for

BFMC Historian, Jim "JQ" Quattlebaum, and Les Haserot's famous '37 Harley Baja bike. JQ figured that, "It was damn well time for a bunch of us to relive some of the adventures that Vern, Les, Wino, Teri, and the rest of them had down in Mexico."

any of us to get lost on our own down there, but just then the cop pulled up to some kind of tin building.

" 'Raul,' the cop said, pointing to the door of the building. 'Raul,' he repeated, and then disappeared back into traffic. We went inside of the tin building. It wasn't a Harley shop. It contained no motorcycles or anything that even resembled a repair place with the slightest clue as to what a generator was, let alone how to repair one. As near as we could figure, it was a paint and body shop with some kind of machine shop toward the rear.

" 'Raul?' I asked one guy.

" 'Nada,' he said, and pointed toward some young teenager that was doing *something* to a piece of sheet metal. I was pretty sure that we had found the wrong dude at the wrong place, but I went up to *Raul* anyway and pointed out my red generator light.

" 'Aw, si,' he said and proceeded to tear my generator off and take it apart. He smelled the coils and then pulled the carbon brushes out. 'No wano,' he said as he showed me how one had worn down. We looked at each other. A lot of that seemed to be happening lately.

"Now what? Raul started pulling on the spring of the brush. He searched around on the greasy concrete floor and found a little piece of what appeared to be aluminum. He bent it, put it into a vise, rounded off the edges with a file, and eventually stuck it into my generator, followed by my burned out brush. 'Wano,' he said, and then put the whole generator back together and remounted it on the bike.

"He motioned for me to crank it up. And, sonofagun, it worked! No more red light. I was back in business, but for how long?

"Raul was happy with the ten-dollar bill I gave him, and we were off again, toward Matamoros and Brownsville and then into the Rio Grande

Valley area. We rode through beautiful fields of every kind of vegetable, orchards, grapefruits, and oranges, and all kinds of bugs, especially this weird kind of huge flying moth.

"Lots of 'em. Lots. Once they started smashing against my windshield, things started getting messy. One of us—Eddie—didn't have a windshield. This got real ugly. And not very tasty. After about an hour of riding through this, Eddie finally motioned for us to pull over. We found a dirt road into a lettuce field and pulled off in there.

"Eddie was completely coated with bugs from head to toe. His glasses were covered—he couldn't see—but he didn't have any trouble seeing the bottle of Tequila that we had. We spread out our sleeping bags right there, killing the bottle of gold as we scraped the bug guts off of Eddie.

"The next morning we found a little cantina in a small town. No lights and a dirt floor But the tortillas, frijoles, and huevos were just fine. And, as usual, our bikes drew a big crowd of onlookers. We figured out how to bypass Matamoros and go straight across the bridge into Brownsville. The Rio Grande never looked as good as it did that day . . . in our rear-view mirrors.

"The generator worked all the way up until the edge of Corpus Christi. The H-D dealer there took care of a permanent repair, but it was *Raul* that got me there. Our ladies flew in and we all camped out on the beach. Then one more night in a motel. I thought again about Les Haserot, about how, on one of his Baja trips, he rolled into Ensenada, in July, after not having a shower for a week, and was mistaken for a fisherman! *We* hadn't seen clean, fresh water in quite a while. The only 'bath' we'd had recently was back in Lake Amistad, four days before.

"The 'adventure,' the spirit of 'the original wild ones' was very, very ripe! But it was perfect—the river of hail, the renting of an entire motel, the mutant worms in the barrel of gas, the mistaken *menudo*, the psycho-speed cop, Raul, Eddie's moth meal, and the community *frijole* pot, complete with June bugs. This all brought us back to 1946 . . . back, as Charlie Brechtel has sung, to 'The Way Things Used to Be' . . . 'people ridin' down the road, just bein' free' . . . back to when men like Les and Vern twisted life's throttle on, and never let go.

CHAPTER 20

The Tale of Teri, Dago, and the Boozettes, Jim Cameron, Earl Carlos, and More Warmth at the All American, a Final Toast to Fat Boy

Somewhere in the genetic goo that makes up the females of this species is a highly charged frayed wire . . . a sharp, loose end that tends to move their emotions like an old west divining rod directly toward men who are, well, *men:* the true antihero types, the lovable bad boys with big hearts, the leathered up, brooding leaders of the packs that ride off with the Barbie-doll queens of the cheerleaders while the clean-cut, baby-faced captain Ken of the football team fights back bewildered tears of confused rejection.

That's not to say that male and female *nerds* don't exist. They do. And they find each other. And they somehow discover how to procreate, producing nerdy kids. They live low-profile lives in their own little low-volume world, and that's fine.

But not in *this* lifestyle.

Teri met Willie Forkner years before Travolta and Olivia Newton-John danced their way through *Grease.* They met long before the Fonz made the chicks swoon at Arnold's Drive-In, long before the Shangri-las cried about the leader of the pack, long before rebels found a cause, long before the weekend in Hollister, and way before Brando and Marvin became Johnny and Chino. But the original wild one, the genuine leader of the pack, was already riding, female hearts were throbbing, and men on the edge were already being widely separated from meek-souled boys.

Teri Forkner in front of a picture of Wino.

Teri was born in Los Angeles on July 22, 1922. Her father came to California from Minnesota in a covered wagon. By 1917 he was riding an Eagle motorcycle. Her mother came west from South Dakota. America, the frontier: real men and women were alive.

Willie and Teri: It was a malt shop romance, in the shadow of L.A.'s Freemont High School, and it worked. Willie's world was fast. He would take Teri to the Big A, to races, and on fishing trips along the coast, south of the border. "We were in Mexico," remembered Teri, "fishing on a small, 36-foot boat called *The Little Dipper*, when a school of whales approached and started to rub against the boat. They'd do that to scrape the barnacles off of their backs but would often capsize boats in the process. Wino shot the gas to the boat motor and tried to out-maneuver the whales. We were zig-zagging through the other boats as the whales kept closing in. I'd point and scream, 'Here comes another one!' and Wino would whip the boat in the opposite direction and belt out this loud laugh!

" 'Missed me again, you SOB!' he'd yell at them. 'Yer gonna have to do better than that!' "

When Wino did his military time as the side machine-gunner on a B-24, Teri worked at Northrop, aiding the war effort as more planes were produced. She recalled, "When Wino returned from the war, he seemed wilder than ever, so much so that the 13 Rebels MC, which he rejoined, had a problem with his loose-cannon attitude and dare-devil actions. Needless to say, that led to his dropping out and subsequently starting the Boozefighters."

Then came the Boozettes. "Naturally, as the guys had their club," said Teri, "we girls had a common bond. Finally, Goldie (C. B. Clausen's lady), Ethelia (Joe Anchando's gal), Sally (I forget who's gal she was), and I got together and discussed having our own club. Pat Manker and some gals joined our Boozettes club later. There was a bunch of us by 1947. Dago wasn't but about 16 at the time, but she'd sneak out of the house and join us when she could. Later, when she got older, she became a regular and eventually married Fat Boy.

"We wore the same shirts as the guys except with 'Boozettes' printed on the back. And then when Wino cranked up the Boozefighters' racing team, we wore the 'Yellow Jackets' T-shirts just like the guys did. We'd have Boozettes shirts on one day, and then at field meets we'd wear the yellow jackets.

"To be accepted in as a Boozette we'd have a meeting and discuss it. If we all agreed to let someone in then we'd decide on her initiation. Usually it would include things like rooting a penny out of a bowl of flour with her nose. Then, with one pant leg rolled up high and the other one down, and wearing fuzzy house shoes, she'd have to walk down along the Pike, an amusement park that was on the beach."

In February of 2001, less than two years before Teri's death, BFMC National Historian Jim "JQ" Quattlebaum had the opportunity to interview her:

JQ: "So how'd y'all handle any problems that might come up amongst the Boozettes?"

Teri: "We'd have a 'saucer party.' We'd sit around a saucer of milk in private. One by one we'd speak our piece to it, whether it was a complaint about another girl or bitching about our guy. We'd have our say without interruption. When we got through we'd pour the milk down the drain, and say, 'The cat drank everything that was said.' It was never to be repeated again!"

JQ: "I heard that the girls handled a lot of the plans for the field meets and parties. Was that true?"

Teri: "Yeah, we'd do most of that. Every time we would put on a race event, I'd go to the county and pay the one dollar per day for the Saturday and Sunday beer permits. We usually had the event in an open field on Rosecrans Street. We would build the beer stand, sell the brew, and then, during intermission, Boozettes would circulate among the cars and spectators asking for a two-bit (25-cent) donation to the race winners. The sponsoring clubs would split the profits of the beer and hamburgers and things we would sell."

JQ: "Did you really break Wino's nose with a wine bottle one time?"

Teri: "Who told you about that?"

JQ: "Wino did!"

Teri: "Well, I sure the heck did, and since he told you about it, I'll tell you the *true* story! He claimed it was an accident but it really wasn't. We were coming back from the Crater Camp Hill Climb, just outside of L.A. back then. A bunch of us were riding on the back of J. D. Cameron's flatbed truck, which was padded with a layer of hay.

"Wino gave me some money to go get another bottle of wine at a local place on the way back. Red Dog hauled me on the back of his bike. When we caught up with the truck, Wino was wallering around with a couple of the girls. It wouldn't have been that big a deal, except I figured that he was trying to make me jealous. As we pulled up beside the truck he rolled over on his side and said, 'Hi honey, pitch me the bottle of wine.'

"Dago wasn't but about sixteen at the time," said Teri, *"but she'd sneak out of the house and join us when she could."*

"When I drew back that bottle everyone around him scrambled out of the way. I guess they read the expression on my face. As Wino raised up I chucked the bottle as hard as I could. It went right through his hands and splattered his nose all over his face!"

JQ: "Did it break?"

Teri: "Not the bottle, but it sure did his nose! He drank the wine anyway. I guess to help the pain!"

JQ: "Y'all had fines for doing certain things back then, didn't you?"

Teri: "Sure. Things like not looking clean. Sometimes we'd spend an hour or two shining our boots before we went to an event. Then we stomped around in the mud and dirt. But we never went anywhere looking dirty. It was kind of a pride thing.

"And if anyone used the 'F word' they were fined five cents. We didn't like dirty talking around other people, either."

JQ: "I heard about some games that the Boozettes would play with the guys, like the butt tracing contest. "

Teri: "Yeah, we had a game where all the girls would sit on a long bench. We'd trace an outline of our butts and one of the guys would have to guess which silhouette belonged to which girl! We had a lot of fun. We were a family!"

JQ: "I gather that the wild ones tamed down a bit as people got older, raised families, followed careers, and moved around. When did you and Wino start to reduce your activity?"

Teri: "About 1953 Wino wanted to go up the coast where there was better fishing. We moved to Trinidad, in upstate California, and he fished with a 52-foot boat named 'Mary LaRocka.' Later we moved to Fort Bragg. However, we always had Boozefighters' reunions—and a *lot of 'em*—on some land that we had at Fort Bragg.

"Once, while we were gathering, a helicopter hovered above and then set down. Wino thought it might be some kind of mistaken raid at first.

Boozette, Jackie.

When people started getting out, Wino charged forward, raising Cain until he realized that it was a bunch of Boozefighters from Santa Rosa. They really pulled one over on him!"

JQ: "How many children did you and Wino have?"

Teri: "We have two daughters named Patricia and Terry, and a son, Bill. There are a total of eight grandchildren, seven great-grandchildren, and three great-great-grandchildren, and all of them have Wino's blood in them!"

JQ: "What's your advice to the Boozefighters and Boozettes of today?"

Teri: "Enjoy yourselves, for life is shorter than you'd think. You only go around once, so you had better enjoy and live it up while you can!"

In 2000, Teri had a reunion with Dago. They hadn't seen one another in years. They met again in Hollister, a regrouping at the magic vortex. The wife of the original wild one again teamed up with the gal who had been blessed with biker blood when she was just 16. In 2004, Randy "Scarface" Mills interviewed Dago, original wild one Jim Cameron, and Earl Carlos, an early member of the 13 Rebels and All American regular. It wasn't a formal round-table discussion, it wasn't Q&A; it was the purest of gold from an era of gold—biker gold.

"Al Jordanelli got me interested in riding," Dago began. "He used to take me out on his Scout. I remember it shifted like an English bike. There was a bar on Vermont that he took me to. I was 16. That's where I really met Teri. We were from the same neighborhood but she was ahead of me in school. I met a lot of the guys there. I met Fat Boy there.

"Later, Teri would come over to the house, and we'd tell my mom that we were going to the malt shop, and, of course, by then we'd go to the All American!"

"I was hanging out at the All American, too," said Jim Cameron, "and I had been in the hospital for quite a while after my bike had caught on

Earl Carlos, early member of the 13 Rebels MC and a regular at the All American.

fire. I'd been out at the Navy Hospital in Corona. It was around Christmas and I finally got out. The very first thing I did was to buy this Indian that Johnny Davis had for sale. I was riding down the street and I happened to notice these two women staring at me from this new Studebaker. They were *really* staring. They looked shocked. Turns out that they were two of the nurses that had been at the hospital where I was. I guess they couldn't believe I'd get right back on a bike after being burned so bad in a motorcycle accident!

"When I got out of the Army I wanted some folks to hang out with. I got out in January and by springtime I was hanging out at the All American. Willie asked me to join the Boozefighters, so I attended my three meetings, but I missed the fourth where they were supposed to vote on my membership. I didn't think I was going to make it, because you had to be *too good* to make it.

"When I showed up again, Willie says, 'Where were you last week?!' I told him that I had something else I had to do. 'Well,' he says, 'we're gonna vote on you *this* week!'"

"They probably needed someone else to buy the beer!" said Earl. "Now *I* started hanging around the All American as soon as I got back, too. It was the kind of place where you could go if you rode a motorcycle and didn't want anyone on your back. Most of the rest of the bars didn't want anyone around who *looked* liked a motorcycle rider let alone anyone who *rode* one. It was like you had a disease. They just didn't want you around. The All American was just kind of a hang-out in an area where a lot of people were riding, a place where if someone came around you could always say, 'Hey let's go down to the All American for a beer.'

"And we could have all of our club meetings in the back room. We were all there anyway, everybody knew everybody. Today it seems like a lot of clubs don't get along but back then we didn't have those problems. I don't remember anything like that ever happening with the Boozefighters or the Rebels."

"Everybody got along mostly," added Dago, "but I do remember that one time at the All American, Tommy Cook got into a fight with someone, a hell of a fight. Nobody else butted in, though. They went outside, falling all over the motorcycles, just kicking hell out of each other. Then they came back in, had their beer, and that was the end of it. It was over.

"There was one time, though, when a bunch of guys from the east came riding into the parking lot at the All American. We counted 16 lights

Dago and Jim Cameron in Huck's backyard, Hollister, 2004.

and reflectors on this one guy's bike. All of our guys had stripped-down bikes. Tommy Cook went out and peed on the guy's bike! He said, 'What are all these lights for!? You guys aren't real motorcyclists!' "

Jim Cameron remembered another *slight* altercation. "The Galloping Gooses were out in the valley and four or five times different members of the Gooses came down and got into it with Willie. Willie would take them down and then they'd go in the bar and shake hands and have a beer. But they were all beat up. Willie never got beat up."

Earl looked at Jim, "He'd be a hard guy to beat up!"

Dago smiled, "He was a pussycat at times, though!

"Teri and I rode our own bikes," said Dago, as the subject of chick riders in the 1940s came up, "and Vivian also rode. Vivian wasn't a Boozette, but she was with us a lot. She had her Scout. She was a good friend always right there for ya!

"But I kept up with the best of them. That old VL I had, it went! I didn't give a damn. One time I was going down the street and my dad was taking my mom someplace in their car, and I turned around and here he was. He says, 'C'mon, go!' I says, 'OK, Old Man, you ain't gonna beat this motorcycle!' But he was racin' me down Florence Avenue. My mother was yelling at him, screaming at him in Italian!"

There was Teri and Wino and there was Dago and Fat Boy.

"Fat Boy proposed to me on his motorcycle one day when we were on the way to the hospital to see Jim Cameron, after he got burned on his bike." She accepted, but this lifestyle sometimes crosses over rough roads. "Fat Boy and I had already divorced, and I didn't know that he had died until my godmother had seen it printed in the paper. He'd had just gotten off of work, going east on Manchester off of Avalon, he and his buddy. This woman was going west. She went to make a left-hand turn into the driveway of a car lot 'cause she wanted to pull out and go the other way. Well, his buddy went on this side of her, and Fat Boy was going to go in front, but she dead-stopped and he took it right there. Someone did find his watch. It had a stretch band and it was completely twisted around. I gave it to Big Jim. He carries it in his pocket now whenever he goes for a ride. If he's havin' a drink, he pours a little drink out for Fat Boy."

CHAPTER 21

The Tale of Kokomo's Big Adventures

"They would knock each other down, jump up and down on the man who was down, then throw buckets of water on the victim, then engage in a free-for-all, with everybody wallowing in the mud."
—From a neighbor's eyewitness account of a party at the 'Frisco
BFMC clubhouse

Whooee! That Kokomo, he sure knew how to have a good time! Of course, "good time" is like "fun"—it's a very relative term and it varies in intensity and, in some cases, *legality*.

"We do not intend to tolerate any hoodlum gangs in Solano County."
—Sheriff John R. Thornton, quoted in a newspaper report of a
"drunken orgy" at the BFMC clubhouse

All things considered, Benny "Kokomo" McKell, the president of the San Francisco Chapter of the Boozefighters Motorcycle Club, was probably the wildest of the wild ones.

If the rest of the boys were kind of the biker equivalent of Jackie Gleason and Red Skelton, then Kokomo was Jonathan Winters, Robin Williams, John

"Kokomo," BFMC San Francisco chapter president,

Belushi, and Jim Carrey all puréed together in one big killer speed blender and poured out in a tall potent cocktail of Boozefighter wackiness at its highest tide.

"Kokomo used to hang out at a bar at 18th and Capp in San Francisco," remembers Vern Autrey. "An old man owned the place, and it was crazy in there. They'd put old socks in the coffee they were serving and all kinds of stuff. And they'd drink beer and fall on the floor and just stay there all sprawled out and the police would come in and ask Rattles—that was the old owner's name—'What the hell's going on here?' And Rattles would say, 'Nothing, officer, just leave 'em alone. Everything's fine!'

"Well, one day up there, Kokomo and this guy were talking at the bar and the other guy says to Kokomo, 'I'm bored. Maybe we should go and beat up a cop or something,' and Kokomo says, 'Yeah, I'm bored, too. I'll be right back.' So he walks out of the bar, went down to the fire department and stole a fire engine! They chased him all over San Francisco. It was all over the newspapers. He's going down Market Street in this fire engine with the si-reen on, going like a sonofagun.

"He was pretty wacky—I confirmed that myself a couple of times—but the guy could ride a motor-sickle like you wouldn't believe. All those guys up there would always hang out at Dudley Perkins' Harley shop in 'Frisco. And you know those guys who ride in those big dromes? Well, Kokomo was one of the guys who'd teach other guys how to ride like that.

"I seen Kokomo in the parking lot of the All American this one morning. We had just came back from Ensenada, and we was all sleeping on our motorcycles. We hadn't got back 'til one o'clock in the morning. And he rode up and woke us up. He says, 'Is Cookie here yet?' I said, 'No, he'll open up in about an hour, I guess.' He says, 'Well, that's good.' And he reached over—he had this sack with him—and he had this bottle of wine. He lays down, takes the cap off the bottle, and drank the whole sumbitch straight down laying on the ground.

"I told ol' Fat Boy, 'Oh hell, and this day has just begun!' "

"Sometimes Kokomo and his boys would come down to L.A. in this old hearse," Jim Cameron said, thinkin' back, rolling his eyes a bit. "They'd be riding in the back and everything and drinking all the way."

Now *there's* a surprise.

But Kokomo's *wardrobe* proved to be one of his more interesting attributes. He generally preferred his "hobo" ensemble or, if he was feeling a bit more formal, he went all out and put on his red admiral's uniform.

"He used to dress in Levis," Vern recalled. "And he'd cut 'em off and slit 'em up the sides about four or five times."

Why not?

He was, however, a bit muddy following the "drunken orgy," another of Kokomo's Big Adventures that made the newspapers in San Francisco.

SIX CYCLISTS PLEAD GUILTY, ONE TO TRIAL

Seven bedraggled motorcyclists, members of the "San Francisco Boozefighters' Club," accused of staging a drunken orgy yesterday at 1195 Benicia road, appeared in justice court today, all on peace disturbance charges, where six pleaded guilty and a not guilty plea was entered by the seventh.

The not guilty plea came from Raymond E. Harrell, 20, of 224 Elmira Street, San Francisco, whose trial was set for Tuesday, Oct. 14. His bail, and that of the six other defendants was set at $500 each.

The six who pleaded guilty included one girl, Alice M. Morris, 19, and her husband, Jim H. Morris, 23, a lumber grader, of 6051/2

West 65th Street, Los Angeles; Benjamin D. McKell, 34, chauffeur, of 1728 O'Farrell Street, San Francisco; Walter W. Wegner, 32, checker, 653 South Van Ness, San Francisco; Earl Warren Heffley, 25, water tender, 3445 20th Street, San Francisco; Walter E. Franklin, 22, merchant seaman, of 941 Benicia Road.

GIRL TO HEALTH CLINIC

The girl was ordered to the Vallejo-Solano County Health Clinic, and investigation by the county juvenile authorities pending sentence Wednesday.

Arrests of the group followed complaints of neighbors, including Howard A. Lyon of Benicia Road, who signed the complaint, and Mrs. Shirley Abbott, 1142 Hargus Avenue, a witness, who described the "orgy" in which the group participated yesterday afternoon, following a ride here from San Francisco.

"They would knock each other down, jump up and down on the man who was down, then throw buckets of water on the victim, then engage in a free-for-all, with everybody wallowing in the mud," neighbors reported.

STILL DIRTY AND MUDDY

Evidence of the battle still was on the defendants' mud-plastered jeans when they were brought into court today.

Judge John J. Bradley warned the accused group: "Your sentence on Wednesday will depend upon your cooperation with the office of Sheriff John R. Thornton."

Sheriff Thornton, in turn, made this statement: "We do not intend to tolerate any hoodlum gangs in Solano county. The hangout of this group on Benicia Road is a disgrace to the community, and will be cleaned out immediately."

Acting on the sheriff's recommendation, the Solano County Department of Health immediately investigated alleged unsanitary conditions, and closed the premises by court order.

Renter of the house is H. C. Barron, Mare Island apprentice who lives with his mother in Sacramento.

Sheriff's records disclosed the clubhouse has been raided three times previously—on July 20, and 27, and again on Aug. 3, when a

SIX CYCLISTS PLEAD GUILTY, ONE TO TRIAL

Seven bedraggled motorcyclists, members of the "San Francisco Boozefighters' Club" accused of staging a drunken orgy yesterday at 1195 Benicia road, appeared in justice court today, all on peace disturbance charges, where six pleaded guilty and a not-guilty plea was entered by the seventh.

The not guilty plea came from Raymond E. Herrell, 20, of 224 Elmira street, San Francisco, whose trial was set for Tuesday, Oct. 14. His bail, and that of the six other defendants was set at $500 each.

The six who pleaded guilty included one girl, Alice M. Morris, 19, and her husband, Jim H. Morris, 23, a lumber grader of 605½ West 65th street, Los Angeles; Benjamin D. McKell, 34, chauffeur, of 1728 O'Farrell street, San Francisco; Walter W. Wegner, 32, checker, 653 South Van Ness, San Francisco; Earl Warren Heffley, 25, water tender, 3445 20th street, San Francisco; Walter E. Franklin, 22, merchant seaman of 941 Benicia road.

GIRL TO HEALTH CLINIC

The girl was ordered to the Vallejo-Solano County Health Clinic, and investigation by the county juvenile authorities pending sentence Wednesday.

Arrests of the group followed complaints of neighbors, including Howard A. Lyon of Benicia road, who signed the complaint, and Mrs. Shirley Abbott, 1142 Hargus avenue, a witness, who described the "orgy" in which the group participated yesterday afternoon, following a ride here from San Francisco.

"They would knock each oth-

er down, jump up and down on the man who was down, then throw buckets of water on the victim, then engage in a free-for-all, with everybody wallowing in the mud," neighbors reported.

STILL DIRTY AND MUDDY

Evidence of the battle still was on the defendants' mud-plastered jeans when they were brought into court today.

Judge John J. Bradley warned the accused group: "Your sentence on Wednesday will depend upon your cooperation with the office of Sheriff John R. Thornton."

Sheriff Thornton, in turn, made this statement: "We do not intend to tolerate any hoodlum gangs in Solano county. The hang-out of this group on Benicia road is a disgrace to the community, and will be cleaned out immediately."

Acting on the sheriff's recommendation, the Solano County Department of Health immediately investigated alleged unsanitary conditions, and closed the premises by court order.

Renter of the house is H. C. Barron, Mare Island apprentice, who lives with his mother in Sacramento.

Sheriff's records disclosed the clubhouse has been raided three times previously—on July 20, and 27, and again on Aug. 3, when a Mrs. B. A. Becker was found lying at the entrance of the building with injuries allegedly inflicted by two members of the motorcycle club. The place has, for some time been used as a rendezvous by cyclists throughout the bay region, deputies said.

Newspaper account of the San Francisco BFMC "drunken orgy."

Mrs. B. A. Becker was found lying at the entrance of the building with injuries allegedly inflicted by two members of the motorcycle club. The place has for some time been used as a rendezvous by cyclists throughout the bay region, deputies said.

"Society is a lot more twisted than I thought," comedian Jim Carrey once said, and that was a long time after a "bedraggled" Kokomo showed up in that San Franciscan court room all covered in mud, a long time after Kokomo tried his fabled tightrope walk along a telephone cable outside of his second-story hotel room during the Hollister Rally, a long time after the 'Frisco cops finally got that firetruck pulled over.

And Carrey was right, of course. But which society? Ours or theirs?

Probably a little (or a lot) of both, but maybe it comes down to which side has more fun, which team gets the most out of the game. Which team gets the muddiest.

CHAPTER 22

The Tale of Jim Hunter, a Tale of Speed, the Brutal Death of a Bultaco, Turn Left, Go Right at 200 MPH

"I feel so lucky that I got to do what I did I wish I could do it all over again!"

—Jim Hunter

Jim Hunter was an intense, claws-first motorcycle racer. And he was honest. "When I first started riding I really wasn't much good at it. Then Gil Armas taught me how to do things the right way. I was always lagging behind. Gil finally asked me what my problem was. I told him that I was afraid I was gonna fall!

"Gil said, 'Well, I need to take you out in the desert and teach you how to fall.' And the next day that's exactly what he did. Gil says, 'Now, I want you to go out there and make a sharp left turn and fall on your ass! It ain't gonna hurt you 'cause it's sand. And you don't have to go too fast just go out there, make a sharp left turn and fall.'

"So I went out there and I made a sharp left turn, but by God, I didn't fall! I kept it up. I *still* didn't *want* to fall! So Gil says, 'OK, go out and make a *right* turn and fall!'"

"So I went out and made a *right* turn but I didn't fall then, either! What I was figuring out was how *not* to fall!

"Then Gil would make me go faster then in big circles then he'd make me do figure eights. After we worked out on that sand for a while, I started to get the hang of this stuff. Then Gil would tell me that I needed to get on up there on the handlebars. 'You can't be sitting your lazy ass way back there, you know!' He really taught me how to ride. Then after that when we went on a ride, by God, I got up with the Boozefighters.

"One thing I never liked, though, was sand in my face. When I got up ahead of everybody, there wasn't any more sand hitting me in the face! I figured out from then on that it's a lot more fun being in front.

"After that, Gil and I talked about racing. Gil was the best racer we had in that area, so he got me out there. Gil always won, but I got to where I was sometimes getting fourth place, third place, then I got up to second place. But I never could beat *him*. I don't know what it was but I could just never get around him. But after he retired, *I* was No. 1! And from then on I pretty well stayed there.

"Before he retired, Gil suggested that I should start racing flat track. I told him that I didn't have the right type of bike for that kind of racing, and I didn't have any money to buy something, either. Gil said, 'You can have my Triumph, It's a good flat track bike.'

"I told him no. If I blow it up or something I couldn't afford to fix it. Gil told me, 'If that happens, you just bring it over to my house and lean it against the garage wall. I'll fix it. Don't worry about anything except winning races!'

"That's how I got started in racing flat tracks, and that's the kind of friend Gil was!

"I started doing pretty well and some guy offered to let me race on his WR Harley. A Harley dealer saw that I was good on it and asked me if I'd ride their new K model that had come out. I did, and everything really took off from there. It was pretty nice having a sponsor providing top-of-the-line bikes, parts, repairs, and all."

Back in 1998, as Jim Hunter approached his 75th birthday, BFMC National Historian Jim "JQ" Quattlebaum, talked to Hunter about his bikes, his racing, his speed:

JQ: "So what ever happened to your old stroker that you were so proud of?"

Hunter: "I sold it to a good friend of mine named Gene Perkins. He has a ranch in Ridgeway, Colorado. He's still got it, and the last time I visited him he got it out and fired it up. It sounded pretty good!

Jim Hunter on his BSA Goldstar.

"In 1976 I went out there and rode in the Colorado 500 Mile Ride, through old ghost towns, mountain trails, and everything. That was fun!"

JQ: "How about your BSA Goldstar that you won so many races on?"

Hunter: "After I quit racing and started my own business, my motorcycle shop, I sold it to a kid just to help him out. Then his father came over and gave me a ration of crap about how much money he was spending. I told him to stick it! And to get out of my shop! And I told the kid not to ever bring his frickin' bike back anymore! I'd been helping him with repairs and only charged him for my cost of the parts. I was pretty POed over that deal, and I never saw the Goldstar again."

JQ: "Did you ever race as a 'Yellow Jacket'?" (*This was the club name that many Boozefighters raced under, due to the "problems" that the BFMC had with the AMA.*)

Hunter: "No. I rode in some of those field events, but mostly by then I was with other racing sponsored teams.

"Some of the other guys tried racing flat track but didn't do too much. There were a few that did pretty good, Bobby Kelton and a couple of other guys. Most of them didn't get too far, but they were just doing it for fun."

JQ: "And *you* took racing pretty seriously?"

Hunter: "Yeah, I was in it to win! I wanted the best equipment, the most horsepower, and whatever it took. There was nothing like the feeling of coming in first place over a bunch of top guys, so I kinda went my own way to get into the big races."

JQ: "I understand that back in those days they didn't pay much prize money."

Hunter: "No. Mostly you just got trophies, and a few bucks now and then."

JQ: "So what did you do to make a living?"

Hunter: "I shagged blueprints (*delivering blueprints on a bike*) for a couple of outfits. Back in those years I could make better money doing that than driving a truck, working freight lines, and stuff like I did when I first got out of the Navy. As a matter of fact, I could clear $80 or more a week and that was pretty good in the 1950s."

JQ: "On your stroker?"

Hunter: "Well, for a little while, but that foot clutch and hand shift didn't work out too good when you're, you know, continuously working 'em! I got a little single BSA, which was easier and got better gas mileage.

"Then a bunch of guys that raced scrambles in the desert would give me their new bikes to break in for them. They'd pay for my gas and everything; it was a heck of a deal!"

JQ: "What do you do for quality time these days, now that you're retired?"

Hunter: "I go to sprint car races, motorcycle races, meet with friends and stuff like that. And I work on old BSAs for a friend who has a cycle shop, especially when he gets in an old Goldstar that needs the engine overhauled. I still love working on 'em!"

Jim Hunter may have always enjoyed working on BSAs, but he considered anything with a two-stroke engine to be abject evil, and his wanton execution of a Bultaco (as reported in the September 1964 issue of *Cycle World*) was a blast of pure, four-stroke adrenaline:

> . . . everyone gets so spread out in the desert's vastness that nobody knows what happened to anybody unless they ask. So they ask, and hear stories that lose nothing in the telling, and some of those stories are good enough to be told again, and again, until they become a part of the desert racers' legends.
>
> Like the one about a guy named Hunter, who hated anything with a two-stroke engine. Some unfortunate dropped his Bultaco on a big rock, punched a hole in its tank, and was trying frantically—with the aid of a couple of other riders who had stopped to lend a hand—to extinguish the fire that ensued. They were all tossing sand on the flames, and making some progress in saving the bike, when Hunter slithered to a stop, jumped off his BSA Goldstar, grabbed up an armload of brush and threw it on the fire.

In 1958, at Bonneville's Salt Flats, Jim Hunter rode a two-wheeled streamliner, named *The Brute*, to a speed of 224.74 miles per hour. After making his run, Hunter had a couple of words for fellow original wild one C. B. Clausen, owner and builder of *The Brute*. "C. B., did you know that SOB steers backward?"

"Oh yeah," said C. B., "I forgot to tell you about that."

"Bull!" said Hunter. "You heard about it and didn't believe it was possible! I didn't either until I figured it out!"

It was time for a physics lesson, one that dealt with the motion of a jet plane. At 200 miles per hour-plus, a jet and a motorcycle streamliner are in the same stretched-out pocket.

After a little research, Jim Hunter was able to explain: "At near 200 miles per hour or so, an airplane's slanted wings and flaps create vertical lift, pulling the plane up. On the salt at those speeds you lose almost all tire traction, but you get horizontal pull in the opposite direction from the wheel's angle because it throws a slipstream of air jetting out around the streamliner's hull on one side. Angle wheel left, get horizontal pull to the right. It's kind of like skidding on ice. It takes a lot of self-discipline to force yourself to turn into the direction you're skidding especially at 200-plus miles per hour."

Hunter had one final comment for Clausen: "As for you, C. B., thanks a lot, you dipstick, for telling me. No wonder those other guys never did attempt to run this squirrelly thing for a second time!"

"Winning isn't everything," Hunter often said, "but it sure does feel a lot better than coming in second place. I'd do whatever it took to win. If someone cut in front of me I'd run him off the track. I had to have the best bike, the most horses, best carb, the best of everything to get me across the finish line first.

"But you'd be surprised how hard it is. There are good riders, with good equipment, who still can't do that. It takes a special desire to win and you can't be afraid to go flat out. Maybe I'm kind of crazy but, man, there's no better feeling than being the best, beating everybody else, and coming in first place! You just can't know how good it is until you've done it. And then you can't wait to do it again!"

It was mentioned to Wino Willie that there were many of Hunter's racing trophies on display at the BFMC clubhouse and museum in Fort Worth, but that some of the awards didn't indicate whether they were for first place or not.

Wino didn't hesitate with his comment: "You can be assured they're for first place! Hunter never kept anything less. I've seen him come in second and chuck the trophy into a ditch on the way home! He was kind of a sore loser that way. Christ! You should see his garage. It's so full of trophies, he hardly has room for his bikes!"

CHAPTER 23

The Tale of Tommie Greathouse

It was 1991. The Boozefighters Motorcycle Club was still regrouping, still unwrapping from a metamorphosis that stoked emotions, club business, and change. But the kind of emotions that were focused on the originals were never subject to change. The love and respect for the original wild ones and for the toughness and freedom-loving spirit of the entire World War II generation was—and is—the hottest brand in the fire of the BFMC.

The war years weaned the originals on strength and brotherhood, traits that were naturally passed down to subsequent generations of the club.

Each original had tales of the war. Wino, gunning out of that B-24. Dink Burns losing both of his legs as his ship went down. Jim Hunter shooting the engine out of a German dive-bomber when he was in the navy. Jim Cameron's army time in the Pacific Theater. Johnny Davis receiving a battlefield promotion to second lieutenant for heroic action under fire. Red Dog surviving Midway. C. B. Clausen's paratroop jumps. J. D. Cameron supplying materials and hardware to the troops, inventing and donating a patent for a bearing knockout tool to the army. Teri working in war aircraft manufacturing. Fat Boy signing up for the navy when he was just 15, helped along by some creative signing of his mother's name by George Manker. Manker enlisted in the navy along with Fat Boy. Les trying his best to enlist in any branch of the service that he could, and being turned down because of the motorcycle injury that he had suffered.

Jack Lilly was also turned down by the Army Air Forces, even though he already had a pilot's license! He was unable to pass the eye exam, but he did join the merchant marines, hoping to have another shot at the air force as the war progressed. "After I spent a lot of time in the Pacific on a freighter delivering war materials and supplies," said Jack, "I figured I'd try another part of the world: the Atlantic Ocean. I got a bus to Houston, Texas, and then on to New Orleans where I got a job on a seagoing tug. We pulled a bunch of barges out in the Gulf, down to—and through—the Panama Canal, and right back out into the Pacific.

"I was assigned to a tanker named the *Roanoke*, delivering oil and gas to warships. Once, Jack Kennedy's PT 109 pulled along side and refueled. I remembered that commander's Boston accent, but didn't catch his name. Years later I put two and two together.

"At one point I was within about 100 yards of the Borneo coast. Japanese soldiers opened fire, but their .25-caliber bullets just bounced off of the ship. Then Australian soldiers ambushed the Japanese and killed most of them while our ship's crew looked on. Bombs were sent our way a few times, but none ever hit a ship I was working on.

"Finally, in the Gilbert Islands, I accomplished a sliver of my dream about flying for the Army Air Corps. I got a hop on a B-24 bomber, and they invited me to sit in as copilot for a while. But when they started taking antiaircraft fire they ran me off into the back. At least I did get to fly in the Air Corps!"

In his book *The Greatest Generation,* Tom Brokaw wrote:

> In the spring of 1984, I went to the northwest of France, to Normandy, to prepare an NBC documentary on the fortieth anniversary of D-Day, the massive and daring Allied invasion of Europe that marked the beginning of the end of Adolf Hitler's Third Reich. There, I underwent a life-changing experience. As I walked the beaches with the American veterans who had returned for this anniversary, men in their sixties and seventies, and listened to their stories, I was deeply moved and profoundly grateful for all they had done. Ten years later, I returned to Normandy for the fiftieth anniversary of the invasion, and by then I had come to understand what this generation of

Americans meant to history. It is, I believe, the greatest generation any society has ever produced.

And they were: Jack Lilly, Wino, Dink, and all the rest. And in 1946 they started a motorcycle club that has survived and has upheld the freedom that they fought for.

But in 1991, amidst some of the club's *re*-growing pains, a Boozefighter came face to face with the legacy of the originals' generation. He began to see what the real priorities in his club were all about. He understood what was *really* important about the life-force that the originals had left for all who came after.

Before World War II there was World War I. And veterans are veterans and heroes are heroes; their guts all share the same warm, liberty-lusting blood.

Like Tom Brokaw, this patch holder also had a "life-changing experience."

History has a way of missing our attention. Occasionally, names like Kaiser Wilhelm II, General Pershing, Hitler, Ike, and Patton get into the history books. We've also heard of dogface heroes like York and Murphy, because of their pure, down-and-dirty bravery. But, for most of us, those heroes hold about the same importance as Batman or Dick Tracy. Much of history is perceived as fantasy unless we have the opportunity to experience it, or to touch some part of the actual stuff that history is made of.

In 1991, while visiting my aged aunt in a nursing home, I shook hands and talked with a magnificent piece of history. His name is Tommie Greathouse.

I first met Tommie while I was sitting on a ledge outside the Denton Nursing Center, impatiently waiting for my mother to come out from taking Aunt Ruth back to her room. An old man came walking up from the street. I thought that he might be coming to visit someone there but he sat down and began talking happily about what "a great day it was and how good it was to be alive." I was surprised to learn that he lived in the facility because he seemed to be too active and too alert to be in a nursing home.

Tommie made a special mention to me that he was born on Christmas Eve, 1892, in the rural area of Greenville, Texas. In 1917, with the United States entering the war, Tommie decided that at 25 years of age he was a man and he made up his mind to join the war effort.

On a cool October Texas morning he and his parents got up early, took their baths and dressed in their best "Sunday-go-to-meetin' clothes." They hitched up the team and headed into town. When they got to the induction center, Tommie said that his father announced to the officials there that, "We are offering the maximum sacrifice, our son, for our nation's defense."

Tommie received some quick training: how to march, how to say "yes, sir," how to shoot a carbine, and, soon after, he was on a troop ship off to war. The Brits and the Huns were engaged in trench warfare, deadlocked in battle. Poison gas was being used and tens of thousands of lives were being lost. "The captain kept reminding us," said Tommie. " 'Boys, no matter what, we've got to protect our cannons. Our artillery fire keeps the Germans on the run. It keeps 'em confused, and that's the only way we're gonna win this war!' " Even though they were young and inexperienced, they actually began to move the Germans back with their artillery. "But troops were dying all around," Tommie remembered. "Some of the men were so scared they could hardly hold their rifles."

Did Tommie get scared?

"You know, I never did. When I first went into battle I made this deal. I said, 'Lord my life is in your hands, and in *my* hands is this carbine. For as long as you keep me going, I'm going to fire this thing.' You know, he kept me going throughout that whole war."

Was he ever hurt?

"Yeah, about two months ago a door slammed on my left arm. But it's doing fine now."

Uh, how about in the war . . . ?

"Oh no, the Lord took care of me and I never even got a scratch!"

While we were talking, another man joined in our conversation. He, too, was a resident of the nursing home. He was much younger than Tommie—he wasn't a day over 80.

The subject flowed from WWI to World War II to motorcycles.

"It seemed," said the *younger* man, "that we Americans could *invent* ways to win. The Germans in World War II always appeared to be bound to strict rules. At times *we* would bend *our* rules a bit to achieve success.

"Now when I was a kid I used to ride the family's old gray mule. Ever ride one?"

I told him that I had, once, but I was only six years old and I got bucked off pretty quick. After that I stuck to riding horses until I got my first motorcycle when I was 14.

He laughed and said, "Let me tell you a motor-*sickle* story. Up there on the front lines it wasn't much fun getting shot at all the time so you'd look for any opportunity to take a break. Well, this courier rode in on one of those green Harley-Davidsons, just as one of those German shells exploded nearby. That poor fellow got blown off his bike and was in kind of bad shape with a shrapnel wound to his chest.

"A little bit later the captain came out of his quarters with that courier's pouch. He asked if anyone knew how to ride a motor-*sickle*. He needed to get the pouch back to headquarters on the double. No one in our group raised their hand. Motor-*sickles* weren't that popular back then, you know. People were mostly afraid of them. Well, I spoke up and told the captain that I thought I could do it.

"He asked me if I had ever rode one of those things. I told him no, but I'd ridden lots of mules and my cousin's bicycle a few times when we went into town. I figured I could ride pretty near anything if I tried. So they strapped that pouch thing on my back, gave me a push start, and away I went. I didn't slow down hardly at all 'til I got to the HQ. It was fun! I liked my *new job*!

"Problem was, however, they turned that bike over to some other fella and made me walk back to the front line.

"I couldn't hardly wait for that war to be over so when I got back home I could get me a motor-*sickle* of my own. And, by golly, I did, too!"

We all shook hands, smiled, and the "younger" gentleman walked off toward the garden, a bona-fide piece of World War II history leaving me there with a bona-fide piece of World War I history, both born with the same thirst for independence and duty as the original wild ones.

Over the past couple of years, Tommie Greathouse came into my mind on the Fourth of July and Veteran's Day and whenever the subject of war was in the news. Recently, I saw a documentary about World War I. They showed the "big guns" firing, and young soldiers, and I remembered how Tommie had mentioned his job of "protecting the cannons." It occurred to me that one of the young men in that old black and white film might have been Tommie Greathouse.

Today, while my mother visited Aunt Ruth, I found Tommie in his room, having just returned from his afternoon walk. Tommie's room displays the memorabilia of his life: newspaper clippings, his framed discharge papers, birthday cards signed by Ronald Reagan and George Bush, a plaque from the Veterans of Foreign Wars, all sharing importance with a picture of his beloved wife. She died after 50 years of marriage.

These days, although Tommie gets around a lot more slowly than he used to, he can still walk without a cane, and even though his hearing has failed somewhat, his mind is starkly clear. He smiles—laughs—and again tells the story of how he and the boys "whipped the Kaiser." He said that on the 11th hour of the 11th day of the 11th month the captain said, "Boys, hold your fire. They say there's an armistice going into effect. But keep your guns loaded and stay ready just in case this thing don't hold."

Then Tommie dug out his Veterans of Foreign Wars cap and put it on. Coming to full attention he asked, "How's that?"

I said, "You look great, sir!"

And with a lump in my throat, I saluted.

In his eyes I saw a young, vibrant soldier who risked his life to preserve freedom and democracy for me and millions of others. I never took the time to thank all those doughboys, and now there was only Tommie left.

Thanks, Tommie, and whenever you get the chance please pass it on to the rest of the boys. Pass it on to the original wild ones.

CHAPTER 24

The Tale of the Sound of Straight Pipes Heard 'Round the World

"Why the BFMC? You are the most authentic symbol of the biker's spirit, and a link between past and present."

—French biker, Marko

"Stopping for breakfast in Fitchville
the joint full of 'Boozefighters' bikers from Appalachia,
tattoos & irongray beards
one momma with designs on both shoulders
'Property of Billy Goat' originals denim her back.
Billy lights a cheroot before he saddles up, she
swinging in behind him.
O Freedom of the grease!
O thumper of asphalt & thundering concrete!
My eggs are here/the parking lot's clear.

en route to Ashland 5 July 91"

—Nick Muska

I met poet Nick Muska while we were drinking on the balcony of an old hotel in the French Quarter of New Orleans. Generally, when two strangers drink *somewhat* together, they talk. We did. The dank, ghost-filled air of the Delta night helped to shorten the friendly fuse that the booze had already lit.

We were both products of the 1960s. That was clear. It was a generation that made it a fun habit to almost always leap long before it looked, and Nick and I obviously had done our share of leaping. But, just as obviously, we had ridden off in slightly different directions after the brightly colored fresh paint of the psychedelic 1960s dried up and began to peel away.

We had both become writers, but our wardrobes were different: Nick in casual cotton, me in worn leather.

It didn't take us long to discover this, either. Some things are simply felt right off the bat. Those are the best things. Those are the things that usually lead to brotherhood. When you look like you ride a motorcycle, the subject of conversation generally turns to, yes, *riding a motorcycle*. But, unless technical grease and micrometer readings are your life's focus, *riding a motorcycle* is a subject that will lead to many, many other topics.

After we explored a few, Nick mentioned that he had written a poem about some Boozefighters he had seen back in 1991 while he was eating breakfast in Fitchville, Ohio.

The idea that years ago, in an Ohio roadhouse, one of America's most creative poets was inspired by the Boozefighter name, a compelling color in this corner of life, this was perfect. I stared out at the crowd along Bourbon Street, realizing that there are so many *layers* to society. Some people just walked by the blues and jazz bars along the Rue. Some people went into them. Some people *lived* in them. Some people were *under* them. It just depended on how deep you wanted to go. And Sinatra was right: "That's life." It's all like this. When a great poet becomes inspired, the object of the inspiration is equally as great. Just walking along Bourbon Street doesn't mean you've truly been to New Orleans. Being able to rhyme "moon" and "June" doesn't make you a poet. Buying a motorcycle doesn't make you a biker.

> " the joint full of 'Boozefighter' bikers from Appalachia,
> tattoos & irongray beards "

The cover of the British book Bikers: Birth of a Modern Day Outlaw *featured the publicity shot of Brando in* The Wild One.

What Wino Willie Forkner and the rest of the original wild ones did in 1946 and 1947—the bloodline that they began—has anchored an inspiration so deep that it has not only transcended years but nations as well.

The true American bikers have inspired the *American Biker,* sure, but the Europeans have also looked to the legend of Hollister, probably for a variety of reasons. But then again, *everyone* needs heroes (or antiheroes), men with purpose.

In 1985 a book was published in England, *Bikers: Birth of a modern day outlaw,* written by Dr. Ian Richard "Maz" Harris. Harris, who died May 31, 2000, at the age of 50 in a motorcycle accident, carefully and clinically chronicles the biker image, beginning back when the term "outlaw" was first applied to bikers.

Maz Harris wasn't just a writer. After taking his degree in sociology from Warwick University, he went on to earn a PhD. He also helped to found the Kent, England, chapter of the HAMC nearly 30 years ago, later becoming the club's press officer.

Harris' book is the European revelation of how the American press electrified public paranoia. Harris expanded what came out of Hollister 1947 to include just how the birth of the American biker hurdled the Atlantic:

> As time went on, a distinctive biker lifestyle began to emerge. Riders affected a similar style of dress and pattern of speech, and the clubs became more tight-knit and divorced from the world of the ride-to-work citizen motorcyclist. Highly structured and highly visible clubs like the Booze Fighters [*sic*], Galloping Gooses, 13 Rebels, Market Street Commandos, Satan's Daughters, Satan's Sinners, Winos, and the Pissed-Off Bastards of Bloomington (later in 1948 to become the Berdoo founder chapter of the Hells Angels), began to travel a little further afield in search of excitement.
>
> It was not long before the media and the law enforcement agencies recognized a potential source of trouble and decided to rise to the challenge posed to their authority by these un-American cycle bums. Their method was systematic harassment. The result was the ostracism of the outlaw bikers from the mass of law-abiding motorcyclists and the subsequent emergence of a new American folk hero or folk devil (depending on your point of view or, more particularly, your social situation).

What occurred on a hot summer's [*sic*] day, July 4, 1947, was an event guaranteed to bring this new kind of motorized outlaw to the attention of the great American public. It was to provoke in moms and dads throughout the land a morbid dread of anyone sporting a leather jacket or driving anything with fewer than four wheels.

The bikers had made it to the big time. They had been discovered in the town of Hollister, California, and branded by the national press as the biggest threat to the American way of life since the Japanese took it into their heads to bomb Pearl Harbor. In the next 10 years the image they created of wild men on motorcycles was to become the subject of numerous books, films, television programmes, newspaper and magazine articles. It was an image which prompted lawmen and elected officials everywhere to take the view that if they didn't want their own town overrun by these degenerate hoodlums, they had better clamp down good and hard on any kid who even looked like he might ride a motorcycle.

The cover of Maz Harris' book features the famous publicity photo of Marlon Brando from the movie, *The Wild One*. It's a perfect cover. Throughout the book the cultural impact and staying power of the 1953 flick is stressed on the biker image in America and in Europe.

The Wild One was far from having been laid to rest, as the onset of the 1960s would show. Outlaw clubs continued to spring up, composed of riders who were proud to be different, imitating not Brando—the image that had been twisted, distorted, and made decent for public consumption—but [Lee] Marvin, the rebel who refused to conform. For the moment the beast had been held in check, but only for the moment. And meanwhile, across the Atlantic, it was only just beginning to bare its teeth.

Harris chronicles how the whole biker image shebang blasts into England at full speed—the teddy boys, the mods, and the rockers—and into the hearts and machines of Europe's real riders.

It may have been just a ripple that began on America's West Coast in 1947, but it soon became a tsunami that engulfed the world, a screamer of a wave that has never crested or broken. It's still churning forward, picking up steam.

Nearly 20 years after Harris' book was published, a French writer named Charlie Lecach contacted those in charge of press and history for the Boozefighters Motorcycle Club. European biker interest in the original wild ones, it seems, had continued to grow. The roots had continued to command respect. A major feature on the BFMC was planned for the heavyweight Italian biker magazine, *Freeway*.

"In my opinion," offered Charlie, "the BFMC is a major part of America's motorcycling heritage and deserves a very special place in its history."

Charlie, who was quickly given the handle, "French Charlie," was subjected to a fairly intense literary anal exam as to just *what* he was going to write about the club, the tone, and the implications.

In 2004, exactly 50 years after *The Wild One* threw gas on the flames of *"The Cyclist's Raid,"* 57 years after Hollister, there was no point in having a midlife image crisis at this stage in the proceedings, no point in having a toxic *déjà vu*.

French Charlie vowed that he would adhere to something rare and porous: the truth.

"This article about the Boozefighters is to be the first article about a motorcycle club that I have written in 14 years of doing this job," said Charlie. "And I did it because of its historical importance, which to my eyes has a direct relationship with American motorcycle history."

He flew from Europe to Daytona and hooked up with some BFMC brothers at Bike Week, conducting interviews, snapping green-and-white pictures. One promise he made was to allow club officers to see the piece before it was published. His word held—he sent proofs of the article . . . *in French*.

"Ensuite les choses se compliquent, certains quittent les Boozefighters pour des raisons familiales, mais beaucoupde nouveaux rejoignent les rangs du BFMC."

Okay, but lines like this were somewhat vague. In its *raw* state the subject matter was pretty much open to speculation. Like, did this have something to do with motorcycling or the biker culture? Or maybe it was accusing the club of really being behind the Roswell UFO conspiracy? Or maybe it was implying that the BFMC had something to do with hanging chads or Michael Jackson's nose?

French translators are tough to find on the spur of the moment but one club member was certain that he could help. Yep. His wife worked in a law

French writer Charlie Lecach: "In my opinion, the BFMC is a major part of America's motorcycling heritage and deserves a very special place in its history."

office where there was a Vietnamese secretary who was "very well educated and speaks five languages."

This really didn't work out well at all. Going from French to Vietnamese to English gave many of "French Charlie's" words meanings that were sort of different than originally intended. Some of the more biker-specific words and phrases didn't have an exact counterpart in Vietnamese, and that left a gaping hole in the French. It wound up sounding like what might have happened if Peter Fonda and Dennis Hopper had found and tried to read the Dead Sea Scrolls *after* they smoked the grass with Nicholson. It just wasn't right.

But then the Vietnamese secretary's husband offered to translate the article. He, too, speaks and reads French. And he's Chinese. Then he too started having some trouble with the more esoteric parts of the article. But he had a friend named Hamid who also, yes, read and spoke French. By now the European presses were rolling. The truth about the aliens at Roswell and the BFMC might just be on the way.

"French Charlie's" article made the cover tease of *Freeway*. It was a major feature, an extremely slick and professional piece that rated six pages, a top flight work.

Then the translation finally came in, a zippy little package that somehow went from French to English via Viet Nam, China, and from wherever Hamid might hang his particular hat . . . or fez.

Thanks, Hamid.

Since this was a long article, he was not able to translate everything, but here's the summary:

> This article is about the young Americans in 1946 who have come back from World War II and founded a motorcycle club. They are different in a way that they do not wear the usual uniform for motorcycle riders. They are changing the rules of the motorcycle riders. As usual the group finds itself in a bar where they discuss the name of their group. They hear a suggestion from a bar client on calling themselves the "Boo-Boo-Boozefighters." They will take the simple version the "Boozefighter."
>
> By July 1947, the newly created club counts between 35 to 40 members. Some quit the group because of family reasons but new members join every day. By 4th of July, 1948, at Riverside, California, they decide to paint their hair in red while gathering as a group.

Boozefighters MC

Les bikers de L'Équipée Sauvage ont quelque chose de pitoyable et manquent de naturel, à commencer par Brando. Tous, sauf Lee Marvin. Dans son rôle de Chino, il s'inspirait directement de Willie Forkner, l'un des membres fondateurs des légendaires Boozefighters !

En 1946, beaucoup de jeunes Américains reviennent du front et se remettent des privations de la guerre. Dans cette quête insatiable de liberté et de joie de vivre, ils sont nombreux à se sentir attirés par la moto. La plupart intègrent sans problème les rangs de l'AMA ou de clubs affiliés à cette vaste organisation. Mais une poignée de durs à cuire, de fêtards bons vivants, refuse de se soumettre aux règlements stricts et souvent peu fantaisistes de ces confréries en uniformes. L'un d'eux, Willie Forkner – ex-mitrailleur de B-24 durant les batailles du Pacifique – part un jour assister à une course. Au guidon de sa moto, il défonce la barrière de sécurité et se joint aux pilotes u beau milieu de l'épreuve, juste pour s'amuser un peu. Les collègues de son club n'apprécient guère ce type de comportement et l'expulsent de leurs rangs. Il se met donc à la recherche de motards plus ouverts d'esprit, de gars dans son genre. Il les trouve très rapidement. Des gens comme Fatboy Nelson, Dink Burns, George Menker et bien d'autres, qui ne demandent qu'à changer les règles du jeu. Ils traînent tous dans le All American Bar de Los Angeles, au point qu'on ne les qualifie tout d'abord pas de motards ayant un problème avec l'alcool, mais d'alcooliques ayant un problème avec la moto ! L'idée même d'un club naît aux environs de mai 1946 dans la Studebaker de Jack Lilly et c'est effectivement Wino Willie (Forkner) qui lance le sujet. Comme toujours, la bande de potes se retrouve le soir au bar et entame une discussion portant sur le futur nom de ce club. On évoque alors des appellations comme les "Bats" ou encore les "Henchmen" (acolytes). De l'autre côté du comptoir, un des piliers de bar écoute la conversation. Il s'agit de Walt Porter, qui roule sur un 750 WLA récupéré au surplus de l'armée et qui fait figure locale d'éponge à bibine. Il leur bafouille alors péniblement « vous pourriez aussi bien vous appeler les Bo-Boo-Boozefighters (Booze = alcool – ndlr), car tout ce que vous faites est de rester scotché au bistrot à batailler pour un verre ! » Porter ne fera lui-même jamais partie du club, mais sera toujours considéré comme un membre honorifique. De plus, sa caricature décore par la suite l'un des logos du BFMC. En attendant, Wino et ses potes ne sont pas convaincus que ce nom soit le meilleur pour ce qu'ils projettent de faire, qu'il mette vraiment en valeur l'ego machiste d'une fraternité motarde. Mais ils

À Hollister, en 1947, trente ou quarante gars le font sortir en force de sa cellule...

The French motorcycle magazine Freeway *featured an article detailing the history of the BFMC. European interest in the club and its legacy gets stronger and stronger.*

Different magazines and publications talk about arrest and disorder by the group at their gatherings. On the other hand the club members consider themselves common citizens and avoid wrong doings and criminal contaminations.

By 1953 most of the club members are becoming family members and they gather professional obligations. Meanwhile, they continue to meet at least once a year. Since the death of Wino (one of the creators of the group) in 1997, the reunions are every year at 4th of July. Meanwhile new younger generations keep joining the group.

Okay, that pretty much says it all: French Charlie's six-page spread neatly packed into a three-paragraph international nut-shell. Thankfully there was nothing about spacecraft, alien body-cavity probes, or, more importantly, Michael Jackson's nose, at least as far as we know. And it's probably a damn good thing about avoiding those "criminal contaminations."

But the point was clear. The American biker is a big deal. A very big deal. Worldwide. Its history is important and the original wild ones rolled right down the middle of it, smoking their tires all the way.

And everybody knows it.

Worldwide.

In another part of France, in the village of Methamis, stands the *"Boozefighters Revenge"* cafe, the word "revenge" actually meaning "come together" in the French idiom. Pierre and Marko are the two Euro bikers who run it. The original wild ones inspired it.

"In order to start on a good basis," wrote Pierre to the offices of the BFMC, "we are going to introduce ourselves and explain our motivations. We are a group of 15 brothers and sisters (our wives or girlfriends), aged 30–45, living in the South East of France. We are independent, having no relationship with any MC, our goals being riding, traveling, and partying as often as possible, trying to make the 1940s and 1950s spirit of freedom revive.

"Some of our bikes are bobbers or choppers, most of them being H-D from Pan to Evo, the others being old European bikes (BMW R50/1955; Triumph Bonneville; Moto Guzzi California).

"The origin of our respectful interest in the BFMC has its source in the conjunction of two passions. Marko has a passion for the 1944 liberation of

France by the U.S. troops, and collects the uniforms and equipment related to it (especially the ones related to the U.S Airborne involved in operation Anvil). His other passion being the American culture and bikes.

"Personally, I am not a collector, but I am deeply interested in the technical and military aspects of World War II, and in the American culture.

"Marko got interested in the first postwar MC created by the vets coming back home after years of tough fighting, mourning the ones who didn't make it, holding onto a powerful spirit of camaraderie and freedom. This must have been a hell of a time!

"Marko nicknamed his bar '*Boozefighters Revenge.*'

"Why the BFMC? You are the most authentic symbol of the biker's spirit, and a link between past and present. Moreover, we have a deep respect for the World War II vets and we would like to perpetuate this tradition in France.

"We are not a MC. We are a group thrilled by the pleasure of riding as brothers, and we are totally free from any commitment. In France, support stickers don't cause any rivalry. All of the MC are respectful of the others; bearing stickers or badges isn't considered as something aggressive or offensive (it's a sort of reminder of the tradition of heraldic arms).

"Our aim is to become an official tribute group in the honor of an historic MC."

England produced a little four-piece band in the 1960s: The Beatles. In the movie *The Wild One*, Chino's (Lee Marvin's) bike "gang" is called the Beetles. A lot of urban legends surround the Fab Four, but how they got their name may just relate in a gritty, leathery way to the original wild ones.

Dave Persails, author of *The Long and Winding Road to the Beatles Anthology*, makes a good case for the connection:

> In more recent years, another theory as to the origins of the Beatles' name has been suggested by George Harrison and Beatles' press man, Derek Taylor. In his second revised edition biography of the Beatles (1985), Hunter Davies intimated that Taylor told him the name was inspired by the film, *The Wild One*. A black leather-clad motorcycle gang is referred to as the Beetles. As Davies put it, "Stu Sutcliffe saw this film, heard the remark, and came back and suggested it to John as the new name for their group. John said yeah, but we'll spell it Beatles, as we're a beat group.'"

Taylor repeated the story in his own Genesis book, *Fifty Years Adrift*.

"At that time, Stuart was into the Marlon Brando type of method acting. There has always been a big thing about who invented the name, Beatles. John had said he invented it. But if you look at a movie called *The Wild One*, you'll see a scene about bicycle *(!)* gangs where Johnny's (played by Brando) gang is in a coffee bar and another gang led by Chino (Lee Marvin) pulls into town for a bit of aggro. The film dialogue printed here shows how Stuart could have thought of the name Beatles."

The story is repeated once more in Pauline Sutcliffe's *BackBeat*, (1994) with a slight twist.

"(Stuart) also dreamt up a new name for the group. Buddy Holly had his Crickets, and, on a forthcoming month-long tour of Britain, Gene Vincent was going to be backed by the Beat Boys. How about 'The Beetles?' One of the motorbike gangs in *The Wild One* was called that, too. A brainstorming session with John warped it eventually to 'The Beatles'—you know, like in 'beat music.'"

Worldwide.

From a poet's inspiration years ago, over a couple of fried eggs, to the most famous rock 'n' roll bunch of all time, to the absolute inside core of the European biker, the original wild ones turned the key. They kicked this engine over.

It's a long ride, and a perfect ride, a ride that just never ends.

CHAPTER 25

The Tale of "Red Dog's" Funeral, Jack Lilly Steps Out From the Past, Echoes of a Last Request

"There was a time when friendship mattered,
I still live in that time,
I'm gonna die in that time."
—"Brotherhood Mystery," Dr. Martin Jack Rosenblum

Edward "Red Dog" Dahlgren was in jail just once. But that was enough to make history. He was the one who was sleeping it off after riding his bike down the sidewalk, inciting the infamous 1947 Hollister "jailbreak" that, well, never really happened.

Fifty-two years later, Red Dog and his wife, Virginia, were the guests of honor at the Boozefighters Fall National in Fort Worth. "Big John" Rogers, the BFMC national president, stood next to Red Dog onstage. They looked out toward the large group. They looked at one another. Two generations of Boozefighter history face to face, a loving brother's look in each one's eyes.

"We all heard about that riot *you* started back in 1947," said Big John, hiding a smile. "Yeah, you're known as a 'trouble maker' so we want you to settle down and behave yourself while you're here!"

It's always stark to look into aged eyes that have never closed to the youthful fire of life. The greatest lesson in life that can be driven into the skulls of the young is the fact that, although the flesh becomes a bit weak, the spirit of pioneers like Red Dog does not. Age will eventually slow and kill the body. Appreciation of what someone is, what he has done, what he stands for, and the desire to continue those traits by the generations that come after—*that* defines immortality.

Red Dog was presented with various awards and tributes but one, in particular, bridged the generations. He, in turn, did some bridging of his own. He was presented with a commemorative patch that had been just designed—the "Red Dog Jailbreak" patch—another link to an important part of the club's history.

But Red Dog proved that history doesn't just apply to things that have passed; it can also have a sharp-edged effect on principles in the present. He gave a short speech. He thanked the club for honoring him, but he also spoke about some of the regrouping that the club had undergone. He spoke about unity, and he spoke about brotherhood.

A few weeks later, Red Dog developed heart problems, needed a pacemaker, and was hospitalized. Another original wild one, Jim Hunter, was admitted to the hospital at the same time for similar problems. Brotherhood.

Red Dog and Hunter needed help. The Boozefighters in Texas took up a collection and wound up with a couple of thousand bucks. There was only one true way to get the money out to Red Dog and Hunter in California: by bike.

But it was the middle of December.

Dancer and JQ rode west with the now very cold cash. Their destination was the California home of another original wild one, Johnny Roccio, and his wife, Jeannine.

When they arrived at the house, Jim Cameron was also there. "That was a special thrill," said Dancer. "Jim Cameron is such a genuinely great guy, always smiling, laughing, telling us the stories of the fun they had in the early days, how he rode his bike into Johnny's Bar. But the best thing of all was when Jim volunteered to be our road captain and escort us over to Red Dog's place. And, man, he could still ride that BSA!"

Red Dog had just been released from the hospital to recuperate at home. His wife knew Dancer, JQ, and Jim were coming. Red Dog didn't. The visit was a surprise for him but his tears were not a surprise to anyone. There is nothing wrong with emotions based in love and brotherhood.

Red Dog was grateful for the money but was reluctant to accept charity. His wife accepted the bucks. She knew of "a good cause to give it to." She also knew that the landlord was after the rent and that the electric bill was overdue.

Before they left, Red Dog made a request of Dancer and JQ. Since they were in Southern California he asked them to go down to see the boys from the San Diego chapter. Red Dog was aware of some of the growing pains that the club had suffered during its regrouping stages. "See the San Diego guys," he said. "You're all good Boozefighters. You believe in the same principles."

The next day Dancer and JQ rode to the convalescent home where Jim Hunter was recovering from *his* hospital stay. But Hunter wasn't in his room. Everyone began to search. The nurses said that they just "couldn't keep a handle on him!" Finally they found him out in the parking lot, advising a visitor on how to fix his flooded carburetor.

A typical Boozefighter.

Dancer and JQ eventually got Hunter to return to his room. They gave him some of the collected funds. The rest was left with Johnny Roccio, who had been looking after Jim Hunter, seeing to his needs.

Brotherhood.

A few days after the visit to the convalescent home, Dancer and JQ learned that Hunter had called a friend, promised him gas money if he'd come and get him, and he "escaped" from the facility in the middle of the night. "I'd rather die at home," Hunter would later say, "than rot away at that Godforsaken old folks' home!"

Perhaps that word *"wild"* is the key to the original wild ones.

San Diego.

Snowman, Buckshot, and others from the Southern California area met up with Dancer and JQ at a local bar. Red Dog's request was met. He was one of the originals whose heart and character was so involved in the early days of this club, and his heart and attitude remained so dedicated to its growth and harmony.

Maybe feeling that his work was done, Red Dog passed away shortly after his visit with the boys from Texas.

A biker's funeral is never a low-profile event.

It was back out to California for Dancer and JQ along with Big John, "Running Bear," and Irish Ed. There was a long procession of bikes from Boozefighters chapters up and down the West Coast.

An older guy walked slowly from out of the middle of the crowd at the cemetery. He was wearing the green and white jersey of the originals.

And from the worn appearance of the shirt, this man—and his colors—were definitely the real thing.

"Who *is* that?" someone asked.

Johnny Roccio and Jim Cameron spoke almost at the same time, "Well, son of a gun, that's Jack Lilly! He's still alive!"

Johnny, Jim, and the other originals hadn't seen Jack in years, but a true brotherhood never fades. Jack was back. Along with his tales and his love for what the Boozefighters were back then, and what they are now.

The evening brought a celebration of Red Dog Dahlgren's life.

Texas Boozefighters, West Coast Boozefighters, the memory of an original wild one, the rediscovery of another, all to the historical backdrop of originals Jim Hunter and Gil Armas shooting pool in a friendly 8-ball rivalry that was begun 53 years before, all to the echo of Red Dog's speech about unity and brotherhood.

CHAPTER 26

The Tale of the Three-Way Deal, the Search for the Lost Crocker

"Outside of a dog, a book is man's best friend.
Inside of a dog, it's too dark to read."

—Groucho Marx

You can hear "Three Blind Mice" playing in the background. The scene had to be in old grainy black-and-white. You can see Larry, Moe, and Curly cooking up an agreement, the Marx Brothers in rapid-fire double-talk, or maybe Bud Abbott hustling Lou Costello: "You got two tens for a five?"

Jack Lilly, George Manker, and Wino Willie, a three-way bike swap, and an in-deep cycle shop owner trying to keep his head above the rising waves of The Deal . . .

Jack got his first bike when he was 12 years old, in 1929; a 1921 one-lunger Cleveland. By 1934, Lilly's dad had passed away and Jack and his mother moved to Los Angeles. In the late 1930s he was riding a Rudge and wanted a bigger bike. Then he met George Manker. Both would become Boozefighters a decade later. Manker was in money trouble. He needed to get rid of the payments he was making on his new 1939 61OV Crocker. He knew that he had to get into a less expensive bike, like an Indian.

Lilly and Manker began to work out *The Deal*, a take-over-payments kind of thing, simple, easy.

(Curly was beginning to chuckle and snap his fingers. "I'm tryin' to think but nothing happens!")

They went down to the shop where Manker had to pay his note and explained to the owner just what they were gonna do. No, it wasn't that easy. Not without some money up front, a $40 "reassignment fee." Jack didn't have $40, but he had the Rudge. How about a trade-in? No.

(The Marx Brothers were in a huddle, thinking "I've had a perfectly wonderful evening. This wasn't it.")

There was another guy who came into the shop, though. He overheard the high-level financial discussion that was going on. His name was Willie Forkner. He had 40 bucks. He bought Jack's Rudge. Jack bought Manker's Crocker. And Manker got an Indian. And down the road a few years they were all wearing green and white and hangin' at the All American.

The Crocker was Jack's dream bike. As time went on he also developed a relationship with Alfred Crocker. "I used to go to his little factory there in L.A. and watch them put bikes together. He had about five employees. Each would start with a frame and completely put a bike together. Alfred changed to war subcontracts during World War II and never could get his motorcycle business going again after the war ended. Those old Crockers are priceless now.

"I'd go out to Rosamond Dry Lake and run my Crocker. In 1940, I clocked 105.1 miles per hour, and that was real good for a stock bike. In those days a Harley wouldn't clock more than about 90 or 91 miles per hour unless you stroked them or something, like C. B. Clausen used to do. Man, I wish I had that Crocker back. It was No. 103, which meant that's how many Alfred Crocker had made to that point.

"As a matter of fact, Red Dog (Red Dahlgren) and I came close to buying out the Crocker plant after the war ended, but the remaining assets were too depleted to arrange adequate financing. The Crocker Company met its demise like many other American-made motorcycles did back then."

But Jack's Crocker faded into the camouflage of wartime America as well. He sold it when he entered the merchant marines during World War II. It was a lost love that haunted him for 61 years. Until . . .

Crocker motorcycle freaks have their own version of Indiana Jones. His name is Markus Karalash and any existing Crocker is his Lost Ark. With a computer for a whip, Markus rolls back a lot of basket-case rocks and deals with a lot of long lost spiders.

Jack Lilly on his Crocker, 1939.

"As a restorer of antique motorcycles," Karalash remembers, "the Holy Grail seemed to me to be the Crocker V-Twin road bike produced between 1936 and 1942. In 1997 I was given the opportunity to cradle two rare Crocker basket cases in my garage. The rarer of the two, and wanting for parts, was a 1938 Small Tank Hemi Head model. I began to make what was missing. Other Crocker owners found out what I was up to and started asking for parts for their own restorations. 'Crocker Motorcycle Company' was born. In 1999 I incorporated the company when a client list became ever expanding, and in 2002 I brought in a partner, Michael Schacht, to accelerate Crocker's expansion.

"Since a restoration requires a great deal of research, especially when a motorcycle as rare as a Crocker is considered, diligent research becomes that much more important. Consequently, in early 2001, I came across the Boozefighters' website and their article on Jack Lilly. After contacting 'History' (aka Jim Quattlebaum) through the website and assuring him that my intention for contacting Jack was for research, he helped to put me in contact with him. I called Jack and told him I knew of the whereabouts of the Crocker that he once cherished so deeply. Like a kid at Christmas, Jack couldn't contain his excitement. He told me stories of how he obtained old No. 103 from another Boozefighter, George Manker, how he knew Al Crocker, and how he actually owned three Crockers in total, his last coming from yet another Boozefighter, Jim Kimball, in 1952. Jack wove story after story about growing up and cycling in Southern California. I learned about the All American Cafe, where they had their club meetings, about Kenny Howard, who Jack knew only as 'Von Dutch.' Jack told me about George Beerup, a well-known L.A. motorcycle dealer, and about Al Crocker himself.

"Jack and I talked and wrote to each other time after time about motorcycles, the Boozefighters, clubs, hot rods, planes, and what life was really like in the 1930s and 1940s. Jack shared so much information that I wrote an article for the Winter 2001 issue of *The Antique Motorcyclist*, titled, 'Crocker Jack.' I could have expanded that article further yet, but was told to keep it under a certain size.

"On November 2–4, 2001, Jack was among the honored guests at the Boozefighters' National Convention in Fort Worth, Texas. I was invited to attend but unfortunately I was not able to. Daniel Statnekov, the present owner of Jack's old No. 103, was able to attend and bring the Crocker with him. By sheer coincidence the motorcycle was restored in the Boozefighters' colors of green and white.

"I promised Jack I would, some day, make a trip out to see him and to shake his hand, but Michael and I didn't make it out to his ranch until March 4, 2004. Jack, excited about our first meeting, put out the BFMC sign on his front gate to greet us. Of course we had to stop there to take photos before we drove up to his house to meet the man himself.

"Like old times never stopped, Jack came out as friendly as ever, telling us of his fantastic exploits of flying and riding like they all just happened yesterday.

"When I reminded him of a certain story he would smile and chuckle, and off he'd go on another ride back into his glory days.

"Jack is in his late eighties, can't see worth a spit and, although he may be frustrated with growing older, he still has a good appreciation for life and all that comes with it. What I found odd was that through it all, Jack was his humble self, exclaiming how he couldn't understand his celebrity. I couldn't find the words to explain it to Jack then but I hope to now. It is his zeal toward living life honestly and enjoying it as much as he could, and then allowing others like Michael and me to look back through his eyes, to show us what his life was like, without polishing it up first.

"Jack's honesty is his virtue and that is why we respect, honor, and celebrate him."

Jack Lilly loved to run that Crocker for time but, unlike original wild ones Jim Hunter and Gil Armas, Jack wasn't exactly a racer.

"I raced briefly—very briefly. In 1951 we went to Culver City to enter the speed track races. I got there too late to run position qualifying races, but when the main race began I was allowed to join at the back of the pack.

"As fate would have it, the leaders got tangled up and fell. Then, like dominoes, the ones that followed also fell. I was one of the few that got around the pile-up and went on to cross the finish line first.

"However, during the next race I hit the rail on turn No. 1 and peeled all the skin off my hand. I picked up my bike and finished the race in last place. When I came into the pit area, my wife—who was dressed like a boy because they didn't let girls in the pits—took one look at my hand and said, 'That's it! No more racing for you!'

"I was glad she took that stand, because that was *my* conclusion, too!"

CHAPTER 27

The Tale of "Boozefighters UP!" Original Minutes, 1946 By-Laws, Ink Smears, "Good Clean Fun," and the "Sour Pickles of the Road"

"We had one rule that said you had to be 'Boozefighters up' at all times. If you passed out, you'd better land on your face 'cause if you landed on your back and covered up that Boozefighters insignia on your back, you were out of the club. We used to tell each other, 'Keep an eye on me. If I crash on my ass, roll me over quick before a (club) officer sees me!' "

—An unnamed old Boozefighter, from an article
by Rip & Trampo, *Easyriders* magazine, October 1983

You've gotta wonder just when it was that the word "attitude" took on a negative meaning . . . when it changed from an actual attitude to a display of power.

The original wild ones had plenty of power. They had just won a war. They were blue-collar boys who were strengthening and straightening the industrial spine of an already-tough nation. They really didn't have to prove anything to anybody in the macho-testosterone department. The only attitude they had was about having fun, enjoying the hell outta life—setting themselves apart from the pasteurized Andy Hardy world that was oozing into postwar America, and the best way to do it was by living on something like a big motorcycle.

Early members of the Gypsy MC. The entire image of the American biker and most of the original clubs has roots in the military and the war years.

In addition to the All American, Curly's, the Pullman, and Shanghai Red, there was another bar down on Avalon (or on nearby South Main Street depending on who's telling the tale) where the boys would sometimes hang out: the Crash Inn.

Lee "Bear" Nolan often told the tale about how Fat Boy Nelson once dumped his bike in front of the joint. The motor kept going and the open primary caught hold on the ground and Fat Boy and his bike became a top, spinning and spinning. Everybody was laughing too hard to help him, of course. Fat Boy was finally able to shut the thing off, but not until the dizziness mixed with the booze from his afternoon at the bar.

"He coulda used the gag box," said "Bear," "but the gutter along Avalon worked, and that made us laugh even harder!"

And laugh they did. Because it was all *fun.* That was the point.

One thing that separates the Boozefighters Motorcycle Club from many of the clubs that began in the 1940s—and especially from the few that still exist—is that so many of the original records and hand-written documents from the founding days have been preserved. That makes the tone of the club inarguable.

And, yeah, it's been mentioned before that fun is a word that's open to many interpretations, but not here. There was no darkness in the fun the originals had on those bikes and in those bars, no double-edged intent.

The first club by-laws from 1946 reveal a lot. They truly are a model for most of the parameters that are held holy by most structured MCs, from back then right through the present: the prospect process—being voted in, kicked out, women and their role, and the absolute esteem for club colors.

But the by-laws also express a clean innocence, too, almost a combination of the seriousness of the brotherhood involved in any legitimate MC, along with the boys-will-be-boys ring of Ralph and Norton at the Raccoon Lodge, and Calvin and Hobbes busting into hysterics over a private joke in their tree-clubhouse.

THE BOOZEFIGHTER BY-LAWS OF 1946

1. To become a Boozefighter a man must attend four meetings consecutively and be voted on by secret ballot by all members present and must not be opposed by three (3) or more members.

2. Club is closed at twenty members.

3. Initiation fee is two (2) dollars. Dues are 50 cents a week. When a member is voted in, he must pay the sum of $2.50.

4. If a member misses three meetings consecutively without a substantial explanation, he will be voted upon again.

5. Any member who is absent without a reasonable excuse from the club activities will automatically be dropped from the club.

6. If a member misses a meeting without a reasonable excuse he will be fined $1.00.

7. Officers will be elected every three months, if they are still living.

8. There will be a fine of one dollar for any member not wearing his sweater to meetings, club activities, races, etc., without a reasonable excuse.

9. Any member leaving or being voted out of the club will either remove the lettering from his sweater, or sell it back to the club.

10. It is strictly against all club rules for any one member to bring more than one case of liquor or one keg of beer or wine to a meeting.

11. There will NEVER be any women in any way affiliated in any way shape or form with the Boozefighters Motorcycle Club or its subsidiaries.

12. If any member of the Boozefighters, or its subsidiaries, is found guilty of crapping out (passing out) on his back, having the club name where it can't be seen, or not having his sweater on when being crapped out, he will be fined $1.00.

13. No member will be completely without a motor for more than six months. If he is, he will be automatically dropped from the club.

BY-LAWS #3-6-8-12, MAY BE AMENDED TO MEET THE ECONOMIC AND SOCIAL TREND OF THE TIMES.

The By-Laws of 1946 are issued in the spirit of fellowship and good-natured fun, and are intended only to form the basis on which to begin local Chapter-Charter operations.

Attitude.

Was America so different back then? Were the people so different? Or were the originals a different breed entirely, the type that could ignore the swirling BS in any era or situation and concentrate on what really mattered: having a good time?

The original minutes of Boozefighters meetings were handed over to BFMC National Historian Jim "JQ" Quattlebaum, to decipher and to put in order. This was like translating Jurassic cave glyphs or restoring the ceiling paintings at the Sistine Chapel. Just like it.

"Wow!" JQ tells the story. "I finally got my hands on the minutes to the meetings. They are precious, intriguing, and inspirational. But I must point out that some of them are not all that legible as their penmanship varied from good and clear note taking to sloppy scribbling, depending on the writer. Apparently old-fashioned fountain pens were used and, in some cases, leaked out splotches of ink on the pages, along with a lot of beer being dripped on them as they wrote.

"Additionally, I had one heck of a time determining what order the pages were supposed to go in. They always dated the meeting notes with the month, day, and usually the time the meeting started and finished, but virtually never thought to put in the year. I guess they never thought about how important that would be to the future Boozefighters 50-plus years later!

"Language was blunt and to the point, using their ex-military style slang and obscenities, but I've done a bit of cleaning up so that theirs, yours, and my grandkids can read what they said without their faces turning red!

"And it takes a lot of detective-type work studying the clues from the minutes, and piecing them together for a clearer, overall picture of the evolution of the club. For example: Wino Willie was not only a charter member, as the founder of the club, but he was shown to have been voted back into the membership three different times. So were Red Dog, J.B., and others. Occasionally these boys would get themselves into trouble for being late or missing meetings, not having a running bike, getting behind in dues, forgetting to bring the beer, losing their temper, or 'crapping out' (passing out) on their colors. Once it was noted that the club 'pres' was replaced because he forgot to pick up the new T-shirts and a frame for the club picture like he'd promised to do!

"As best as I can determine, these minutes cover a span of time from April 1947 through October 1950. I haven't located the 1946 minutes (if they ever did exist), nor years in the early 50s. I do have a couple of pages that appear to be from February through August of 1951. I understand from a talk that I had with Jim Hunter (the last active president of the old-time BFMC) that the club slipped into inactivity by 1954, with get-togethers becoming more like reunions.

"Over the years since, these reunions would occasionally take place at some special old-timer's race, motorcycle rally, or family visitation, with some members traveling up to 2,500 miles to make it. These usually included old riding buddies from other friendly clubs that became like adopted Boozefighters."

And the minutes tell a story, the story of that good, clean fun, the tale of a simple bond among brothers that really didn't provide much fodder for exposés, police infiltration, or enemy turf wars.

Just a slight glance into the inner circle of club business:

Apr 47—Discussion ref beer bust, put money in bank, Jim Smith to get picture frame. Beer bust run 25th Apr. JB wants to join club—1st meeting Apr 16.

Whee! A dandy little discussion is now going on about how the gooses talk. It appears there are five words in their vocabulary: mother f_____, c____, f___ and __it.

June 4—Very few here this week—I guess we'll just drink the beer & stumble around a lot. We'll never make it—a visitor just brought in another case of beer.

Mar 5—There's $15.00 left out of the taco feed to be split up among the three clubs. Put $5.00 into the collection glass for Frenchy. Can't take the trailer to Mexico because the Mexicans will take it away from us. Club paid 50 cents for 50 copies of our by-laws.

Apr 2—We hear there's no use trying to get the IMA in this country. Sure hope somebody finds Toot's sweater. Our pres f____d up and didn't order the 'T' shirts or the picture frame. Nominations for pres were opened.

July 9—Article in L.B. Press Telegram read to club. Feeling running high over article Red, Root Beer, Duke, Sergent are all visitors. Beer's gone! Meeting closed. Meeting reopened (more beer).

Oct 8—No f_____g minutes. Beer by Manker.

Oct 22—Beer by Bobby.

Nov 12—John Davis makes motion we kick Manker out of meeting for wanting to tear up the trailer.

Apr 7—Fat Boy fined 25 cents for being passed out on the same day & while the meeting was being held, no class at all. Discussion about getting new pins. John D has pink on.

May 5—Meeting called to order by s__t head Cameron. Tues night all Boozefighters will indulge in a spaghetti feed. Hunter was much loaded and acts like a G. D. Texan. Meeting closed—no beer.

May 26—Smoe bought beer. Boozefighters got beat last Sunday by Sharks in baseball. Everybody must wear sweaters from now on or it's the belt line.

Dec 17—C. B. must be p___y whipped. Hasn't made it to meeting yet. Just got here. Motion made to convert hearse into water wagon.

Preserved in the pages and pages of minutes like these is the essence of the Boozefighters, the essence of a true brotherhood that was founded on the joy of life's basic pleasures: a bike, some booze, and guys you could count on . . . even if they did forget things like ordering the damn T-shirts!

And maybe it *was* a special breed that was spawned in those years, a breed that was able to balance the ability to laugh with the ability to try their best to shed the image that society had on the horizon for them.

There are few surviving clubs that are as old as the Boozefighters MC. The Gypsy MC is one of them. They began in 1932, and even then society's perception of the American biker was beginning to claw at the door. When their riders were called "the sour pickles of society" by the local citizenry, they countered by making their patch into just that: a pickle. It's an important club ensign that is still worn by their members today.

Image, attitude . . .

Norm "Raoul" Flynn, president of the Gypsy MC Houston chapter, describes the origin of his club, a story that extends well beyond just the Gypsy MC, a story that adds to the entire mix of that special breed: the first American bikers. Like any family, they, too, have had to deal with some inner conflict, but the ultimate concepts of family and brotherhood, the concepts that were so valued by all of the original wild ones, have kept them alive.

"In 1932," Raoul says, "in a small mountain town in Eastern Tennessee named Maryville, the Gypsy Motorcycle Club was born. During this time, several adventurous souls were beginning to venture out on public roads on their two-wheeled machines. Among these brave souls was a young man named Lee Simerly, who was Papa Jack's father. Lee would get several of his friends and acquaintances together and do some serious riding through the mountains and towns of Tennessee. As this group of daring young men grew, they took on the name of Gypsy and formed a club, with Lee Simerly being its first president. Thus the Gypsy Motorcycle Club was born.

"As the group grew larger and rode a greater number of miles, the people who did not understand this daring and fun loving group of bikers called them 'The Sour Pickles of Society.' This is how the idea for the 'pickle patch' came about, and it is still proudly worn on the back of all Gypsys today.

"Some sixteen years later, in 1948, Lee's brother Chuck took over as president and remained so until Lee's son Jack became president in 1960. Jack Simerly, known as 'Papa Jack,' moved to Aransas Pass, Texas, where he started the first chapter in Texas, in Corpus Christi in 1964. The club was reorganized in 1966 to be the Gypsy Motorcycle Club, with the main intent of establishing a family-oriented motorcycle club and to build a better public image of bikers. Papa Jack began this by first chartering the club with the AMA in 1968 and changing the cutoff Levi jacket once worn by that daring group of young men to the Gold Mississippi Riverboat Gambler vest still worn today. Papa Jack passed away in 1998. After Papa Jack's death, Hap Simerly, Papa Jack's brother, became the chairman of the board.

"In 2004 the Gypsy MC continues as a family-oriented motorcycle club with chapters or members in three countries and at least five states. The Gypsy MC vision is to continue the traditions established during our more than seventy-year history, to promote the concepts of family and brotherhood, to support the freedom of the road and rights of all motorcyclists, and to contribute to the communities where we live.

"We are a proud group and have the right to be. We've seen a lot of other organizations come and go, and we're still riding strong. We wear the gold with pride."

That sounds like attitude to me, the attitude that in order to survive you'd better have your priorities straight. And family, brotherhood, and freedom are pretty damn good priorities, priorities that have obviously driven the American biker from the very beginning, the priorities of the original wild ones, the priorities that will ensure that this lifestyle will never have an end.

CHAPTER 28

The Tale of Wino's Open Letter to the Club, Insights into a Holy Heritage

Wino Willie Forkner poured a double shot of blast-furnace hooch into life.

Men like Wyatt Earp, Doc Holiday, and Wild Bill Hickok grabbed the mainstream public's vicarious psyches over a century ago, firing up their imaginations, wrapping them in wide-eyed nights filled with dime-novels, read by candlelight, kerosene lamps, and dim electric bulbs.

Willie did the same thing in the 1940s and 1950s, but this time it was a different kind of pioneer on a different kind of horse. Every hero has his tools of the trade. It's all about the man and the aura that surrounds him, whether it's the hand-tooled leather of a speed-slick, low-slung holster; the pearl handles on a pair of bad .44s; a giant, muscled stallion that looks like God's own thoroughbred; or loud, chromed, and pumped-up Milwaukee iron.

But there is one more tool of the American biker, a sanctified emblem, the holy symbol of brotherhood: the patch. The brand that binds. The never-ending handshake. The loving hug that conveys so much.

Recently I heard Mike "Porkchop" Preston, president of the Sierra Mountains Chapter of the Top Hatters MC (another club that was there in Hollister with the original wild ones in 1947) say, "It isn't so much about the patch on your back as it is about the man in front of it." And he's right, of course, but it does all begin to become one as a brotherhood gains strength.

Symbols don't make the man, but the man definitely makes the symbol. He wouldn't be allowed to wear it otherwise.

In an open letter to the Boozefighters MC on December 1, 1988—a rebuilding and regrouping time for the club—Wino Willie candidly discussed what he felt about changes in the club's patch, his comments about history of the original club patch, and more. He looks at the volatile subject of black club members and the somewhat disturbing evolution of import bikes. He speaks from the hip, direct and straight, kind of like Doc Holiday and his big gun:

> Bros, the patch in the picture enclosed was designed by Terry the Tramp in Bellingham, Washington. I had one made for myself. I like all the designs that all of you submitted. Terry wanted me to pick one for all charters. But I'm not going to dictate to you what patch you should wear. As long as it has 'Boozefighters MC' on it. I further suggest you get your charters up to 15 members or more and let them vote on what patch they prefer.
>
> The other picture enclosed is the first Boozefighters shirt I had made to submit to the club for approval. It's now 42 years old. The only one in existence. (As you can see, I'm a fat old man. The shirt doesn't fit so good anymore.) They didn't approve of the lettering. They preferred block lettering—they didn't approve of the shirt. They wanted wool turtlenecks, long sleeves, Kelly green sweaters, with a zipper in the front of the turtleneck. That was our winter sweater, which we voted on. The next summer we came up with the two-tone football T-shirts. This, of course, is in Southern California, where the climate is pretty even. The sweaters were great, but would be out of sight pricewise now-a-days.
>
> In regards to 'Terry the Tramp's' letter of 11-10-88 about blacks in the club. Now the input I get from all the old Boozefighters from the 1940s and 1950s is as follows:
>
> When we formed the club in 1946 and took off the khaki colors, and put on the green and white with Boozefighters MC on the back, we immediately went from heroes to outlaws and a-holes. So we think we know a little bit about persecution. We didn't have many black riders in Southern California at that time. We never had one ask to join the club. We raced in hundreds of open

events. We never had a black join us in competition and we still think it's pretty much that way. We could be wrong. We didn't have much time for racist thoughts. We were too busy promoting all kinds of races, from field meets to half-milers and a party or two along the way. We never went into a bar that the owner didn't want bikers. We never went to a town that we weren't invited to and when we left we were invited back. To every damn one of them, including Hollister.

Also, should some of you might be too young to remember or haven't read the history of the last four wars. The black dudes fought along side of the white dudes in every damn one of them. To preserve the rights for all of us, to be free and ride free. So that's why we say to you bros, do what you have to do to preserve this heritage. In the future we would appreciate it if you wouldn't write to us about any arbitrary BS—solve these problems amongst the active charters. Love to hear from you about the progress of the charters. And about any big parties you're going to have. Keep it light so us old a-holes don't get our blood pressure up.

When we fired up the Boozefighters in 1946 there wasn't any Jap bikes in this country. The only thing besides Harleys and Indians was English machines. So we really didn't pay much attention to what a bro rode. The only thing we were really interested in was if he wanted to participate in all the club activities.

"We don't remember what year the first Honda 50s were sold in this country, but we do remember that they sold for $149, and we didn't think at that time that this little piece of shit that looked like a girl's bicycle would ever take hold in this country. Neither did the car companies think that the little Jap cars would ever be accepted. So for a few more years we didn't pay any attention to the importing of this shit. As you well know, today it's completely out of hand.

The first good thing that happened was two years ago the government put a tariff on the larger Jap bikes that were coming into this country, and it's really starting to show here in California. Some of the smaller Jap dealers have gone belly-up. There's more Harley dealers in California than in history. Selling so fast the factory hasn't been able to keep up with the demand. Harley-Davidson finally had to have the government lift the tariff.

We all buy something from Japan, because less merchandise is being built in America. Now we are all trying to point our finger at somebody to blame. Our bros who ride ricegrinders are only exercising their American right to freedom of choice. Maybe we should all pull together to get our bros back in the mainstream by buying American.

In closing, I want to say that all of us old a-holes have had our day in the wind.

Carry on in the true Boozefighters tradition.

Wino & Friends

CHAPTER 29

The Final Tale

The final tale in the story of the original wild ones has not been written yet. It never will be.

As *Easyriders* magazine's Dave Nichols said in his foreword to this book: "This is a story that is as old as humankind; it is a true story about men, boundaries, brotherhood, society, and freedom of expression. It is a tale of rebellion, of fire and magic, remembrances, and embellishments that make legends."

These prime cuts from the human essence are immortal. They have no end, and they began when man began, deep in his soul, his spirit. But these things, this "brotherhood" and "freedom of expression," this "fire and magic," are evidently meant only for the elite. They are obviously there for the taking by anyone, but so few make the effort. Is it because of fear? Is it intimidation? Or is it just pure laziness that keeps most of humanity in a safe little box? A 9-to-5, lame-sitcoms-every-evening, four-door-sedan, missionary position, just-a-social-drink-when-necessary-not-to-offend kind of box.

The original wild ones not only reached out and grabbed life's elusive brass ring, they leapt at it. They wrestled it to the ground and came up laughing. They drank bottle after bottle of life dry and always came back for more. And they left plenty of full ones for those of us who have chosen to follow in their footsteps.

And, sure, in the opinion of some members of society, bikers may not be the elite. But talk is cheap. The proof in this particular 100-proof pudding is not in talk; it's in the feeling, the feeling of big-cat freedom in the wind, the feeling of being just inches above the asphalt, hammer-down on a razor-straight interstate, unchained and invulnerable. And it's the feeling of a brotherhood that most people will never know or understand.

Is this what it means to be a part of society's true elite?

Just ask any real biker.

Ask the original wild ones.

INDEX